SUSPICION AND FAITH

Suspicion and Faith

THE RELIGIOUS USES OF MODERN ATHEISM

Merold Westphal

WILLIAM B. EERDMANS PUBLISHING COMPANY
GRAND RAPIDS, MICHIGAN

Copyright © 1993 by Wm. B. Eerdmans Publishing Co.
255 Jefferson Ave. S.E., Grand Rapids, Mich. 49503

Printed in the United States of America

Library of Congress Cataloging-in-Publication Data

Westphal, Merold.
    Suspicion and faith: the religious uses of modern atheism /
Merold Westphal.
        p.   cm.
    Includes bibliographical references and index.
    ISBN 0-8028-0643-0 (paper)
    1. Christianity and atheism. 2. Apologetics — 20th century.
3. Christianity and atheism — History — 19th century. 4. Christianity and
atheism — History — 20th century. 5. Freud, Sigmund, 1856-1939 —
Religion. 6. Marx, Karl, 1818-1883 — Religion. 7. Nietzsche, Friedrich
Wilhelm, 1844-1900 — Religion. I. Title.
BR128.A8W47   1993
261.2'1 — dc20   93-19541
                                                                                 CIP

Unless otherwise noted, scripture quotations are from the Revised Standard
Version of the Bible, copyrighted 1946, 1952 © 1971, 1973 by the Division of
Christian Education of the National Council of the Churches of Christ in the
U.S.A., and used by permission.

for my students and colleagues
    in the Senior Seminar program at Hope College
    where this project had its birth

Contents

Preface

This book was written more for the church than for the academy. I hope my academic friends and colleagues will find it of interest, since it deals with topics that are being discussed among us. But my main concern is that these topics are not being discussed *in the church* as much as they should be.

So I have written for pastors more than for philosophers and for theologians who think of themselves as pastors of a certain kind more than for theologians who think of themselves as philosophers of a certain kind. I especially hope, therefore, that this book will be read and studied in theological seminaries, where those who become pastors and church theologians receive decisive spiritual and intellectual formation. Needless to say, I also hope that literate and reflective laity will be among its readers.

While this book is thus addressed to Christian readers by a Christian writer, I hope for readers outside the church. I think that believing souls from other religious traditions and those estranged from all traditions of faith will find it edifyingly disturbing.

What I have written here is a sequel, in a way, to *God, Guilt, and Death*.[1] There I tried to let the believing soul speak in order to understand, from the inside, as it were, the meaning of the religious life. But I acknowledged the incompleteness of that strategy and the need to complement it with cross-examination of the believing soul from the perspective of suspicion. This book is now my attempt to portray that cross-examination as it comes from three modern atheists, Freud, Marx, and Nietzsche.

1. *God, Guilt, and Death: An Existential Phenomenology of Religion* (Bloomington: Indiana University Press, 1984).

My central thesis is that from a religious point of view the atheism of Freud, Marx, and Nietzsche should be taken seriously as a stimulus to self-examination rather than refuted as an error. This is because their critique of religion seems to be (1) all too true all too much of the time and (2) a modern echo of an ancient assault on the devotion of the devout, the one developed by Jesus and the prophets of Israel. Since (1) it is not the task of religious apologetics to refute the truth and since (2) it is the task of theology to understand its canonical norms, religious thinkers and thinking believers might do well to listen humbly to the admittedly arrogant assault on their faith and practice by this unholy trinity. Our spiritual vitality may depend on our willingness to listen and to learn.

Both books grew out of courses I have taught repeatedly. I want to thank the undergraduate students at Hope College and at Loyola College in Maryland and the graduate students at Fordham University who have read these modern atheists and discussed their critique of religion with me. I am also grateful to St. Olaf College for the opportunity to present an early version of these ideas as the Belgum Lectures, to the Institute for Christian Studies in Toronto for a similar opportunity in their annual Lectureship on Christianity and Learning, to Bethel College and Cedarville College for opportunities to present these ideas under the Visiting Philosopher Program of the Council for Philosophical Studies, and to the Senior Seminar Workshop at Hope College for some of the earliest and most helpful feedback on the project. All these conversations have helped me clarify the project and have confirmed my original sense of its importance.

Over the past few years several short pieces of this project have seen the light of day. I would like to thank the publishers of the following items for permission to incorporate significant portions of them in this book:

"The Hermeneutics of Lent," *Perspectives* 1/2 (February 1986), pp. 8-11.

"Barth's Critique of Religion," *Perspectives* 1/8 (October 1986), pp. 4-6.

"Taking Suspicion Seriously: The Religious Uses of Modern Atheism," *Faith and Philosophy* 4/1 (January 1987), pp. 22-42.

"The Challenge of Liberation Theology," *The Acts and Proceedings of the 182nd Regular Session of the General Synod, Reformed Church in America* (Reformed Church in America) LXVIII (1988), pp. 357-80.[2]

---

2. This essay was presented to General Synod as a report from the Theological Commission. In keeping with denominational practice, no author was

"Paranoia and Piety: Reflections on the Schreber Case," *Psychoanalysis and Religion,* ed. Joseph H. Smith and Susan A. Handelman (Baltimore: Johns Hopkins University Press, 1990), pp. 117-35.

The abbreviations used in the text for the works of Marx (with Friedrich Engels) and Nietzsche are explained in the first footnote in the first chapter of the sections on each of the two men (chapters 20 and 35). Abbreviations for the works of Feuerbach are explained in n. 4 of chapter 20. References to Freud are given by volume and page number from *The Standard Edition of the Complete Psychological Works of Sigmund Freud,* ed. and trans. James Strachey (London: Hogarth, 1953-74).

MEROLD WESTPHAL

---

specified, since the Commission adopted the report as its own. In fact I wrote both the original draft and the revisions that grew out of feedback given both by and to the Commission.

I The Hermeneutics of Suspicion

1 Atheism for Lent

". . . Yes, you heard me right. I propose the serious and sustained reading of Marx, Nietzsche, and Freud as a Lenten penance."

"You've got to be kidding. That's positively outrageous."

"Perhaps it is. But I'm not kidding. I'm quite serious."

"But you've named three of the most militant atheists of modern times, three founding fathers of secular humanism."

"I know, though I like to think of them as the great modern theologians of original sin. In any case, it is precisely their critique of religion that I recommend for Lenten reflection, more specifically their critique of the Christianity of the Christendom in which they lived as unbelievers."

"But isn't the purpose of Lent to aid the victory of the Spirit over the flesh, the religious over the secular in us?"

"Now we're getting somewhere."

The conversation is imaginary, but what Marx, Nietzsche, and Freud can help us see, if we let them, is that the distinction between the flesh and the Spirit does not coincide with the distinction between the secular and the sacred for the simple reason that religion, too, can be a work of the flesh. If "*all* our righteous deeds are like a polluted garment" (Isa. 64:6), why should we suppose our religious life to be otherwise? If "the heart is deceitful above all things, and desperately corrupt" (Jer. 17:9), why should it not put the respectability of religion to work for devious purposes?[1] Isn't Karl Barth right when he

---

1. Mike Martin tells us that the first book-length study of self-deception he can find, Daniel Dyke's *The Mystery of Selfe-Deceiving,* takes Jeremiah 17:9 as its theme. See *Self-Deception and Morality* (Lawrence, KS: University Press of Kansas, 1986), p. 32.

3

reminds us that it was the church and not the world that crucified Christ?[2]

Let's back up to more familiar territory. The movement of Lent is from penance to penitence to repentance. Acts of penance such as fasting (or reading) are an important part of Lenten observance, but they are not ends in themselves. Their goal is to lead to penitence, true sorrow for our sins. Thus the traditional "epistle" lesson for Ash Wednesday from Joel 2 begins with the admonition to "rend your heart, and not your garments." That is prophetic parlance for the challenge to let all our external acts of penance serve only to melt the inward hardness of our hearts.

While true sorrow for our sins is valuable in itself, it is not complete by itself. Just as faith without works is dead, so penitence without repentance is sterile. To the initial movement from outward act to inward feeling there must be joined the movement back to outward act. This is why Paul rejoiced, not that the Corinthians were grieved, but that they were "grieved into repenting. . . . For godly grief produces a repentance that leads to salvation and brings no regret" (2 Cor. 7:9-10). Thus the traditional collect for the first Sunday in Lent asks, with reference to fasting, "Give us grace to use such abstinence, that our flesh being subdued to the Spirit, we may ever obey thy godly motions in righteousness, and true holiness." This means it is even possible to define Lent as "the time when Christians are called upon to change their opinion and practice in the light of Christ's person and message."[3] So understood, of course, Lent is not so much a distinct time of the Christian year as a necessary dimension of the life of faith at any time of the year.

It is easy to understand (if not to practice) the idea that Lent is every day, that the call to repentance is as permanent as the good news of grace. But how shall we understand the strange idea that the works of the flesh that need to be subdued to the Spirit include our piety and that our religious opinions and practices are among those that need changing? Having finally gotten clear about the relation between faith and works, are we now to repent of both our faith and our works?

We might jump right in and start reading Marx's, Nietzsche's, and Freud's critiques of religion. But since that might be a little too much

2. Karl Barth, *The Epistle to the Romans*, trans. Edwyn C. Hoskyns (New York: Oxford University Press, 1933), p. 389.

3. L. W. Cowie and John Gummer, *The Christian Calendar* (Springfield: G. and C. Merriam, 1974), p. 61.

like learning to swim by jumping off the end of the dock, let us turn first to (apparently) less threatening writers: Luther and Barth. In opposition to the rationalist and idealist views of human nature, which assimilate the contrast of flesh and spirit to that of body and mind or sense and reason, Luther regards reason itself as an expression of the flesh, repeatedly explaining this in terms of reason's role in "the presumption of religion," in which "they select acts of worship and works that they themselves like." Where such "self-chosen works and forms of worship" prevail, we witness "the invention of an idol in the heart." Instead of true worship of the true God, religion becomes "superstition."[4]

Since Luther's enemies were primarily religious, it is not surprising that he discovered that religion, too, can be a work of the flesh. Nor is it surprising that he did not frequently transcend the natural (fallen) tendency to assume that such false religion was "their" religion. In his case, "they" are primarily Jews, Muslims ("Turks"), and Roman Catholics ("papists").

Barth takes us beyond this Lord-I-thank-Thee-that-I-am-a-Protestant-Christian complacency into which Luther habitually falls. Instead of separating himself from the target of the Pauline polemic against the religion of human choice and human achievement, he lets that critique include him first of all. When he speaks of "the criminal arrogance of religion" in which people become preoccupied with "their religious needs" to "surround themselves with comfortable illusions about their knowledge of God and particularly about their union with Him," it is he and his own Reformed tradition of which he primarily speaks. The illusory god that we create in our own image to conform to our knowledge and our values provides us with confidence and security; but as we are secretly the masters of this god, it turns out to be "No-God" at all, but rather, on closer examination, just idols such as "Family, Nation, State, Church, Fatherland." Since idolatry is inherently polytheistic, it is not surprising that, just as Zeus and Hera once squabbled on Mount Olympus, so today's "No-God" presents itself to us as the conflict between "Nature and Civilization, Materialism and Idealism, Capitalism and Socialism, Secularism and Ecclesiasticism, Imperialism and Democracy," all of which express our willingness to make ourselves ultimate. "The cry of revolt against such a god is nearer the truth than is the sophistry with which men attempt to justify him."[5]

4. Martin Luther, *Lectures on Galatians* (1535), trans. Jaroslav Pelikan, in vols. 26-27 of *Luther's Works*, ed. Jaroslav Pelikan and Walter A. Hansen (St. Louis: Concordia, 1963-64), 26:309, 229, 397; 27:54-57.
    5. Barth, pp. 37-52.

It is in this context that Barth seeks to guard against an anti-Semitic reading of the Gospels' critique of religion. Instead of saying that it was the Jews and not the Romans who crucified Christ (which leaves us out, since we are neither), he says that it was the church rather than the world that did it. The implication is that the sophistry which seeks to justify the "No-God" in its various incarnations is to be found in the church, and that since the atheism of Marx, Nietzsche, and Freud can be understood as a cry of revolt against such a god, we would do well to pay close attention to them. But this claim is not identical to these atheists' claim that they have the truth and that the church knows nothing but error, superstition, and illusion. It is rather the claim, scarcely less disturbing, that there is an atheism which is closer to the truth than a certain kind of religion, not the religion of "somebody else," but quite possibly our own.

It is not surprising that an early edition of Barth's commentary on Romans received a very negative review in the official organ of the Dutch Reformed Church. The members of that church were warned that the book was too "negative" and thus "foreign to their piety."[6] I am not in a position to dispute the factual accuracy of this latter claim. Insofar as it is correct, I suspect that it does not distinguish the Dutch church from most churches in the English-speaking world. There is surely a discrepancy between Barth's Lutheranism, which sees even our own religion as a work of the flesh, and the prevailing piety of most Christian churches, Protestant, Catholic, and Orthodox. The question unavoidably arises, however, whether this reflects negatively on Barth's critique or on that piety.

Perhaps we need to see Marx, Nietzsche, and Freud, along with Luther and Barth, as expressing a Promethean protest against all the Zeuses of *instrumental religion, the piety that reduces God to a means or instrument for achieving our own human purposes with professedly divine power and sanction.*

To see what such piety looks like in the flesh, consider the devout Salieri of Peter Shaffer's *Amadeus*. By the age of twelve, he tells us, "My one desire was to join all the composers who had celebrated [God's] glory through the long Italian past." At sixteen, he prays, "I will honor You with much music all the days of my life. . . . I am your servant for life. . . . Let your voice enter me! Let me conduct you." As a suitable moral context for this fervent devotion, he takes on vows of chastity and charity. "I will live with virtue. I will strive to better

6. Barth, p. 21.

the lot of my fellows."[7] How beautiful the faith of youth, how inspiring its passion!

Not quite. This soaring self-transcendence has a flip side of sordid self-interest. Salieri gives himself to God, but not exactly as a gift. His merchant parents thought of God as "a superior Habsburg emperor, inhabiting a Heaven only slightly farther off than Vienna. All they required of Him was to protect commerce, and keep them forever preserved in mediocrity. My own requirements were very different. [Pause] I wanted Fame. Not to deceive you, I wanted to blaze like a comet across the firmament of Europe! Yet only in one special way. Music! Absolute music!" Conveniently, the frescoed God Salieri saw in church every Sunday was

> staring at the world with dealer's eyes. Tradesmen had put him up there. Those eyes made bargains, real and irreversible. "You gave me so — I'll give you so! No more. No less!" . . . The night before I left Legnago forever, I went to see Him, and made a bargain with Him myself! . . . I knelt before the God of Bargains, and I prayed through the moldering plaster with all my soul. [He kneels] "Signore, let me be a composer! Grant me sufficient fame to enjoy it. In return . . .

Then follows Salieri's pledge of allegiance, and he hears God say, "Bene. Go forth, Antonio. Serve Me and mankind, and you will be blessed" (pp. 11-12).

At thirty-one we find Salieri as an upwardly mobile, "prolific composer to the Habsburg court." He was very much in love, "or at least in lust," with his prize pupil, Katherina Cavalieri, "a bubbling student with merry eyes and a sweet, eatable mouth. . . . But because of my vow to God I was entirely faithful to my wife. I had never laid a finger upon the girl — except occasionally to depress her diaphragm in the way of teaching her to sing" (pp. 14-15). He was keeping his bargain.

But God was not keeping his. As if to repudiate the idea that he was the God of Bargains in the first place, he created Mozart at precisely the wrong time and place. The perfection of Mozart's music revealed the mediocrity of Salieri's. Even when the latter became "the most famous musician in Europe" after the former's death, the divine mes-

---

7. Peter Shaffer, *Amadeus* (New York: New American Library, 1984), pp. 11-12, 30. Subsequent pages, given in the text, are from this edition. Soon enough it becomes clear that by virtue Salieri means sexual virtue.

sage lost none of its sting. "I was to be bricked up in fame! Embalmed in fame! Buried in fame — but for work I know to be *absolutely worthless!* This was my sentence: I must endure thirty years of being called 'Distinguished' by people incapable of distinguishing" (p. 147).

Salieri's response? All-out war on God. With all the anger and sarcasm of which he is capable, he prays once again.

> Grazie, Signore! You gave me the desire to serve You — which most men do not have — then saw to it the service was shameful in the ears of the server. Grazie! You gave me the desire to praise You — which most men do not feel — then made me mute. Grazie tanti! You put into me perception of the Incomparable — which most men never know! — then ensured that I would know myself forever mediocre. . . . You know how hard I've worked! Solely [sic] that in the end, in the practice of the art which alone makes the world comprehensible to me, I might hear Your Voice! And now I do hear it — and it says only one name: MOZART! . . . [Savagely] Grazie e grazie ancora! [Pause] So be it! From this time we are enemies, You and I! I'll not accept it from You — do you hear? . . . [ellipsis in the text] They say God is not mocked. I tell you, Man is not mocked! . . . [ellipsis in the text] I am not mocked. . . . And this I swear: To my last breath I shall block You on earth, as far as I am able! [He glares up at God. To audience] What use, after all, is man, if not to teach God His lessons? (pp. 73-75)

To complete the retraction of his original promise to God, "I am your servant for life," Salieri canceled the moral vows that had accompanied it.

> The next day, when Katherina Cavalieri came for her lesson, I made the same halting speech about "coins of tenderness," and I dubbed the girl La Generosa. . . . She consumed twenty "Nipples of Venus" — kissed me with brandied breath — and slipped easily into my bed. . . . She remained there as my mistress for many years behind my good wife's back. . . . So much for my vow of sexual virtue. [Slight pause] The same evening I went to the Palace and resigned from all my committees to help the lot of poor musicians. So much for my vow of social virtue. (pp. 80-81)

Salieri presents us with a vivid picture of the piety that reduces God to a means to the believer's own ends. Freud, Marx, and Nietzsche find this sort of piety to be the rule rather than the exception. Behind what professes to be love of God and neighbor they regularly find love of self, disguised beyond recognition, at least to those who perpetrate this pious fraud. To see our three atheists as critics of instrumental religion could be to make them instruments for self-examination and sanctification. Reading them at any time of the year could be a Lenten spiritual exercise that could lead to godly sorrow and the repentance "that leads to salvation and brings no regret."

2 On Learning When Not to Refute Atheism

Marx, Nietzsche, and Freud for devotional reading! The idea is strange, even weird. But our trio has at least one conspicuous advantage over the authors we more easily turn to for spiritual edification: Because they write in the language of psychology and sociology, it is easier to see that they are talking about real people in the real world.

But our trio has an even more conspicuous disadvantage. They are atheists. Worse, they are militant atheists. Worse yet, they are among the most influential and widely read atheists of our time. Few writers can claim to have contributed as deeply and decisively to the secular humanism that permeates the world we live in. It is "out there" shaping the way "they" think and act, and it is "in here" shaping the way we think and act, even in our battles with secular humanism. And they have contributed to the spread of this virus more than almost anyone else. How can we possibly come to think of them as God-given instruments of our own cleansing and renewal as individual Christians and as the church? How can we be enabled to recognize in the diatribes of these enemies of the faith the painful truth about ourselves?

I believe the final answer to this question is found in recognizing the profound parallel between the critique of religion in Marx, Nietzsche, and Freud and the critique of religion found in the Bible. Faith as fraud? Devotion as deception? These are strong charges, but modern atheism is not the first to make them. What about Amos, whose God cannot stand the music offered in his praise (Amos 5:23)? What about Isaiah (Second or Third), for whom "all our righteous deeds are like a polluted garment" (Isa. 64:6)? And what about Jesus, who considers the most pious people of his day "whitewashed tombs" (Matt. 23:27) and the temple run by the chief priests a "den of robbers" (Mark 11:17)?

We need only recall Jesus' critique of the Pharisees, Paul's critique of works righteousness, James's critique of cheap grace, and the Old Testament prophetic critiques on which these are based to be reminded that biblical faith has built into it a powerful polemic against certain kinds of religion, even if they are practiced in the name of the one true God. These biblical diatribes against false religion are addressed to the covenant people of God in their worship (as they think) of the God of the covenant; indeed, in the case of James and Paul, these sharp critiques are addressed to the Christian church.[1] They cannot be neutralized by appeals either to metaphysical orthodoxy or to ritual rectitude and zeal or to the combination of sound doctrine and proper worship.

But perhaps the most frightening critique of instrumental religion in the Bible is the portrayal of Jesus' own disciples in the Gospel narratives. I am not referring here to the prayerlessness that made the power over evil spirits that Jesus gave them useless (Mark 9:14-29), the insensitivity with which they scolded parents who brought their children to Jesus (10:13-16), the overconfidence with which Peter denied that he would deny Jesus (14:27-31), the lethargy that made it possible for Peter, James, and John to sleep through Jesus' agony in Gethsemene (14:32-42), the cowardice they showed when "they all forsook him and fled" (14:50), or even the disloyalty with which Peter eventually denied even knowing the one he had confessed as Messiah (14:66-72).

These are all signs of weakness, evidence that the faith of the disciples had the awkward habit of running out of gas at crucial moments. But there is also evidence that their faith had a venal quality to it, that even when it was present it was corrupted by instrumental interests. We see this on the three occasions when Jesus tried to tell them of the suffering and death awaiting him in Jerusalem:

Mark 8:27–9:1 Immediately after Peter's dramatic confession, "You are the Christ," Jesus speaks of his suffering and death. Peter rebukes him, but Jesus responds, "Get behind me, Satan! For you are not on the side of God, but of men." The subsequent episodes suggest that it is not cowardice but ambition that speaks here. If Jesus is the Messiah, Peter is in line for a top job in the new administration.

Mark 9:30-41 Again Jesus tries to tell the disciples what lies ahead, but they are unable to understand and afraid to ask about it.

---

1. See the fascinating suggestion by Juan Luis Segundo that James and Paul can be harmonized on the basis of their complementary critiques of religion. *Faith and Ideologies*, trans. John Drury (Maryknoll, NY: Orbis, 1984), pp. 120-30.

What do they find to talk about in the episode that Mark and Luke record next? They have a debate about which of them is the greatest. Who will have the most prestigious positions in the kingdom? And to keep the inner circle conveniently small, they try to silence a man who is casting out demons in Jesus' name, "because he was not following us."

Mark 10:32-45 Jesus tries again. James and John respond by coming forward with a painfully honest confession of what motivates their discipleship: "Grant us to sit, one at your right hand and one at your left, in your glory." The text does not say which of the two brothers wanted to be Secretary of State and which one Secretary of Defense, but it does tell us that the other ten disciples were very upset at this attempt to get an inside track on the spoils of victory.

It is in these texts that Jesus' profoundest teachings about the meaning of discipleship occur. He speaks of self-denial, cross-bearing, servanthood, losing one's life for the sake of the gospel, and giving one's life for others. The contrast between his understanding of what it means to be a bearer of the kingdom and the disciples' self-centered discipleship is as powerful a critique of instrumental religion as anything to be found in Freud, Marx, and Nietzsche.

But because their critique of religion is so deeply biblical, in spite of their own unbelief, Freud, Marx, and Nietzsche can help us to recover the meaning of the biblical critique of religion if we will let them. The Spirit that speaks to the church also blows where it will. Is it possible that the Spirit would speak to the church through its worst enemies?

We can more clearly see the powerful parallel between Marx, Nietzsche, and Freud, on the one hand, and Amos, Jeremiah, Jesus, James, and Paul, on the other, if we become more precise about the nature of the atheism being recommended for our devotional meditation. For it is not every form of modern atheism that I have in mind. To focus on Marx, Nietzsche, and Freud requires a simultaneous broadening and narrowing of the meaning of "atheism."

"Atheism" can be used of religious unbelief in a broad and inclusive sense. It thus includes both the atheist proper, who claims to know that God does not exist, and the agnostic, who, with a kind of Socratic ignorance, claims only that we do not or cannot know whether God exists. Further, atheism is no longer limited to the issue of God's mere existence, but also includes major claims about the nature and activity of God. Nor are its negations limited to the propositional content of the religious life. They extend from religious theory to religious practice with the claim that the liturgical, devotional, and ethical practices of the religious life are rationally impermissible or at best unwarranted, in either case irrational.

There is a narrowness, however, that corresponds to this broadness of usage. Marx, Nietzsche, and Freud represent a type of atheism different from the atheism that has dominated European philosophy of religion from at least the time of Gaunilo through Hume and Kant and that continues to this day to hold center stage in Anglo-American discussion. This atheism we can call "evidential atheism." It is nowhere better summarized than in Bertrand Russell's account of what he would say to God if the two were ever to meet and if God were to ask him why he had not been a believer: "I'd say, 'Not enough evidence God! Not enough evidence!' "[2]

By contrast, Marx, Nietzsche, and Freud have been called the masters of the school of suspicion.[3] What unites them in spite of important and possibly irreconcilable differences is their joint practice of the *hermeneutics of suspicion, the deliberate attempt to expose the self-deceptions involved in hiding our actual operative motives from ourselves, individually or collectively, in order not to notice how and how much our behavior and our beliefs are shaped by values we profess to disown.* While our trio develops and applies the hermeneutics of suspicion with primary emphasis, respectively, in the spheres of political economy, bourgeois morality, and psycho-sexual development, they also each subject the religion of Christendom to the critique of suspicion.

This suspicion is to be distinguished from skepticism, which gives rise to evidential atheism. Skepticism is directed toward the elusiveness of things, while suspicion is directed toward the evasiveness of consciousness.[4] Skepticism seeks to overcome the opacity of facts, while suspicion seeks to uncover the duplicity of persons. Skepticism addresses itself directly to the propositions believed and asks whether there is sufficient evidence to make belief rational. Suspicion addresses itself to the persons who believe and only indirectly to the propositions believed. It seeks to discredit the believing soul by asking what *motives*

---

2. Quoted by Alvin Plantinga in *Faith and Rationality: Reason and Belief in God,* ed. Alvin Plantinga and Nicholas Wolterstorff (Notre Dame: University of Notre Dame Press, 1983), pp. 17-18.

3. Paul Ricoeur, *Freud and Philosophy: An Essay on Interpretation,* trans. Denis Savage (New Haven: Yale University Press, 1970), p. 32. This is without doubt the best book in English on Freud, but it is heavy going since it presupposes considerable knowledge of Freud and the philosophical tradition. Perhaps the best general introduction is Philip Rieff's. See below, p. 34 n. 5.

4. Cf. Ricoeur, p. 33.

lead people to belief and what *functions* their beliefs play, looking for precisely those motives and functions that love darkness rather than light and therefore hide themselves. Where Hume and Kant challenge the soundness of the arguments for the existence of God, Marx, Nietzsche, and Freud seek to show how theistic belief functions both to mask and to fulfill forms of self-interest that cannot be acknowledged.

While skepticism (along with evidential atheism) has its origins in Platonic-Cartesian doubt, suspicion arises from Francis Bacon's critique of the Idols of the Tribe and Cave. "The human understanding is no dry light," writes Bacon, "but receives an infusion from the will and affections; whence proceed sciences which may be called *'sciences as one would.'* For what a man had rather were true he more readily believes." With reference to impatience, hope, superstition, arrogance, and pride, Bacon comments, "Numberless in short are the ways, and sometimes imperceptible, in which the affections colour and infect the understanding." This leads to the advice that every seeker of truth adopt the rule "that *whatever his mind seizes and dwells upon with peculiar satisfaction is to be held in suspicion. . . .*"5

The style is different, to be sure, but Schopenhauer clearly makes the same point when he says that by will he does not mean a power guided by knowledge and under the direction of reason. Instead, he says, we should think of the will by analogy with blind instinct, which uses reason as its instrument. Reason gives fictitious accounts of our behavior for the sake of moral appearances, or, even better, under the guidance of the will becomes entirely unable to notice unwelcome facts about the self. In short, the will is substance and master, the intellect only accident and servant.6

In his masterful book on Freud, Paul Ricoeur makes the point with similar generality. Suspicion is necessary to keep before us "the nonautonomy of knowledge, its rootedness in existence, the latter being understood as desire and effort," that is, as the will and affections of which Bacon and Schopenhauer speak. "Thereby is discovered not only the unsurpassable nature of life, but the interference of desire with intentionality, upon which desire inflicts an invincible obscurity, an ineluctable partiality."7

---

5. Francis Bacon, *Novum Organum,* XLIX, LVIII, emphasis added.
6. Arthur Schopenhauer, *The World as Will and Representation,* trans. E. F. J. Payne (New York: Dover, 1966), I, 111, 114, 292, 368-69; II, 126-28.
7. This corruptibility of knowledge means that "representation obeys not

As we shall see in more detail, Freud sees dreams and neurotic symptoms as the disguised fulfillment of repressed wishes. He then suggests that religious beliefs are like dreams and religious practices like neurotic symptoms. In both cases the claim is that we can neither understand nor properly evaluate the belief or behavior in question until we discover the hidden drives and motives that shape them. In other words, suspicion easily transfers its critique from beliefs to practices.

The resulting evaluation of the religious life is as a whole devastating for at least two reasons. First, to an even somewhat impartial observer the critique seems *all too true all too much of the time.* The prominence of various self-serving motives in our piety, or at least in that of others, is all too easy to notice. Who can fail, for example, to see the self-deception in the Afrikaner attempt to portray apartheid as a divine mandate or in the "white man's burden," "manifest destiny," and "anti-Communist" theologies that have shaped the colonial domination and even extermination of indigenous populations in North, Central, and South America? Or who can fail to notice the instrumental character of the piety of the politicians, especially at election time? Do they serve God for nought (Job 1:9)?

Second, by its nature suspicion discredits the believer and the believing community even if their beliefs should turn out to be true and their practices in themselves good. Even orthodoxy becomes idolatrous when belief in the triune God serves to sanctify the flaunting of his purposes in the world. The God of the Bible repudiates metaphysical compliments, however orthodox, ritual tributes, however splendid, and moral rectitude, however rigorous, when they are set in the context of instrumental religion, offered to a god we hope to domesticate.

So it is not surprising that almost invariably our first reaction to Marx, Nietzsche, and Freud is to seek to refute or discredit them. It is comforting to think (though at this reference to comfortable thoughts suspicion begins to get suspicious) that Marx can be blamed for the Soviets, that Nietzsche can be blamed for the Nazis, and that American (scientific) psychology treats Freud as beyond the pale.

---

only a law of intentionality, which makes it the expression of some object, but also another law, which makes it the manifestation of . . . desire. It is because of the interference of the latter expressive function that representation can be distorted." This interference and this distortion are what call for the hermeneutics of suspicion, "an exegesis of the desires that lie hidden in that intentionality." Ricoeur, pp. 457-58.

While this temptation is largely a defensive reaction to the exposé suspicion is likely to generate, it gains the appearance of legitimacy from a failure to distinguish the two kinds of atheism. No doubt the proper response of Christian thinkers to evidential atheism is to seek to refute it. This can be done by trying to show that there is, in fact, sufficient evidence to warrant religious beliefs and practices rationally. Or it can be done by challenging the way in which the evidentialist demands evidence.

I shall not discuss the relative merits of these strategies here.[8] My thesis here is that an entirely different response is called for by the atheism of suspicion. The first task of Christian thinkers as they face the likes of Marx, Nietzsche, and Freud is not to refute or discredit them. It is to acknowledge[9] that their critique is *all too true all too much of the time* and to seek to discover just where the shoe fits, not "them" but ourselves.

In short, I am calling on the philosophers, theologians, and above all the pastors and lay teachers of the Christian community (1) to be the prophetic voices that challenge the church to take seriously the critique of religion generated by suspicion and (2) to lead the way in using it as an aid to personal and corporate self-examination. The emphasis of Christian spirituality on personal self-examination and the emphasis of Hebrew prophecy on corporate self-examination make it possible to speak of the *religious uses of modern atheism* when we speak of the atheism of suspicion.

---

8. I am willing to predict, however, that the recent challenge of "Reformed" epistemology to evidentialism as such is likely to be as central to the discussion of evidential atheism for the foreseeable future as discussion of invisible gardeners was a few decades ago. A clear and powerful version of this challenge is to be found in Plantinga and Wolterstorff, *Faith and Rationality.* On the problems posed for "Reformed" epistemology by the hermeneutics of suspicion, see my essay "Sin as an Epistemological Category," in *Christian Philosophy,* ed. Thomas P. Flint (Notre Dame: University of Notre Dame Press, 1990), pp. 200-226.

9. Since the hermeneutics of suspicion is concerned with the processes by which we manage not to notice things of which we are by no means unaware, questions of knowledge can never be separated from questions of acknowledgment. Thus Mike Martin defines self-deception as "the purposeful or intentional [but not deliberate] evasion of fully acknowledging something to oneself." *Self-Deception and Morality* (Lawrence, KS: University Press of Kansas, 1986), p. 6. Cf. p. 13, where Martin links acknowledging with admitting or confessing. With similar voluntarist overtones, Karl Barth relates faith not as opinion in relation to knowledge (*epistēmē/Wissenschaft*) but as acknowledgment in relation to knowledge. Because revelation comes to us from without and beyond our capacities, "Knowledge in this case means acknowledgment. And the utterance or expression of this knowledge is termed confession." *Church Dogmatics* I/2, ed. G. W. Bromiley and T. F. Torrance (Edinburgh: T. and T. Clark, 1956), pp. 172-73.

When we have eliminated the logs of self-deception from the theory and practice of our own piety, then we can seek to correct the specks of error in the theories of Marx, Nietzsche, and Freud (Matt. 7:1-5).[10] Perhaps, we may hope, there will no longer be the need to do so, our lives having already refuted them more effectively than our arguments ever could.

10. Our tendency to admit that we are not without fault while insisting that their errors are surely greater and more dangerous than our own identifies us as the hypocrites to whom Jesus addresses these words.

3 Help from Gilbert and Sullivan

When philosophers talk about "sciences as one would" or "the inter-ference of desire with intentionality," they may give the impression that suspicion is the esoteric practice of an intellectual elite. But it is not. Just as we all ask the skeptical question "How do you know?" meaning "What evidence do you have for that claim?" so we all engage in suspicion, at least of others. For example, we may not suspect that the concept of rationalization comes to us from the Freudian tradition,[1] but we easily recognize as rationalizations such pseudo-justifications of "petty" theft as "But everyone does it" or "They'll never miss it" or "They can afford it better than I" — at least when these are offered by someone other than ourselves. When we see through the self-deception involved in holding to such beliefs in order to hide from oneself the fact that one is a thief, we practice the hermeneutics of suspicion, even if we are suspicious of anyone who uses the term "hermeneutics."

My own favorite example of suspicion in everyday life comes from my favorite Gilbert and Sullivan operetta, *The Pirates of Penzance*. (It is Gilbert's lyrics and not Sullivan's music that will be helpful here, but if this chapter were entitled "Help from W. S. Gilbert," who would have known whom I had in mind?) Our story concerns a certain Frederic.

> When Frederic was a little lad he proved so brave and daring,
> His father thought he'd 'prentice him to some career seafaring.[2]

So he instructed the boy's nursemaid, Ruth, to apprentice him to a pilot. Unfortunately Ruth was hard of hearing, and she apprenticed

1. Ernest Jones, "Rationalization in Every-Day Life," in *An Outline of Psy-choanalysis,* ed. J. J. Van Teslaar (New York: Boni and Liveright, 1924), pp. 98-107.
2. W. S. Gilbert, *The Pirates of Penzance or The Slave of Duty,* Act I.

him to a pirate instead. Act One opens on the day Frederic's appren-
ticeship is to expire. Ruth, who has accompanied him throughout his
career as a pirate, hopes he will take her with him as his wife. He has
his doubts, however, thinking that a young man of twenty-one usually
looks for a wife of seventeen rather than forty-seven. Since he has seen
no other woman since he was eight, he wonders whether Ruth is
beautiful or "on the whole, plain."

She tells him that she has been told she is beautiful, but admits
that this was years ago. Still, she is just about to convince him that she
is "a fine woman," when a "bevy of beautiful maidens," all sisters,
appears on the Cornish beach where the pirates have left them. After
berating Ruth as a false and faithless woman who played upon his
innocence, Frederic sets out to meet the nubile strangers. As he begins
to tell them his story, their response is twofold:

How pitiful his tale! How rare his beauty!

He is indeed (if he has been properly cast) a hunk. But he also
understands (we're not supposed to ask how) the Victorian upbringing
the girls have received. He senses that an appeal to his pitiful tale is more
likely to win him a wife than an appeal to his rare beauty. So he sings

Oh, is there not one maiden breast
    Which does not feel the moral beauty
Of making worldly interest
    Subordinate to sense of duty?
Who would not give up willingly
    All matrimonial ambition,
To rescue such a one as I
    From his unfortunate position?

All of the girls decisively reject his proposal, knowing that a
recently retired pirate, however handsome, is not a suitable match for
any daughter of a Modern Major General — all of them, that is, except
Mabel, who is (if she has been properly cast) the most beautiful. Before
offering her heart to the "poor wandering one," the ex-pirate whom she
has met but moments before, she scolds her morally insensitive sisters.

Oh, sisters, deaf to pity's name,
    For shame!
It's true that he has gone astray,
    But pray

Is that a reason good and true
    Why you
Should all be deaf to pity's name?

To which the other girls reply in chorus

The question is, had he not been
    A thing of beauty,
Would she be swayed by quite as keen
    A sense of duty?

This is the hermeneutics of suspicion in a nutshell. Frederic speaks of duty, and Mabel speaks of pity. But the sisters, along with us, see through this moral facade. They recognize the force actually directing the behavior of Frederic and Mabel, nature's elective affinity, which is known colloquially as sex appeal. They are suspicious of the moralism with which the two lovers feel compelled by social convention and the desire for respectability to hide from themselves what everyone else can plainly see, to rationalize their behavior by deceiving themselves about its real character. The sisters' pointed questions unmask the not very lofty function played by the lovers' discourse on lofty ideals.

It is plainly suspicion and not skepticism that is at work here. The beliefs of Frederic and Mabel are not themselves challenged, either by an argument denying the importance of duty and pity in general or by an argument denying the specific claims the lovers make about what duty and pity call for in the present situation. No doubt there are circumstances in which the worldly interest of matrimonial ambition should take a backseat to duty, and perhaps those with a properly cultivated sense of pity will recognize Frederic's predicament as just such an occasion. These are the kinds of issues the skeptic would like to debate. But not Mabel's sisters. It is sufficient for them to recognize that whatever the moral truth about the situation may be, objectively speaking, Frederic and Mabel have lapsed subjectively into hypocrisy and self-deception, pretending to be what they are not and managing at the same time not to notice the pretense.

There is a difference between the spontaneous suspicion of Mabel's sisters and the more reflective suspicion of our lyricist, W. S. Gilbert. The sisters are not concerned to enlighten Frederic and Mabel. Their questions are specifically labeled as an aside. They are addressed to the audience and, more importantly, to each other. The purpose of their suspicion is simply to justify their own response to Frederic by discrediting Mabel's. Gilbert, by contrast, offers this scene to his Victorian audience in hopes of enlightening them. He hopes that they will recognize themselves and their culture in Frederic and Mabel and will come to a more honest understanding of their preoccupation with duty and virtue. His suspicion is more a gesture of friendship than of self-justification, or so it seems to me. For while his satire is biting, it does not strike me as bitter.

And yet there is an important similarity between Gilbert's suspicion and that of the sisters. In both cases it is easy suspicion, seeing through the self-deceptions of others. How good Gilbert may have been at the harder kind, practicing suspicion on himself, we have no way of knowing.

If we turn from light opera to moral philosophy we will regularly find philosophers to be just as suspicious as Mabel's sisters and in just the same way. They suspect that the moral values of which we are often so proud are all too often servants of the very interests that they are supposed to regulate, just as government agencies all too often serve those special interests that they are supposed to constrain, rather than the common good that they are supposed to embody. We will do well to keep Mabel's sisters in mind as we note a few examples.

Who better to begin with than Kant? He knows that "innocence is a glorious thing," but also that it is "easily led astray." Because inclinations represent a "powerful counterweight" to duty, there "arises a natural dialectic, i.e., a propensity to quibble with these strict laws of duty, to cast doubt upon their validity . . . and to make them, where possible, more compatible with our wishes and inclinations. Thereby are such laws corrupted in their very foundations. . . ."[3]

This is the beginning of the reversal in which duty becomes the servant of inclination. But it is not just by such amendments to the moral law that self-interest corrupts the moral life. Even when we do the right thing, we do not always do it for the right reason. Sometimes,

> after the keenest self-examination we can find nothing except the moral ground of duty that could have been strong enough to move us to this or that good action and to such great sacrifice. But there cannot with certainty be at all inferred from this that *some secret impulse of self-love, merely appearing as the idea of duty,* was not the actual determining cause of the will. *We like to flatter ourselves with the false claim to a more noble motive;* but in fact we can never, even

3. Immanuel Kant, *Grounding for the Metaphysics of Morals*, trans. James W. Ellington (Indianapolis: Hackett, 1981), p. 405. I have given the Academy edition pagination, which is to be found in most editions of the *Grundlegung*.

by the strictest examination, completely plumb the depths of the secret incentives of our actions.

Thus we need not be an "enemy of virtue" but merely a "cool observer" (like Mabel's sisters) to notice that "we everywhere come upon the dear self, which is always turning up, and upon which the intent of our actions is based rather than upon the strict command of duty."[4]

Needless to say the second corruption often depends on the first. That is, if my behavior is actually determined by self-interest but masquerades to others and, more importantly, to myself as morally motivated, it may be quite useful to have available a version of the moral law that has been amended to suit this purpose. But it is not always necessary. Sometimes I can mask my real motives with reference to a version of the moral law that is as pure as my operative motives are impure. As we have already seen, this may well have been the case with Frederic and Mabel. Still, it is important to note how easily the content of the moral law is jeopardized once its function has changed from regulator to servant of the inclinations.

Ever the son of his pietist upbringing, Kant focuses our attention on the inner recesses of the self, in biblical language, the heart. By contrast, Rousseau alerts us to the same phenomena in public, political discourse. Describing the final stages of political decline, he writes:

> Finally, when the State, close to its ruin, continues to subsist only in an illusory and ineffectual form; when the social bond is broken in all hearts; *when the basest interest brazenly adopts the sacred name of the public good,* then the general will becomes mute; all — *guided by secret motives* — are no more citizens in offering their opinions than if the State had never existed, *and iniquitous decrees whose only goal is the private interest are falsely passed under the name of laws.*[5]

In our own time suspicion plays a prominent role in Anglo-American moral philosophy. It is what leads R. M. Hare, for example, to challenge anything more than a *prima facie* reliance on our *prima facie* moral intuitions in asking what rights I may possess.

> For people who ask this latter question will, being human, nearly always answer that they have just those rights, whatever they are, which will promote a distribution of goods which is in the interest

4. Kant, p. 407, emphasis added.
5. Jean-Jacques Rousseau, *Social Contract,* book IV, chapter 1, emphasis added. Cf. Psalm 94:20 and Isaiah 10:1ff. in relation to Rousseau's comment on "iniquitous decrees . . . under the name of laws."

of their own social group. *The rhetoric of rights,* which is engendered by this question, *is a recipe for class war, and civil war.* In pursuit of these rights, people will, because they have convinced themselves that justice demands it, inflict almost any harms on the rest of society and themselves.[6]

The most widely discussed theory of justice in our time starts from just this assumption. John Rawls suggests that we can find an account of justice that will be more than a rationalization of special interests only behind the "veil of ignorance." We are invited to perform the following thought experiment. Imagine a kind of moral constitutional convention in which the rules for life together will be agreed upon. Deprive all the delegates of that knowledge of themselves that would make it possible for them to argue for rules that would be to their advantage at the expense of others. In other words, no one knows whether he or she is male or female, black or white, highly gifted and skilled or largely unendowed with intellect and talent, and so forth. The rules freely agreed to under these conditions would be fair.

Ronald Dworkin calls our attention to the suspicion that motivates this theory, the perceived need to filter out the self-deceptive self-interest which otherwise co-opts our moral discourse. The theory that places us behind the veil of ignorance in order to discover what justice really is "supposes, reasonably, that political arrangements that do not display equal concern and respect are those that are established by *powerful men and women who, whether they recognize it or not, have more concern and respect for members of a particular class, or people with particular talents or ideals, than they have for others.*" Needless to say, the principles of "justice" that legitimize such "political arrangements" will be rationalizations rather than genuine moral insights. The veil of ignorance is designed to make it impossible (within the thought experiment) for powerful people "to design institutions [or propagate principles], consciously or unconsciously, to favor their own class."[7]

Alasdair MacIntyre goes even farther. In his view it is not only

6. R. M. Hare, "Justice and Equality," reprinted in *Justice: Alternative Political Perspectives,* ed. James Sterba (Belmont, CA: Wadsworth, 1980), p. 119, emphasis added.

7. Ronald Dworkin, *Taking Rights Seriously* (Cambridge: Harvard University Press, 1977), p. 181, emphasis added. Rawls's theory is found in *A Theory of Justice* (Cambridge: Harvard University Press, 1971). Dworkin's notion of people designing institutions (and theories) that favor their own class is precisely the interpretation Rousseau gives to any Lockean type of social contract in his *Discourse on Inequality.* In such contexts he detects "jealousy" masquerading as "benevolence." See *Rousseau's Political Writings,* ed. Alan Ritter and Julia Conaway Bondanella (New York: Norton, 1988), pp. 42-45.

the concepts of rights and justice but a broad spectrum of our moral concepts that can be labeled moral fictions. Although MacIntyre does not use the concept of irony in this connection, we will best understand him if we think of moral fictions as concepts whose use is ironical but is not known to be so by those who use them. Irony in its simplest form involves a discrepancy between the purported (official, manifest) meaning and the actual (operative, latent) use of discourse. The refrain from Mark Antony's funeral oration is a familiar example: "Brutus is an honorable man."[8] In its "official" meaning the statement praises Brutus, but it actually functions to raise doubts and eventually to accuse.

Similarly, according to MacIntyre, key concepts in contemporary moral discourse often claim to offer objective and impersonal criteria while their actual use is that of rhetorical manipulation in the service of unavowed interests. In the modern world, moral causes typically "offer a rhetoric that serves to conceal behind the masks of morality what are in fact the preferences of arbitrary will and desire. . . ."[9] Thus the rhetoric of revolution is often the venting of hatred and resentment, the rhetoric of property rights is often a thinly veiled defense of economic privilege, and the rhetoric of family is often an ironic expression of racism or homophobia.

The difference between this irony and that of Mark Antony is that Antony's is fully conscious and intentional, while the former conceals the truth from those who speak ironically (and possibly from no one else, as in the case of Mabel and Frederic). MacIntyre thus comes down clearly on the "un-" side of Dworkin's "consciously or unconsciously" and the "or not" side of Dworkin's "whether they recognize it or not." *Moral fictions are, to repeat, concepts whose use is ironical but is not known to be so by those who use them.*

8. William Shakespeare, *Julius Caesar*, act III, scene ii.
9. Alasdair MacIntyre, *After Virtue* (Notre Dame: University of Notre Dame Press, 1981), p. 69. See chapters 6 and 9 for the full discussion. MacIntyre's thesis "that all rational vindications of morality *manifestly* fail and that therefore belief in the tenets of morality needs to be explained in terms of a set of rationalisations" (p. 111, emphasis added) suggests that suspicion comes to the fore and moral fictions are more easily unmasked where confidence in demonstrable objective truth is in decline. But if, as sometimes seems the case, he also wants to suggest that periods of skepticism and epistemological relativism are what give rise to the false consciousness that suspicion seeks to expose, this is doubtful. Belief in truth that is at once objective and discoverable provides fertile soil for rationalization. See my essay "Orthodoxy and Inattention," *Reformed Journal* 30/1 (January 1980), pp. 13-15.

4 Religious Fictions Too?

The lesson that Mabel's sisters and moral philosophy seek to teach us is that our morality can easily do less to expose our faults than to blind us to them. But our theme is religion rather than morality. Are there religious fictions as well as moral fictions? Is Martin Buber right when he says, in agreement with Luther and Barth, that just as "there is nothing that can so hide the face of our fellow-man as morality can" so also "religion can hide from us as nothing else can the face of God"?[1]

That there are such religious fictions is precisely what Marx, Nietzsche, and Freud claim. They are not the first, however, to direct the critique of suspicion toward religion. Their claim to fame in the present context is not the originality of their ideas but the impact they have given to those ideas. A brief look at an earlier version of their project will provide the final preparation for our exploration of the religious uses of their modern atheism.

David Hume is best known for his philosophical skepticism, and this is true in his philosophy of religion as well. In his *Dialogues Concerning Natural Religion* and in sections X and XI of *An Enquiry Concerning Human Understanding* he asks the familiar questions about whether there is sufficient evidence to provide rational support for belief in God and miracles. His skeptical answers to these questions, along with Kant's more comprehensive but similar project, shook the foundations of both the deists, who wanted to find a religion within the limits of reason alone, and the orthodox, who wanted to establish as much as possible on the basis of general revelation, understood as rational proof, and leave as little as possible dependent upon faith in biblical special revelation.

1. Martin Buber, *Between Man and Man* (New York: Macmillan, 1965), p. 18.

But in his lesser-known *The Natural History of Religion* Hume turns from skepticism to suspicion. There he distinguishes the questions "concerning [religion's] foundation in reason" from those "concerning its origin in human nature."[2] He gives skeptical answers to the questions about the foundation of religion in reason in his most familiar writings on religion. But the questions concerning religion's origin in human nature give rise to the hermeneutics of suspicion in the *Natural History*.

Questions of origin turn out to be, in the first instance, questions of motive. Belief in an "invisible intelligent power" to whom prayers and sacrifices could be directed does not arise from "speculative curiosity" or "the pure love of truth." To lead people's attention beyond the immediacy of the here and now, "they must be actuated by some passion, which prompts their thought and reflection; some motive, which urges their first inquiry." Such motives include "the anxious concern for happiness, the dread of future misery, the terror of death, the thirst of revenge, and appetite for food and other necessaries."[3] In short, the originating motive for the religious life is the hopes and fears of ordinary life, especially the fears.

The hopes and fears that come to our attention in this way are not, at least not primarily, those that have been fashioned in the school of moral ideals. They are rather the hopes and fears of more or less immediate self-interest. Hume sees the "selfish view" they express at the heart of "idolatry or polytheism."[4] But since the negative effects that Hume sees stemming from this "selfish view" belong to popular religion as such and are not limited to polytheism, it appears that Hume is working toward a definition of idolatry or superstition — he uses the terms interchangeably — that depends more on the motivation of the believing soul than on the propositional content of belief. For him idolatry resides more in the heart than in the head.

Hume calls our attention to the structure of instrumental religion, the piety that is primarily motivated by the believing soul's self-interest. Like Luther and Barth he describes it as idolatry, superstition, and polytheism, and like Barth he refuses to exclude the practice of

2. David Hume, *The Natural History of Religion*, ed. H. E. Root (Stanford: Stanford University Press, 1957), p. 21. For a contemporary account of origin as precisely what raises suspicions rather than providing hoped-for legitimation, see Michel Foucault, "Nietzsche, Genealogy, History," in *The Foucault Reader*, ed. Paul Rabinow (New York: Pantheon, 1984), pp. 76-100.

3. Hume, pp. 27-28, 31.

4. Hume, p. 47.

metaphysically and liturgically orthodox Christianity from these descriptions.[5]

The first mark of instrumental religion, on Hume's account, is flattery. Where our relation to someone of superior power is primarily based on our hopes and fears concerning what we might get out of the relationship, the temptation to resort to flattery is all but unavoidable. The believing soul will naturally speak of adoration, but Hume's suspicion detects adulation. The difference is subtle but profound. Real adoration is extraordinarily difficult and rare, because it involves a self-forgetful transcendence of normal self-preoccupation.[6] Words and deeds of adulation may be externally indistinguishable from those of genuine adoration, but they are in fact exactly the opposite, for in them self-seeking knows nothing about self-forgetfulness. They are religious fictions, ironical hymns, creeds, and rites.

To the degree that Hume's suspicion is well founded on this point, the relation between believer and deity shows itself to be dishonest, founded on the falsehoods of flattery.[7] Naturally, if the believer is not utterly shameless and cynical, it will be necessary to hide this dishonesty not only from the deity but also from the believing soul. Piety becomes inseparable from self-deception.

The second mark of instrumental religion to which Hume calls our attention reveals that this dishonesty and self-deception are not restricted to the relation between believer and deity. My neighbor becomes its victim as well. Hume notes that idolatrous worship is "liable to this great inconvenience, that any practice or opinion, however barbarous or corrupted, may be *authorized by it*" and that "the greatest crimes have been found in many instances, *compatible with* a superstitious piety and devotion." At the conclusion of his study he finds

5. John Stuart Mill similarly notes that content does not render any doctrine immune from abuse. "But is utility the only creed which is able to furnish us with excuses for evil-doing and means of cheating our own conscience? They are afforded in abundance by all doctrines which recognize as a fact in morals the existence of conflicting considerations, which all doctrines do that have been believed by sane persons." *Utilitarianism,* ed. George Sher (Indianapolis: Hackett, 1979), p. 25.

6. No one has shown this more clearly than Gabriel Marcel. He describes a writer for whom admiration was "a humiliating state which he resisted with all his force." In this attitude Marcel detects "a burning preoccupation with self" that would best express itself by asking "but what about me, what becomes of me in that case?" *Creative Fidelity,* trans. Robert Rosthal (New York: Farrar, Straus, and Giroux, 1964), pp. 48-49. I have argued that true religion involves a "useless self-transcendence" that is the exact opposite of this posture. See *God, Guilt, and Death: An Existential Phenomenology of Religion* (Bloomington: Indiana University Press, 1984), chapter 8.

7. Hume, pp. 43, 65-67.

himself forced to ask, "What so pure as some of the morals, included in some theological systems? What so corrupt as some of the practices, to which these systems *give rise?*" And he immediately identifies such systems as "comfortable views."[8]

It is no accident that idolatrous and superstitious religion gives rise to crimes and corrupt practices. For the essence of instrumental religion on Hume's account is the self-seeking that makes the sacred a means to its own ends. Once again it looks as if he is giving a contextual definition of idolatry and superstition as the comfortable views that provide moral and religious legitimation for the barbarous and criminal behaviors which self-interest often generates.

Hume has intolerance and persecution particularly in mind. But the issue is obviously more general than crusades, inquisitions, and pogroms, dramatic as these examples may be. It concerns the origin of religion in human nature. To ask about this *origin* is at first to ask about the *motives* of the religious life, and thus about the inwardness of the believing soul. But it is also to ask about the *function* of the religious life, and thus about the public practices to which religion "gives rise."

Hume's suspicion of religion culminates in this question about the function of faith. Before Marx and Weber he insists that we notice religion's role in legitimizing social practices. On his view the philosophy of religion can be neither serious nor complete until this question is asked: What practices (life-styles, institutions, laws, customs) do these beliefs in fact (that is, in real life) serve to legitimate? And he calls our attention to the fact that religion *gives rise* to or legitimates social practices either actively, by authorizing them, or passively, merely by being compatible with them. Religion can give rise to anti-Semitism, apartheid, imperialistic nationalism, and revolutionary or counter-revolutionary terrorism either by giving explicit justifications for such practices, or, more subtly, by silent compatibility. In the latter case all that is necessary to legitimate the practices is an understanding that one can be, for example, a good Christian while engaging in them.

The question of the *origin* of religion in human nature is thus a question about both the *wishes* that lead to piety and the *work* that piety does for the faithful. But the question of function is not a second question in addition to the question about motive. For in a context where self-deception is all too real a possibility, function is often the best and sometimes the only clue to motive. We do not discover the real motives that direct our lives by looking to see what seems to be motivating us.

8. Hume, pp. 48, 72, 76, emphasis added.

For wherever there are grounds for suspicion those apparent motives will be false motives; they will be part of the rationalization by which we manage not to notice what is really going on. (Remember Frederic and Mabel!) Only when we find out what role our beliefs actually play in our lives will we discover what our really operative motives are. As Paul Roazen writes with reference to Freud, "It is a basic psychoanalytic rule that the result of an action, whatever the conscious motive, sheds light on the underlying intention; 'in human affairs the effect of an action frequently betrays the motivation of that action.' If religion has led to intolerance and aggression, may it not be that these were the very forces underlying religion in the first place?"[9]

No doubt most of us need help in distinguishing our apparent motives from our operative motives by careful attention to the actual role religion plays in our personal and public lives, thereby identifying the superstitious and idolatrous elements in our piety. Strange as it may still seem, Marx, Nietzsche, and Freud may offer us more help for this task of self-examination than almost anyone else.

9. Paul Roazen, *Freud: Political and Social Thought* (New York: Random House, 1968), p. 131. The internal quotation is from Kurt Eissler. A good example is found in one of Freud's most famous case studies. The "Rat Man" was faced with a "conflict as to whether he should remain faithful to the lady he loved in spite of her poverty, or whether he should follow in his father's footsteps and marry the lovely, rich, and well-connected girl who had been assigned to him . . . , [a conflict] between his love and the persisting influence of his father's wishes." In order to avoid this difficult choice, he fell ill with the obsessional neurosis Freud was treating. "The proof that this view was correct lies in the fact that the chief *result* of his illness was an obstinate incapacity for work, which allowed him to postpone his education for years. But the *results* of such an illness are never unintentional; what appears to be the *consequence* of the illness is in reality the *cause* or *motive* of falling ill" (10:198-99, first two sections of italics added, last three Freud's). References to Freud are given in the text by volume and page number in *The Standard Edition of the Complete Psychological Works of Sigmund Freud*, ed. and trans. James Strachey (London: Hogarth, 1953-74), 24 vols.

II Freud and the Psychoanalysis of the Believing Soul

5 Freud's Pessimism

Freud believes that religion is false. We will explore this belief briefly in the next chapter. But his best-known discussion of religion is not entitled "The Future of an Error," but *The Future of an Illusion* (1927). With this title he designates suspicion rather than skepticism as his primary mode of critique. Though his positivism entails that religion is without evidential warrant, his focus is on motive and function rather than evidence.[1] His account of the motives that lead to religion and the function it plays in believers' lives revolves around a single concept: consolation. It is his understanding of the nature and urgency of the need for consolation that I refer to in speaking of Freud's pessimism.

The categories developed by Robert Brustein in *The Theatre of Revolt* for interpreting much of modern drama can be helpful in locating that pessimism. Brustein distinguishes three kinds of revolt. "*Messianic revolt* occurs when the dramatist rebels against God and tries to take His place. . . . *Social revolt* occurs when the dramatist rebels against the conventions, morals, and values of the social organism. . . . *Existential revolt* occurs when the dramatist rebels against the conditions of his existence."[2] What distinguishes existential revolt from the other two and makes it a helpful concept for understanding Freud is precisely its pessimism. Where messianic revolt is defiant, existential revolt is resigned. Where social revolt is hopeful, existential revolt is despairing. Resigned despair permeates Freud's thinking.

Thus we cannot disagree with Erik Erikson's suggestion that

---

1. Paul Ricoeur, *Freud and Philosophy: An Essay on Interpretation*, trans. Denis Savage (New Haven: Yale University Press, 1970), pp. 26, 33, 234-35.
2. Robert Brustein, *The Theatre of Revolt: An Approach to the Modern Drama* (Boston: Little, Brown and Company, 1964), p. 16.

Freud's view of life is essentially tragic.[3] We should think of Arthur Miller's Willy Loman and Chekhov's three sisters rather than Oedipus and Antigone. For the hero of existential revolt is the antihero, and in spite of the Oedipus complex, we probably gain more insight from Freud into Dostoyevsky's Underground Man than into Oedipus.[4]

Philip Rieff relates Freudian bleakness to the issue of religion. "The permanence of conflict is Freud's leading theme, and part of his hostility to religion stems from an awareness that religion somewhere assumes a fixed point . . . at which conflict is resolved. In contrast, Freud maintains an intractable dualism; self and world remain antagonists, and every form of reconciliation must fail. Indeed, nothing so well represents Freud's own irreligion as his feeling for the irreconcilable."[5] Thus emerges the distinction between the consolations offered by religious illusions and the resignation implied by scientific truth.[6]

The world that is intractably antagonistic to the self is the dual world of nature and of culture, and religion is to be understood as rooted in the need for help in dealing with these powers (21:21).[7] Unlike civilization, nature "does not demand any restrictions of instinct from us, she would let us do as we liked; but she has her own particularly effective method of restricting us. She destroys us — coldly, cruelly, relentlessly, as it seems to us, and possibly through the very things that occasioned our satisfaction." After showing herself to us as earthquakes, floods, storms, and diseases, she finally appears as "the painful riddle of death," earning for herself the name of Fate (21:15-16; cf. 29, 72).

Civilization comes on the scene as our ally against the over-whelming and indifferent power of nature. Perhaps it is with Freud in mind that Peter Berger writes, "Every human society is, in the last resort, men banded together in the face of death."[8] But civilization is as indifferent to the individual's happiness as nature (21:140), and we pay a high price for its assistance. At every turn it demands renunciation

3. Erik H. Erikson, *Childhood and Society* (2nd ed.; New York: W. W. Norton, 1963), p. 280.

4. Brustein, pp. 28-29.

5. Philip Rieff, *Freud: The Mind of the Moralist* (Garden City, NY: Doubleday, 1961), p. 292.

6. Rieff, pp. 326-27. Cf. Freud, 21:32-33, 145. For references to Freud, see p. 29 n. 9.

7. See previous note.

8. Peter Berger, *The Sacred Canopy: Elements of a Sociological Theory of Religion* (Garden City, NY: Doubleday, 1967), p. 52. A similar motif, developed in much greater detail and with explicit reference to psychoanalysis, is found in Ernest Becker, *The Denial of Death* (New York: Macmillan, 1973).

of instincts, and it never hesitates to support its demands with coercion (21:5-11, 95). It demands that we channel large portions of our energy into work, and its primary taboos, those against incest and murder, are signs of the more general restrictions it places on our desire for satisfaction of our sexual and aggressive instincts (21:11-13, 101-15): "Civilized man has exchanged a portion of his possibilities of happiness for a portion of security" (21:115).

Not only does civilization demand that we negate our aggression by sublimating sexual energy into the aim-inhibited form of friendship and even the irrational and impossible form of universal neighbor love (21:109-11, 143), it also seeks to enforce its demands with the guilt that it helps to shape and that punishes the wish even when the act does not follow. In this way civilization brings about "permanent internal unhappiness" (21:123-28). Thus "guilt is the most important problem in the development of civilization and . . . the price we pay for our advance in civilization is a loss of happiness through the heightening sense of guilt" (21:134).[9]

Nature and culture are thus the devil and the deep blue sea, the rock and the hard place between which our longings for happiness are caught. But the reference to guilt indicates that the story is not quite as simple as is suggested by the picture of the self over against the worlds of nature and culture. For in guilt culture takes up internal residence to resist and restrict my pursuit of happiness, and it turns out that nature is also as much an internal as an external problem.

Freud develops this more complex and complete account in *The Ego and the Id* (1923) and in *New Introductory Lectures on Psychoanalysis* (1933). There he portrays the "poor ego," the I, the self, as serving "three tyrannical masters . . . [:] the external world, the super-ego and the id." The ego, that which I think of as I myself, is "driven by the id, confined by the super-ego, [and] repulsed by [external] reality. . . . If the ego is obliged to admit its weakness, it breaks out in anxiety — realistic anxiety regarding the external world, moral anxiety regarding the super-ego and neurotic anxiety regarding the strength of the passions in the id" (22:77-78; cf. 19:56).

We have already noted nature's threats of disaster and death and culture's demands for renunciation of instincts. We need now to look

9. These statements about guilt come from *Civilization and Its Discontents* (1930), emphasizing a theme Freud says was insufficiently developed in *The Future of an Illusion* (1927). Freud's formula for civilization's constraints on sex and aggression is the following: "When an instinctual trend undergoes repression, its libidinal elements are turned into symptoms, and its aggressive components into a sense of guilt" (21:139).

at the ways in which nature and culture become internal threats as id and superego respectively.

The id is nature as instinct or drive. With Plato, Freud distinguishes ego and id as reason and passions, and with Hume he notes that reason is the slave of the passions.[10] Thus he pictures the ego as a weak rider on a powerful horse, the id. The energy comes from the horse, the guidance from the rider (22:76-77; 19:25). Or so we would like it to be. Frequently, however, "a rider, if he is not to be parted from his horse, is obliged to guide it where it wants to go; so in the same way the ego is in the habit of transforming the id's will into action as if it were his own" (19:25). It is with reference to this impotence of the ego that Freud approvingly refers to Groddeck's claim that "we are 'lived' by unknown and uncontrollable forces" (19:23).[11]

So dominant is the id and so subordinate the other parts of the self that Freud even speaks of the id as "the whole person" (22:105; cf. 19:24-25). As early as The Interpretation of Dreams (1900), before Freud developed the language of id, ego, and superego, he saw instinctual drives as primary and the processes that would direct or restrain them as a secondary overlay (5:603-4).

If the id is nature internalized as instinct or drive, the superego is culture internalized as conscience. As the voice of culture, which can be thoroughly unreasonable, conscience is not to be identified with either the voice of reason or the voice of God. It is rather the voice of violence, and Freud goes out of his way to stress its "extraordinary harshness and severity towards the ego" (19:53).

The cruelty of the superego is especially manifest in the intense feelings of guilt that are so fundamental to obsessional neurosis and melancholia (depression). In the latter case

> we find that the excessively strong super-ego . . . rages against the ego with merciless violence, as if it had taken possession of the whole of the sadism available in the person concerned. Following

10. Hume writes, "Reason is and ought only to be the slave of the passions, and can never pretend to any other office than to serve and obey them." *A Treatise of Human Nature*, ed. L. A. Selby-Bigge (Oxford: Clarendon Press, 1888), p. 415. Freud accepts the description but does not agree that this is as it ought to be. Like Plato, he sees it as our task to increase the power of reason vis-à-vis the passions. It is his unwillingness to identify reason and the superego that permits him to be as critical of Plato as of Hume.

11. Freud borrows the term "id" from Groddeck and adds in a footnote, "Groddeck himself no doubt followed the example of Nietzsche, who habitually used this grammatical term [*das Es*, the it] for whatever in our nature is impersonal and, so to speak, subject to natural law" (19:23).

our view of sadism we should say that the destructive component had entrenched itself in the super-ego and turned against the ego. What is now holding sway in the super-ego is, as it were, a pure culture of the death instinct, and in fact it often enough succeeds in driving the ego into death, if the latter does not fend off its tyrant in time by the change round into mania. (19:53; cf. 22:60-61)

Of course, not everyone experiences suicidal depression. But each of us is, on Freud's view, an ego seeking to preside over an utterly unruly assembly, or, to change the metaphor, trying to mediate negotiations between implacable enemies, the demands of instinctive nature on the one hand and the external pressures of social requirements along with the internal pangs of guilt on the other. Whether we simply think in terms of the self confronting the worlds of nature and culture, or use the more complex model of the ego threatened by external reality (natural and cultural), the id, and the superego, the result is the same. The chances for human happiness are dim.

Freud identifies happiness with pleasure and finds the purpose of life in the pleasure principle. But the program of the pleasure principle "is at loggerheads with the whole world. . . . There is no possibility at all of its being carried through; all the regulations of the universe run counter to it. One feels inclined to say that the intention that man should be 'happy' is not included in the plan of 'Creation' " (21:76).

This pessimism is not quite as absolute as it seems. Freud acknowledges a "reduced sense" in which happiness is possible and thus a problem or task for the ego (21:83). The goal of therapy, in fact, is to give the patient's ego greater freedom, to enable it to move "from perceiving instincts to controlling them, from obeying instincts to inhibiting them. . . . Psycho-analysis is an instrument to enable the ego to achieve a progressive conquest of the id" (19:50n.1, 55-56). Hence the watchword of therapy: "Where id was, there ego shall be" (22:80).

We must not forget, however, that the happiness of the therapeutically empowered ego is a "reduced" happiness, not at all the fulfillment of the pleasure principle. It is a bad situation made a little better, as if slaves were no longer to be whipped or prisoners were to get better food. But there is no talk of emancipation or pardon. Thus Freud never really moves beyond the very early formulation in *Studies in Hysteria* (1895), addressed to patients wondering about the efficacy of therapy: "But you will be able to convince yourself that much will be gained if we succeed in transforming your hysterical misery into common unhappiness. With a mental life that has been restored to health you will be better armed against that unhappiness" (2:351).

6 Freud's Scientism

If Freud is the existential rebel who reacts to this human condition with resignation and despair, the believing soul seeks in religion a far deeper consolation. Freud is content to seek the minor ameliorations of the slave who is no longer whipped, though still a slave, or the prisoner who gets better food, while still in prison. But the religion of the "common man" is a

> system of doctrines and promises which on the one hand explains to him the riddles of this world with enviable completeness, and, on the other, assures him that a careful Providence will watch over his life and will compensate him in a future existence for any frustrations he suffers here. The common man cannot imagine this Providence otherwise than in the figure of an enormously exalted father. Only such a being can understand the needs of the children of men and be softened by their prayers and placated by the signs of their remorse. The whole thing is so patently infantile, so foreign to reality, that to anyone with a friendly attitude to humanity it is painful to think that the great majority of mortals will never be able to rise above this view of life. (21:74)

Of course, religion is not the only human strategy for dealing with the human predicament described in the previous chapter:

> Life, as we find it, is too hard for us; it brings us too many pains, disappointments and impossible tasks. In order to bear it we cannot dispense with palliative measures. 'We cannot do without auxiliary constructions,' as Theodor Fontane tells us. There are perhaps three such measures: powerful deflections, which cause us to make light of our misery; substitutive satisfactions, which diminish it; and

intoxicating substances, which make us insensitive to it. Something of the kind is indispensable. (21:75; cf. 16:372)

Actually Freud proceeds to identify seven "auxiliary constructions" in wide use: (1) chemical intoxicants, which serve as a "drowner of cares," (2) yoga techniques to kill off the instincts, (3) work as a displacement or sublimation of aggressive and sexual energy, (4) the illusions of art, which provide temporary escape to another world, (5) delusional negation of reality as in paranoia or religion, (6) unconstrained pursuit of sexual satisfaction, and (7) escape into neurotic illness (21:78-84).[1]

It is far from clear how this list of seven maps onto the earlier list of three, but that is hardly important. Freud's view is that all of these painkillers have serious limitations (no emancipation or pardon here), but that for each of us some will work better than others. "There is no golden rule which applies to everyone: every man must find out for himself in what particular fashion he can be saved" (21:83).

Actually, Freud is not the latitudinarian that he presents himself as here. In very early personal correspondence he expresses an utterly aristocratic contempt for the "mob," the "common people" who try the first and sixth of the strategies just listed.[2] But in his mature published writings, it is religion alone to which his personal hostility is directed. Philip Rieff opens his discussion of Freud on religion with the following perceptive paragraph:

> It is on the subject of religion that the judicious clinician grows vehement and disputatious. Against no other stronghold of repressive culture are the reductive weapons of psychoanalysis deployed

1. Freud's listing of religion and chemical pain killing as alternative strategies for dealing with the same problem (cf. 21:49) calls to mind Marx's oft-quoted identification of religion with the opium of the masses. We will look at that text later on in its context. Here it is worth noting that Nietzsche sees things the same way. Speaking of Germany he writes that "nowhere have the two great European narcotics, alcohol and Christianity, been abused more dissolutely." *Twilight of the Idols*, in *The Portable Nietzsche*, ed. and trans. Walter Kaufmann (New York: Viking Press, 1954), p. 507. Cf. Nietzsche's *The Gay Science*, trans. Walter Kaufmann (New York: Random House, 1974), p. 147.

2. Ernest Jones, *The Life and Work of Sigmund Freud*, one-volume edition by Lionel Trilling and Stephen Marcus (Garden City, NY: Doubleday, 1963), pp. 122-23. Freud's identification of the "common man" with the "poor" in this letter makes it clear that he has in mind a hierarchy as much economic as cultural. On the positive side, he seems to favor the third and fourth strategies: work — especially his kind of work, science — and art. He quotes Goethe: "He who possesses science and art also has religion; but he who possesses neither of those two, let him have religion" (21:74n.1).

in such open hostility. Freud's customary detachment fails him here. Confronting religion, psychoanalysis shows itself for what it is: the last great formulation of nineteenth-century secularism, complete with substitute doctrine and cult. . . . What first impresses the student of Freud's psychology of religion is its polemical edge. Here and here alone, the grand Freudian animus, otherwise concealed behind the immediacies of case histories and the emergencies of practical therapeutics, breaks out.[3]

No doubt there are biographical factors at work here, including the Christian anti-Semitism that Freud experienced from boyhood on. Furthermore, Freud's tolerance extends only to strategies that are themselves tolerant of other strategies, and he does not find this in religion. In the paragraph immediately following his announcement that we must each find our own path to salvation, he writes, "Religion restricts this play of choice and adaptation, since it imposes equally on everyone its own path to the acquisition of happiness and protection from suffering" (21:84).

But Freud has little to say on either of these points. The brief against belief that he develops at considerable length is rather summarized in the passage cited at the beginning of this chapter. There he repudiates the consolations of religion because belief in the Heavenly Father is "so patently infantile, so foreign to reality. . . ." We need to explore these two critiques, which, as we shall see, are quite distinct from each other. The former expresses Freudian suspicion, the latter Freudian skepticism. As I argued in chapter 2, these two types of intellectual assault on religion call for entirely different responses.

It is on epistemological grounds that Freud finds religion "so foreign to reality." His skepticism takes the form of scientism or positivism or empirical verificationism. Geography teaches that "Constance lies on the Bodensee," and a student song continues: "If you don't believe it, go and see" (21:25). Religious beliefs cannot be confirmed in this way. Freud formulates the general point as follows: "But scientific work is the only road which can lead us to a knowledge of reality outside ourselves. It is once again merely an illusion to expect anything from intuition and introspection; they can give us nothing but particulars about our own mental life, which are hard to interpret, never any information about the questions which religious doctrine finds it so easy to answer," for ex-

---

3. Philip Rieff, *Freud: The Mind of the Moralist* (Garden City, NY: Doubleday, 1961), p. 281.

ample, questions concerning God and immortality (21:31-32). In his *New Introductory Lectures on Psychoanalysis* (1933) Freud specifically asks whether psychoanalysis entails any specific *Weltanschauung*. No, he says, "as a specialist science . . . it is quite unfit to construct a *Weltanschauung* of its own: it must accept the scientific one. . . . It asserts that there are no sources of knowledge of the universe other than the intellectual working-over of carefully scrutinized observations — in other words, what we call research — and alongside of it no knowledge derived from revelation, intuition or divination" (22:158-59).

Religion is distinguished from the other auxiliary constructions to be picked on by Freud because religion alone makes unwarranted truth claims in the search for happiness. These truth claims are the basis for religion's attempt to prescribe a single path for all and for the deeper ground of "the grand Freudian animus." Thus art, religion, and philosophy may seek to contribute to human happiness in ways that make them rivals of science. But of the "three powers which may dispute the basic position of science, religion alone is to be taken seriously as an enemy" (22:160). For art is content to be illusion and makes no truth claims, while philosophy either restricts itself to the scientific *Weltanschauung* and becomes positivism or makes pretensions to supra-scientific truths but has no significant impact on the great mass of the people.

In the concluding chapter of *The Future of an Illusion* Freud formulates the following objection against his project: "That sounds splendid! A race of men who have renounced all illusions and have thus become capable of making their existence of earth tolerable! I, however, cannot share your expectations. . . . We seem now to have exchanged roles: you emerge as an enthusiast who allows himself to be carried away by illusions . . ." (21:51). In reply, Freud seeks to defend his faith in science. "Our God Λόγος" is not illusory, he claims. "We believe that it is possible for scientific work to gain some knowledge about the reality of the world, by means of which we can increase our power and in accordance with which we can arrange our life. If this belief is an illusion then we are in the same position as you. But science has given us evidence by its numerous and important successes that it is no illusion" (21:54-55).

Many contemporary philosophers of science have raised questions about the claim that science gives us "knowledge about the reality of the world."[4] But for the moment we can put such doubts aside. There

---

4. I have in mind the work of Duhem, Poincaré, Kuhn, Feyerabend, Hanson, and Foucault, among others.

can in any case be no question that scientific "knowledge" increases our power. What Freud fails to notice is that even if science is indeed not an illusion, scientism is another matter entirely. Freud has not given us the logic by which "Science gives us knowledge of reality" becomes "*Nothing but science* gives us knowledge of reality." It would not make much of a school ditty, but if we append "if you don't believe it, go and see" to either of the formulations of Freudian positivism given three paragraphs before this one, the result is embarrassing for Freud: It is far from clear where one would look for empirical, scientific verification of his claim about science, which turns out itself to be no scientific claim and hence, on Freud's own terms, to give us no knowledge about reality. Freud lacks the sophistication of later positivists who acknowledged that their own dogmatic[5] formulations were useful nonsense or merely recommendations of policy.[6]

This self-referential refutation of scientism is as familiar as it is forceful. Neither nineteenth-century positivism of truth nor twentieth-century positivism of meaning (logical positivism) has offered a cogent defense against it. My own favorite formulation of the point comes from William James's famous essay "The Will to Believe." He writes that "*a rule of thinking which would absolutely prevent me from acknowledging certain kinds of truth if those kinds of truth were really ther_, would be an irrational rule.*" A few pages earlier James identifies such a view as "an insane logic."[7]

---

5. I use "dogmatic" here in two senses. On the one hand it connotes an uncritical acceptance of belief, while on the other it suggests that a belief functions like a religious doctrine. Freud's scientific *Weltanschauung* is the framework for what Rieff refers to as his "substitute doctrine." See p. 40 n. 3 above.

6. See Carl Hempel, "Problems and Changes in the Empiricist Criterion of Meaning," in Leonard Linsky, ed., *Semantics and the Philosophy of Language* (Urbana: University of Illinois Press, 1952).

7. William James, *Essays on Faith and Morals*, ed. Ralph Barton Perry (Cleveland: World, 1962), pp. 59, 56.

7 Freud's Suspicion I: Dreams and Wish Fulfillment

It is because of Freud's positivism that he finds belief in Providence "so foreign to reality." Insofar as his atheism rests on his scientism it can be classified as skeptical or evidential atheism. As such it deserves to be refuted, and I believe it is best refuted by noting with James what an "insane logic" it practices, what an "irrational rule" it represents. It says, in effect, "Anything my net doesn't catch isn't a fish,"[1] and thereby ends up revealing both its dogmatism and its incoherence.

It is quite a different story when Freud finds belief in a heavenly father to be "so patently infantile." Here we encounter the dimension of Freud's atheism that particularly concerns us, his suspicion. In keeping with the suggestion that we treat suspicious unbelief differently from skeptical unbelief, I will devote much more attention to Freudian suspicion than to Freudian skepticism. The aim of this attention will not be to refute Freud, but to learn to take him seriously.

As "foreign to reality," religion is an error; as "so patently infantile," it is an illusion. We move, therefore, from an epistemological category to a psychological category. Since illusion will be defined in terms of wish fulfillment, and since wish fulfillment is at the heart of Freud's theory of dreams, we can say not only that "*interpretation of dreams is the royal road to a knowledge of the unconscious activities of the mind*" in general, but also that it provides the path to understanding Freud's critique of religion in particular (5:608). We must turn our attention briefly to *The Interpretation of Dreams* (1900) and to the popular summary of the dream theory in *Introductory Lectures on Psychoanalysis* (1916-17).

Freud introduces the notion of wish fulfillment while exploring

---

1. I am indebted to John E. Smith for this helpful formulation.

the "underlying kinship between dreams and mental disorders," a linkage hinted at by Kant and Schopenhauer. He quotes the following from Radestock's book on dreams:

> A man tormented by physical and mental suffering obtains from dreams what reality denies him: health and happiness. So too in mental disease there are bright pictures of happiness, grandeur, eminence and wealth. The supposed possession of property and the imaginary fulfilment of wishes . . . often constitute the chief content of a delirium. A woman who has lost a loved child experiences the joys of motherhood in her delirium; a man who has lost his money believes himself immensely rich; a girl who has been deceived feels that she is tenderly loved.

Freud comments that this passage "shows quite clearly that ideas in dreams and in psychoses have in common the characteristic of being *fulfilments of wishes*. My own researches have taught me that in this fact lies the key to a psychological theory of both dreams and psychoses" (4:90-91).[2]

Daydreams provide an important hint in this direction. Their content is "dominated by a very transparent motive. They are scenes and events in which the subject's egoistic needs of ambition and power or his erotic wishes find satisfaction" (15:98). Since daydreams (1) "are in fact wish-fulfilments, fulfilments of ambitions and erotic wishes which are well known to us," (2) lack the linkage to sleep and the hallucinatory character of dreams, and (3) are nevertheless called dreams, Freud concludes, "Linguistic usage, therefore, has a suspicion of the fact that wish-fulfilment is a chief characteristic of dreams" (15:130).

Children's dreams are often indistinguishable from daydreams, providing a *"direct, undisguised fulfilment of [some] wish"* (15:128). Thus a boy who had to give a basket of cherries to someone else as a birthday gift, most unwillingly, dreamed that night that he had eaten the cherries. A girl who had been unable to eat all day because of illness dreamed of strawberries and other favorite foods (15:127, 132). Freud is reminded of the proverb "What do geese dream of? Maize" (4:130-32).[3]

---

2. The intimate parallel between dreams and the symptoms of mental disorders is utterly fundamental for Freud. It already appears in the "Preliminary Communication" to *Studies in Hysteria* (1893, in vol. 2 of the *Standard Edition*) and in the "Project for a Scientific Psychology" (1895, in vol. 1). It is basic to both of the works currently under consideration. See 4:xv, xix, xxiii, xxix, 101-2, 303; 5:568-69, 607-8 for a few sample statements.

3. Freud cites a collection of related proverbs, reminding us that pigs dream

Some adult dreams are also, like daydreams, undisguised wish fulfillments. These are often, but not always, related to pressing physical needs such as hunger, thirst, and sexual desire. Among the examples cited by Freud is the grandmother of the girl who dreamed of strawberries. When *she* was unable to eat because of illness, she, like the girl, dreamed of eating an unusually delicious meal (15:132).

More important, however, is the obvious fact that many dreams of both adults and children, so far from being undisguised wish fulfillments, are extremely unpleasant sources of fear and anxiety. No one is likely to confuse a nightmare with a daydream. This does not lead Freud to abandon the wish fulfillment theory, only to formulate it more carefully. All dreams, he continues to insist, perform a wish-fulfilling function, but this can be seen in most dreams only after they have been interpreted, since their manifest content and their latent content are not identical (15:214, 222, 168). The proper definition is: *A dream is a (disguised) fulfillment of a (suppressed or repressed) wish* (4:160). The crucial distinction between manifest and latent content points to the crucial topic of distortion in dreams.

Much of what we need to understand on this topic can be found by looking at the first two dreams that Freud gives detailed interpretations to in *The Interpretation of Dreams,* the dream of Irma's injection and the dream of the uncle with a yellow beard. Like so many of the dreams Freud discusses in detail, these two are his own.

The circumstances in which Freud dreamed about Irma's injection are the key to its interpretation. Freud was treating Irma for hysteria and was especially anxious about the therapy because Irma and her family were personal friends and because Irma was resisting his therapeutic suggestions. During a vacation break in therapy, Freud received a report from a medical colleague, Otto, who had seen her: "She's better, but not quite well." Freud thought he detected a reproof in this report, both from Otto and from Irma's family. "The same evening I wrote out Irma's case history . . . in order to justify myself" (4:106). And the same evening he dreamed about Irma and Otto, with the same goal of self-justification.

In the dream Freud offers a fourfold defense. (1) It is Irma's fault. Freud reproaches her for not accepting his solution to her problems and gives her characteristics that identify her with two other women whom

---

of acorns and hens of millet as well. While in *Dreams* the proverb about geese and maize is related to the boy's dream of eating the cherries, in the *Introductory Lectures* it is related to daydreams (15:130-31).

Freud thinks would be recalcitrant patients. He actually says, *"If you still get pains, it's your own fault"* (4:108-10). (2) Her problems are organic. Since Freud is only treating her for hysteria, he is not responsible for the illness if it has an organic basis. (3) Dr. M., who suggests an organic diagnosis, does not understand hysteria or take it seriously. He is not as good a doctor as Freud. (4) It is Otto's fault. Irma's problems come from an unwise injection administered by Otto, probably with an unsterile syringe.

Freud (awake) recognizes that it is not entirely consistent to take comfort from the organic diagnosis and then ridicule Dr. M. for offering it.

> The whole plea — for the dream was nothing else — reminded one vividly of the defence put forward by the man who was charged by one of his neighbours with having given him back a borrowed kettle in a damaged condition. The defendant asserted first, that he had given it back undamaged; secondly, that the kettle had a hole in it when he borrowed it; and thirdly, that he had never borrowed a kettle from his neighbour at all. (4:119-20)

But Freud is desperate and willing to try anything.

It is not just logic that he is willing to suspend; it is decency as well. Freud speaks of the *consolation* (a central concept in his critique of religion) offered in his dream (4:114-15), but only the second self-justification offers an innocent consolation. The keynote of the other three is revenge (4:115, 119). Freud's dream is his revenge on Irma, Dr. M., and Otto for failing to agree with Freud's therapy or for reporting the fact that his patient was not wholly well. The blame for her illness is specifically attributed to Irma and Otto. While there may be grounds for the reproach against Irma, that against Otto, the primary target of the dream, is entirely fabricated.

Not all of this is immediately obvious, but Freud's revenge on Irma and Otto is right on the surface, and Freud uses this dream much as he uses daydreams and children's dreams. The closing words of the chapter are the title of the following chapter: *"A dream is the fulfilment of a wish"* (4:121). It is, then, only the next chapter after that that is titled "Distortion in Dreams." But we already have in hand the clue to distortion in Freud's thirst for revenge. In itself the desire for consolatory vindication in the face of doubts about one's work is not so bad. But the vindictive spirit in which Freud carries it out is not pleasant to behold. In real life some of us are shamelessly vindictive, but most of us try to hide our uglier motives from others and from ourselves. Even

in our dreams, as Freud will try to show, we often disguise from ourselves motives that we can acknowledge only with shame.

That is what happens in the dream of the uncle with a yellow beard
(which Freud tells in the chapter on distortion in dreams). The background is the good news that Freud has been recommended by two
professors for a much-desired academic appointment and the unpleasant
reminder that others at least as well qualified have not been appointed
"due to denominational considerations" that apply to Freud as well,
which is to say they were all Jewish (4:136-37). In the dream Freud's friend
R. is his uncle, for whom (in the dream but not in real life) Freud has great
affection. His uncle's face is elongated and he has a yellow beard.

There is no transparent wish fulfillment in this dream. In fact,
Freud found it at first to be sheer nonsense. But then he thought,

> If one of your patients who was interpreting a dream could find
> nothing better to say than that it was nonsense, you would take him
> up about it and *suspect* that the dream had some disagreeable story
> at the back of it which he *wanted to avoid becoming aware of.* Treat
> yourself in the same way. Your opinion that the dream is nonsense
> only means that you have an internal resistance against interpreting
> it. (4:138, emphasis added).

This suspicion proved to be well founded.

The uncle in question was Freud's Uncle Josef, who had been
punished for a criminal offense in connection with a business deal. His
brother, Freud's father, deeply wounded by the event, had said that
Josef was more a simpleton than a criminal. By identifying R. with
Uncle Josef, Freud makes R. into a simpleton. But why? The clue comes
from a conversation several days earlier with another friend, N. Like
R., N. was one whose hoped-for appointment had run into "denominational" difficulties. In discussing this with Freud, N. mentioned a
legal action brought against him earlier by a woman attempting to
blackmail him. The case was thrown out of court. But N. thought that
this might be the excuse used against him by the government. So he
said to Freud: "*You* have an unblemished character" (4:139).

The dream is now clear to Freud.

> My Uncle Josef represented my two colleagues who had not been
> appointed to professorships — the one as a simpleton and the other
> as a criminal. I now saw too why they were represented in this light.
> If the appointment of my friends R. and N. had been postponed for
> "denominational" reasons, my own appointment was also open to

doubt; if, however, I could attribute the rejection of my two friends to other reasons, which did not apply to me, my hopes would remain untouched. (4:139)

But Freud remains troubled "over the lightheartedness with which I had degraded two of my respected colleagues in order to keep open my own path to a professorship." He realizes that the "well-designed slander" with which he does this, like that of Otto in the previous dream, represents not his beliefs but his wishes. In the mirror of his dream Freud sees a man who wishes his friends were simpletons and criminals so that his own career might advance. The ugliness of these wishes is the clue to the intensity of the affection Uncle Josef (= friends R. and N.) suddenly receives in the dream.

> The affection in the dream did not belong to the latent content, to the thoughts that lay behind the dream; it stood in contradiction to them and was calculated to conceal the true interpretation of the dream. And probably that was precisely its *raison d'être*. . . . My dream-thoughts had contained a slander against R.; and, in order that I might not notice this, what appeared in the dream was the opposite, a feeling of affection for him. (4:140-41)

To generalize,

> there are some dreams which are undisguised fulfilments of wishes. But in cases where the wish-fulfilment is unrecognizable, where it has been disguised, there must have existed some inclination to put up a defense against the wish; and owing to this defense the wish was unable to express itself except in a distorted shape. . . . A similar difficulty confronts the political writer who has disagreeable truths to tell to those in authority. . . . A writer must beware of the censorship, and on its account he must soften and distort the expression of his opinion . . . must conceal his objectionable pronouncement beneath some apparently innocent disguise. . . . (4:141-42)[4]

4. When Freud first introduced the censorship metaphor in 1895, he identified it with two concepts that are utterly central to psychoanalytic theory, resistance and defense. Ideas that get censored are those "of a distressing nature, calculated to arouse the affects of shame, of self-reproach and of psychical pain, and the feeling of being harmed; they were all of a kind that one would prefer not to have experienced, that one would rather forget." Censorship is thus a defense against noticing them. By the same token, the same energy that seeks to hide them in the first place will not welcome subsequent attempts to bring them to light. Thus therapy is bound to meet with resistance precisely when it gets close to the heart of the matter (2:313; cf. 327).

Dreams are the *disguised* fulfillment of *repressed* wishes because there are two "forces" or "agencies" at work in their production, one that generates wishes and one that censors them (4:143-46). Not surprisingly, just as daydreams are fulfillments of egoistic or erotic wishes (15:98, 130), so our psychic censorship is directed against "an unbridled and ruthless egoism" that, "freed from all ethical bonds, also finds itself at one with all the demands of sexual desire, even those which have long been condemned by our aesthetic upbringing and those which contradict all the requirements of moral restraint. . . . These censored wishes appear to rise up out of a positive Hell" (15:142-43).

Freud has not yet developed the language of id, ego, and superego for talking about all this, but it is already clear that wish fulfillment gets caught up in the conflict between the superego on the one hand and the amoral wishfulness of the id and the ego on the other. The result is a dissimulation of our actual operative motives that evokes systematic suspicion in Freudian thought.

8 Freud's Suspicion II: Doctrines and Wish Fulfillment

One of Freud's hysterical patients is called "Dora" in the case study devoted to her. She was a brilliant young woman, whose intellectual gifts were placed in the service of resistance to Freud's interpretations of her symptoms. Philip Rieff writes, "In this earnest debate, Freud's tactic was not to dispute Dora's logic but to suspect her motives."[1]

We have just seen that this is the form Freud's suspicion takes in interpreting his own dreams as well. Recognizing that his opinion that the dream about the uncle with a yellow beard was nonsense was resistance rather than insight, he decides to "suspect that the dream had some disagreeable story at the back of it which he wanted to avoid becoming aware of" (4:138). And when he discovers a dubious logic in the dream about Irma's injection, ridiculing Dr. M. for offering a diagnosis that he offers himself in his own defense, he uses this irrationality not to refute the dream but to uncover its hidden motivation. For he recognizes that the unity and coherence of the dream lie in its motive, not in its logic. Its logic, rather, is in the service of its motive.

Ouch! That goes against the philosophical anthropology that with Plato sees reason as supreme and with Descartes sees the mind as fully transparent to careful introspection. But Freud thinks that "the interpretation of dreams may enable us to draw conclusions as to the structure of our mental apparatus which we have hoped for in vain from philosophy," and in the presence of a mind capable of producing the kind of distortion he finds in his own dreams and then resisting its exposure, he says, "Psycho-analysis is justly suspicious" (4:145; 5:517).[2]

---

1. Sigmund Freud, *Dora: An Analysis of a Case of Hysteria*, ed. Philip Rieff (New York: Macmillan, 1963), p. 18. For the concept of resistance see above, chapter 7, n. 4.
2. Actually, we have noted in chapters 2 through 4 that an anti-Platonic,

It is important to note that it is not just dreams which evoke Freudian suspicion; it is the mind capable of producing them. Freud does not just generalize from his dreams to yours and mine; he generalizes from dreams to non-hallucinatory thought. He believes that the interpretation of dreams provides striking confirmation of Bacon's claim that "the human understanding is no dry light," that "what a man had rather were true he more readily believes," and "that whatever his mind seizes and dwells upon with peculiar satisfaction is to be held in suspicion" (see chapter 2 above).

Thus in the famous seventh chapter of *The Interpretation of Dreams*, where Freud tries to develop the full ramifications of his discovery, he describes "all thinking" as "no more than a circuitous path" from the memory of a satisfaction to a repetition of that satisfaction.

> Accordingly, thinking must aim at freeing itself more and more from the exclusive regulation by the unpleasure principle [the desire to maximize pleasure and minimize pain] and at restricting the development of affect in thought activity. . . . As we all know, however, that aim is seldom attained completely, even in normal mental life, and our thinking always remains exposed to falsification by interference from the unpleasure principle. (4:602-3)

That reason is, even if it should not be, the slave of the passions, as Hume has said, can hardly be expressed more forcefully than this. "Thought is after all nothing but a substitute for a hallucinatory wish; and it is self-evident that dreams must be wish-fulfilments, since nothing but a wish can set our mental apparatus at work. Dreams, which fulfil their wishes along the short path of regression, have merely preserved for us in that respect a sample of the psychical apparatus's primary method of working, a method which was abandoned as being inefficient" (5:567). It is important to recognize that what is abandoned in rational, wakeful adults is neither the wishes nor the demand that they be satisfied, but only the attempt to do so through hallucination, a method to which we revert in sleep and in psychosis.[3]

If we underestimate the degree to which our thinking serves not

---

anti-Cartesian suspicion is to be found in numerous non-Freudian philosophers (or should we call them Freudian?).

3. This formulation obviously brings thinking into close proximity with daydreaming. The differences are that thinking, like dreaming and unlike daydreams, is not satisfied with what it knows to be imaginary and also that thinking, again like dreaming, is subject to the distortions of censorship, the absence of which is essential to daydreaming. In both respects thinking is subject to self-deception.

truth but wish fulfillment, and if we overestimate the degree to which our reason has freed itself from the mastery of passion, desire, and affect, Freud thinks this is primarily due to our moral decency. The force that censors the amoral wishes of ego and id, forcing them to travel in disguise, then resisting all attempts to bring the masquerade to an end, is nothing but our moral disapproval of those wishes. Our morality tends less to expose our deepest desires than to blind us to them. With the help of the disguises that our intellect can always provide, including rationalizations, we manage not to notice whatever our conscience cannot approve. Self-deception would be as impossible as it would be unnecessary if we had no moral scruples.

For example, Freud believes that children envy parental privileges and regularly direct death wishes toward their parents, especially the parent of the same sex. While interpreting his own dreams he found this to be true of himself. He was deeply ambivalent toward his father, loving and hating him at the same time. But this is not usually noticed. "We must distinguish," he writes, "between what the cultural standards of filial piety demand of this relation and what everyday observation shows it in fact to be. More than one occasion for hostility lies concealed in the relation between parents and children — a relation which affords the most ample opportunities for wishes to arise which cannot pass the censorship." With specific reference to the relation between father and son he writes, "The sanctity which we attribute to the rules laid down in the Decalogue has, I think, blunted our powers of perceiving the real facts. We seem scarcely to venture to observe that the majority of mankind disobey the Fifth Commandment" (4:256).

What we "scarcely venture to observe" in the majority of our fellow humans we are even less likely to notice in ourselves. It is in self-consciousness above all that the Decalogue shines darkness on the deceitfulness of the human heart. It is for this reason that in seeking to interpret a dream or neurotic symptom, Freud must make two demands of his patients: "an increase in the attention he pays to his own psychical perceptions and the elimination of the criticism by which he normally sifts the thoughts that occur to him . . . since it is precisely his critical attitude which is responsible for his being unable, in the ordinary course of things, to achieve the desired unravelling of his dream or obsessional idea or whatever it may be" (4:101; cf. 101-3).[4]

Rational thought is in the service of amoral desire, and moral

---

4. Prior to *The Interpretation of Dreams*, while he was developing the method of free association in treating hysteria, Freud discovered the importance of suspending the critical faculty. See 2:148-49.

commitment tends to keep us from noticing this. It is especially in *The Future of an Illusion* that Freud develops his claim that religious thought is no exception to this principle. We have already seen (in chapter 5) the basis for an overwhelming desire for consolation, the overwhelming power of nature and culture and our "infantile helplessness" before them (21:5-20, 72-74). Accordingly Freud tries to show "that religious ideas have arisen from the same need as have all the other achievements of civilization: from the necessity of defending oneself against the crushingly superior force of nature. To this a second motive was added — the urge to rectify the shortcomings of civilization which made themselves painfully felt" (21:21; cf. 17-18).

The way it works is quite simple. What we want is someone strong enough to protect us from death and friendly enough to compensate us for the renunciations demanded by our culture. Would not eternal life in paradise do both jobs quite well? Accordingly, "We shall tell ourselves that it would be very nice if there were a God who created the world and was a benevolent Providence, and if there were a moral order in the universe and an after-life; but it is a very striking fact that all this is exactly as we are bound to wish it to be" (21:33; cf. 30).[5]

Actually Freud thinks it striking only in the sense that it is noteworthy, not that it is surprising. With reference to the idea that religious ideas are motivated by needs, he writes, "I do not find that so striking. Do you suppose that human thought has no practical motives, that it is simply the expression of a disinterested curiosity? That is surely very improbable" (21:22; cf. 47). Here we find the general suspicion of the human intellect that emerged from *The Interpretation of Dreams* explicitly applied to its religious operations.

Freud's conclusion is that religious ideas "which are given out as teachings, are not precipitates of experience or end-results of thinking: they are illusions, fulfilments of the oldest, strongest and most urgent wishes of mankind. The secret of their strength lies in the strength of those wishes." Here we discover that Freud uses the term "illusion" as a technical term. "Thus we call a belief an illusion when a wish-fulfilment is a prominent factor in its motivation, and in doing so we disregard its relations to reality, just as the illusion itself sets no store by verification." It was, for example, "an illusion of Columbus's that he had discovered a new sea-route to the Indies. The part played

---

5. It is because this "benevolent Providence" is grounded in the adult's "infantile helplessness" and has "the father . . . hidden behind every divine figure as its nucleus" that Freud finds religion to be "so patently infantile" (21:17-19 and 72-74).

by his wish in this error is very clear." Indo-Germanic racial superiority and the asexuality of children are also illusions (21:30-31).

Freud is careful to distinguish illusions, in this technical sense of the term, from delusions.

> What is characteristic of illusions is that they are derived from human wishes. In this respect they come near to psychiatric delusions. But they differ from them, too, apart from the more complicated structure of delusions. In the case of delusions, we emphasize as essential their being in contradiction with reality. Illusions need not necessarily be false. . . . For instance, a middle-class girl may have the illusion that a prince will come and marry her; and a few such cases have occurred. That the Messiah will come and found a golden age is much less likely. . . . To assess the truth-value of religious doctrines does not lie within the scope of the present enquiry. It is enough for us that we have recognized them as being, in their psychological nature, illusions. (21:31, 33)

Paul Ricoeur underscores this truth neutrality of the illusion label: "The essential characteristic of illusions is not their similarity to error in the epistemological sense of the word but their relationship with other fantasies and their inclusion within the semantics of desire." This is why "what is involved is *not the truth* of the foundation of religious ideas *but their function* in balancing the renunciations and satisfactions through which man tries to make his harsh life tolerable."[6]

It will not be long before Freud seems to forget this distinction. In *Civilization and Its Discontents,* just three years later, he simply identifies religious beliefs with delusions (21:81-85). But, given his careful definition of illusion, we can recognize that he can do so only by combining the suspicion that identifies religious beliefs as illusions with the skepticism that identifies them as errors.[7] But that skepticism rests on Freud's scientism, his elevation of science from a practice to a *Weltanschauung.* Having already noticed the self-referential contradiction of claiming truth for the unscientific proposition that "Science is the only way to truth," the believing soul is likely at this point to find the temptation to refute Freud all but irresistible once again.

---

6. Paul Ricoeur, *Freud and Philosophy: An Essay on Interpretation,* trans. Denis Savage (New Haven: Yale University Press, 1970), pp. 234-35, emphasis added.

7. Thus when Freud writes in *Totem and Taboo* that "it would be another matter if demons really existed. But we know that, like gods, they are creatures of the human mind . . ." this is a premise and not a conclusion of his psychoanalytic analysis (13:24).

9 On Remembering When Not to Refute Atheism

But once again this temptation should be resisted, though Freud is not invulnerable to critique. Two objections can be raised against his treatment of religious beliefs as illusions.

The first concerns its logic. Freud's critique is an *ad hominem* critique, directed against the believer's believing, not against the believer's belief. He is careful to point out that an illusion is not necessarily an error and may in fact be true. By doing this he avoids the genetic fallacy of discrediting a belief because of the way it comes to be held. "My mother told me so" may not be a very reliable epistemological principle, but many of the things our mothers have told us are in fact true. Up to this point all is in order.

But when Freud suddenly (in *Civilization and Its Discontents*) forgets all about his own carefully drawn distinction between illusions and delusions, he falls prey to the *ad hominem* and genetic fallacies, illegitimately suggesting that we should reject religious beliefs because of some flaw in the believing soul. For the sake of the truth and for the protection of the logically unsophisticated, the believing soul may be more than happy to point out this carelessness on Freud's part and to remind Freud that without his (indefensible) scientism, his suspicion cannot show religious beliefs to be delusory, that is, false.

This objection is well founded. Kant serves as a helpful example. He seeks to free his own moral ideals from precisely this pseudo-refutation, which goes by the name of "realism" in ethics. Those who teach ethics to today's young people will surely have discovered how important and difficult it is to preserve ethical norms from the ultimate put-down, which is: "But people don't really act that way." As if, for example, the sexual revolution had rendered the seventh commandment obsolete. Kant was keenly aware of the problem. We have already seen (in chapter 3) that his suspicion in the moral realm is much like that of Mabel's sisters. But while he insists that one need not be an "enemy of virtue" but only a "cool observer" to notice that "we everywhere come upon the dear self" trying to put the facade of morality on its egoistic deeds and motives, he insists that the strict imperatives of duty are not in the least bit discredited by this fact. Rather, "reason unrelentingly commands actions of which the world has perhaps hitherto never provided an example and whose feasibility might well be doubted by one who bases everything upon experience; for instance, even though there might never yet have been a sincere friend, still pure sincerity in friendship is nonetheless required of every man. . . ."[1]

Just as the validity of moral norms is not affected by the immorality of those who espouse them, so the truth of beliefs is not affected by the irrationality of those who believe them. Ricoeur makes clear the implication of the distinction between illusions and delusions in this regard. He assumes

> that psychoanalysis is necessarily iconoclastic, regardless of the faith or nonfaith of the psychoanalyst, and that this "destruction" of religion can be the counterpart of a faith purified of all idolatry. Psychoanalysis as such cannot go beyond the necessity of iconoclasm. This necessity is open to a double possibility, that of faith and that of nonfaith, but the decision about these two possibilities does not rest with psychoanalysis. . . . The question remains open for every man whether the destruction of idols is without remainder; this question no longer falls within the competency of psychoanalysis.[2]

It is in the very next sentence that Ricoeur makes the point, cited above in chapter 8, that psychoanalysis involves the function rather than the truth of religious beliefs. The suspicion that brings to light the role of wish fulfillment in holding religious beliefs cannot settle the question of their truth value.[3]

---

1. Immanuel Kant, *Grounding for the Metaphysics of Morals*, trans. James W. Ellington (Indianapolis: Hackett, 1981), p. 407.

2. Paul Ricoeur, *Freud and Philosophy*, trans. Denis Savage (New Haven: Yale University Press, 1970), pp. 230, 235. Cf. *The Conflict of Interpretations: Essays in Hermeneutics*, ed. Don Ihde (Evanston: Northwestern University Press, 1974), pp. 144-45, 190, 440. Erik Erikson agrees: "Clinical knowledge, then, like any knowledge, is but a tool in the hands of a faith or a weapon in the service of a superstition." Erik H. Erikson, *Childhood and Society* (2nd ed.; New York: W. W. Norton, 1963), p. 417.

3. Of course, it does not follow that religious beliefs are true just because

The second objection to Freud's talk of religious belief as illusion is psychological. We can call it the *tu quoque* strategy for discrediting Freud, the Latin phrase meaning, in most straightforward terms, "it takes one to know one." Again it may be helpful to begin with an example from ethics rather than with the critique of religion. Suppose a conservative like F. A. Hayek is tired of hearing about justice when he wants to talk about liberty and would like to use suspicion to discredit egalitarian appeals for fairer distribution of society's wealth and other advantages. To this end he first quotes Oliver Wendell Holmes, Jr., "I have no respect for the passion for equality, which seems to me merely idealizing envy." Then he adds his own commentary: "When we inquire into the justification of these demands, we find that they rest on the discontent that the success of some people often produces in those that are less successful, or, to put it bluntly, on envy. The modern tendency to gratify this passion and to disguise it in the respectable garment of social justice is developing into a serious threat to freedom. . . . It is probably one of the essential conditions for the preservation of [a free] society that we do not countenance envy, not sanction its demands by camouflaging it as social justice. . . ."[4]

In this attempt to unmask the envy that masquerades as justice we recognize the cunning of Mabel's sisters. It is not easy to deny the presence of envy or even, as Nietzsche will suggest, the spirit of revenge in the cries of the wretched of the earth. But it is very easy to turn the tables on Holmes and Hayek. Is it not obvious that all this noise about liberty is but a mask for the greed of those most highly favored by the natural and social lotteries that have distributed both the abilities to do what our society most generously rewards and the rewards themselves, not always without violence? Is it not probably one of the essential conditions for the preservation of a just society that we do not countenance greed, not sanction its demands by camouflaging it as love of liberty?

It is just as easy to play this tit for tat game with Freud. He considers theistic belief to be infantile wish fulfillment, an illusion derived from our sense of helplessness before the indifference of both nature and culture to our happiness. In our helplessness, he believes, we say to

---

Freud or someone else cannot prove them false. And Freud rightly protests against the notion that we have a right to believe whatever we would like to be true, so long as no one can prove such beliefs false (21:32).

4. F. A. Hayek, *The Constitution of Liberty* (Chicago: University of Chicago Press, 1960), pp. 85, 93.

ourselves: Wouldn't it be nice if there were a loving heavenly father to take care of us. This is the origin, in the Humean sense, of the biblical God.

But there are very powerful forces at work within us that lead in exactly the opposite direction. God, if there were such a being, would be a power we would envy and an authority we would resent. Wouldn't it be nice, we say to ourselves, if there were no God. We could be in charge without any unsolicited divine interference. Ironically, Freud calls attention to these forces both biographically and theoretically. When he interpreted his own dreams in the years following his father's death, he discovered a powerful resentment and hatred of his father. And his theory of the Oedipus complex insists that this phenomenon is virtually universal, portraying parents as resented rivals of children, whose death wishes toward their parents are one of the first texts of psychic life to be censored and thereby rendered unconscious.[5]

It begins to look as if *The Future of an Illusion* is a case of the pot calling the kettle black. If the theism of the believing soul is, in psychoanalytic perspective, infantile wish fulfillment, is not Freud's own unbelief equally infantile (Oedipal) wish fulfillment superimposed on adolescent rebellion against all authority? As Dostoyevsky has pointed out, the psychological argument does indeed cut both ways.[6]

It is unquestionably possible to score points against Freud and his atheism of suspicion using either or both of these two strategies. But the title of this chapter and its first eight words suggest that this is a temptation for the believing soul to resist. Why, since it has been conceded that in each case the point is well taken? Because if one's first and primary response to Freud is to try to discredit him, one risks winning the battle and losing the war. Or, to use another military metaphor, one risks winning only Pyrrhic victories in this manner, ending up dead right, which is just as dead as dead wrong.[7]

Consider the setting of the story of the Good Samaritan. It grows out of an exchange between Jesus and a lawyer about eternal life. The

---

5. For fascinating biographical details and a fuller analysis of Freud's account of children's resentment toward their parents, see my discussion in *God, Guilt, and Death* (Bloomington: Indiana University Press, 1984), section 3B.

6. Fyodor Dostoyevsky, *The Brothers Karamazov*, book XII, chapter X.

7. My mother used to cite the following poetic gem (on occasions that seemed appropriate to her, but never to me):

Here lie the remains of Jonathan Jay,
Killed in maintaining his right of way.
He was right, dead right, as he sped along,
But he's just as dead as if he were wrong.

lawyer, a Pharisee, is able to give the same magnificent twofold summary of the law that Jesus himself gives on another occasion. But when Jesus tells him simply to do this and he will live, he gets defensive. "But he, desiring to justify himself, said to Jesus, 'And who is my neighbor?' " In itself this is a perfectly legitimate question, and in fact anyone seriously interested in the command of neighbor love is bound to ask it. But in the four simple words "desiring to justify himself" the narrative levels a devastating critique at the Pharisee.[8]

We open ourselves to precisely this same critique when our first response to Freud (or Marx or Nietzsche) is to try to score points against them by either of the two strategies just discussed. With reference to the first I spoke of the believing soul eager to discredit Freud "for the sake of the truth and for the protection of the logically unsophisticated," but the suspicion unavoidably arises that it is more a matter of the desire to justify oneself.

Both objections raise points worthy of being noted. But in the circumstances we discredit ourselves more than our trio of unbelieving brothers by raising these points. For we stand accused by their critique of being Pharisees, of practicing a self-serving religion that is idolatrous by our own standards. And this critique may be true even if (1) our own beliefs are true, and (2) the unbelief of the critics is of suspicious origin with regard to its own motives. If our first response is to defend ourselves by attacking them, we invite the impartial observer to say, "But they, desiring to justify themselves, began to talk about *ad hominem* and genetic fallacies and to turn suspicion against the suspicious."

We can put the same point a little differently. Peter Homans has asked: "Has theology's preoccupation with philosophy in effect obscured its capacity to engage those contemporary modes of thought and experience that are predominantly psychological in character?"[9] The question is not as innocent as it seems. For it suggests the further question whether theology's preoccupation with apologetics and questions of truth is self-deceptive and defensive, a repression of awkward questions about motive and function. When the believing soul's immediate response to Freud is to insist either that religious beliefs may nevertheless be true or that Freud cannot establish the truth of his own atheism, the suspicion is naturally aroused that this response is not the expression of a disinterested love of truth.

---

8. Luke 10:29. It is Matthew 22:35 that identifies the lawyer as a Pharisee.
9. Peter Homans, *Theology After Freud* (Indianapolis: Bobbs-Merrill, 1970), p. x. Cf. pp. xii-xiii.

Just as Jesus taught us, on pain of being hypocrites, to attend to the speck in our neighbor's eye only *after* removing the log from our own, so there will be plenty of time to make the points that need to be made against the atheism of suspicion *after* we have taken its critique seriously.[10] Already we have allowed the exploration of these two objections to distract us from feeling the full force of Freud's theory of illusions, the analogy between dreams and religious beliefs. For while we have been talking about wish fulfillment, we have not been talking about distortion.

10. See above, p. 17 n. 10.

10 Freud's Suspicion III:
Doctrines and Distortion

From what has been said so far it might seem that Freud develops an analogy between religious beliefs as illusions and daydreams or children's dreams as relatively transparent wish fulfillments. The element of distortion implied by the definition of a dream as a *disguised* fulfillment of a *repressed* wish has not come to the fore. But in Freud's eyes distortion is the very heart of the matter. For he believes that religious beliefs as well are the disguised fulfillment of repressed wishes.

In dreams we represent the world to ourselves, not as we have good reason to believe it to be, but simply as our egoistic or erotic desires would like it to be. Then, since we are not proud either of the driving motives or of our willingness to play fast and loose with evidence and truth in the service of those motives, we do our best to hide from ourselves what we have done.

Irma is to blame, Otto is to blame, R. is a simpleton, and N. is a criminal. This is Freud's dream belief (see above, chapter 7) in spite of the fact that he knows (1) that resistance is a normal part of therapy, (2) that he has no reason at all to suspect Otto of using a contaminated syringe, (3) that R. is anything but a simpleton, and (4) that N. has been cleared of the charges brought against him. He is willing to invent and believe slanders against his friends in order to satisfy his own ego. No, I am not to blame. Yes, I will get the appointment.

Freud was closer to being thoroughly shameless in the case of Irma's injection, leaving his shifting of the blame pretty much on the surface. But in his dream about the uncle with a yellow beard we see the distortion involved in repression and disguise. First, Freud distorts reality to make it more to his liking; then, because he is ashamed of this, he distorts the representation that performs this function so as not to notice what he has done. By disguising the wish fulfillment in the

61

dream he represses the motives that formed the dream, leaving them and the meaning of the dream unconscious, unavailable to immediate interpretation.

This is the kind of distortion Freud finds in religious illusions. We represent God to ourselves, not in accordance with the evidence available to us but in accordance with our wishes; in other words, we create God in our own image, or at least in the image of our desires. Now we have three things to be ashamed of: (1) the desires that govern this operation, (2) our willingness to subordinate truth to happiness, and (3) our hybris in making ourselves the creator and God the creature. If we are not utterly shameless, we will do our best to distract attention, especially our own, from what is going on.

This is how it works in more specific terms: I am looking for consolation in the face of death and compensation for the renunciations imposed by culture. My credo comes to look like this: "Over each one of us there watches a benevolent Providence . . . which will not suffer us to become a plaything of the overmighty and pitiless forces of nature. Death itself is not extinction . . . but the beginning of a new kind of existence which lies on the path of development to something higher." What is more, "the same moral laws which our civilizations have set up govern the whole universe as well, except that they are maintained by a supreme court of justice with incomparably more power and consistency. In the end all good is rewarded and all evil punished. . . . In this way all the terrors, the sufferings and the hardships of life are destined to be obliterated. Life after death . . . brings us all the perfection that we may perhaps have missed here." Accordingly Jewish mono-theism has good reason to be proud of uniting all this in a single figure, thereby laying "open to view the father who had all along been hidden behind every divine figure as its nucleus" (21:19).

Here, then, is the daydream of the human race. But where is the distortion? Actually, this wonderful story is not quite what we want. We do not wish to see all good rewarded and all evil punished. For ourselves we would prefer mercy to justice, and even mercy has its down side, for there is humiliation as well as relief in hearing "You deserve to be punished but I will cancel the punishment."

Freud describes two ways in which we edit the text of our credo to solve this problem. The first comes to light when the first ellipsis two paragraphs back is filled in. "Over each one of us there watches a benevolent Providence *which is only seemingly stern . . .*" (italics added). We do not really want a Heavenly Father whose strength may be matched by strictness, who, if he is good, is more committed to the good and to our becoming good than to our momentary happiness and who therefore turns against us when we turn against the good. What we really want is a doting, spoiling grandfather of the kind implied by a wall hanging I recently saw. It was a cotton garden glove, overstuffed with cotton balls and attached to a dowel about a foot long. On it were embroidered the words "Grandpa's Paddle." Or, as a Rhodes Scholar I had the privilege of teaching has put it, "I tend to create a God whose demands are relative, few, and negotiable."

The second editing strategy reinforces the notion of the parental wimp with that of the favorite child. Having neutralized the notion of punishment, it focuses on that of reward.

> Now that God was a single person, man's relations to him could recover the intimacy and intensity of the child's relation to his father. But if one had done so much for one's father [apparently a reference to whatever good one had done], one wanted to have a reward, or at least to be his only beloved child, his Chosen People. Very much later [after the Jewish origins of covenantal monotheism], pious America laid claim to being "God's own Country"; and, as regards one of the shapes in which men worship the deity, the claim is undoubtedly valid.

This mode of worship Freud immediately identifies as "the final form taken by our present-day white Christian civilization" (21:19-20).

If I can be the favorite child of a thoroughly domesticated parent, I need fear no punishment and can count on rewards, both quite independently of what I deserve. But if *we* do this collectively by becoming God's chosen people, that is even better. For in this way we can salvage the justice of the moral order after all, in the form of the punishment we wish upon our enemies. The enemies of the chosen people are the Canaanites, destined by divine decree either for extinction or for slavery as hewers of wood and drawers of water for the chosen people (Joshua 9). Central casting has discovered that dark-skinned native populations and Communists are especially convincing in the role of the Hittites, the Amorites, the Canaanites, the Perizzites, the Hivites, the Jebusites, and the Gibeonites.

Freud, it seems, is willing to make this an away game. He has shifted the discussion from his positivistic turf to the believing soul's biblical turf. From his point of view, which he knows the believing soul does not share (and which he may suspect he cannot defend), merely to believe in divine Providence of any sort is to commit an epistemological sin, to allow desire to dictate doctrine against the evidence. But when the believing soul fashions a God who is only seemingly stern and who plays favorites with me and with my people, such a soul does so against a different kind of evidence, the biblical evidence so proudly and piously appealed to when it is found convenient.

Freud was not the world's best biblical scholar, but he knew that, Marcion notwithstanding, the God of both the Old and the New Testaments is a God of tough love. He knows that covenantal relation implies special responsibility rather than special exemption. "You only have I known of all the families of the earth; therefore I will punish you for all your iniquities" (Amos 3:2). And he knows that under the new covenant the nation of Israel has been replaced by the international church as the covenant people of God, invalidating in advance the claim of America or any other nation to view its enemies as Canaanites.

This is why Freud sees doctrine as dreamlike in the full sense, which includes distortion. In "the final form [of religion] taken by our present-day white Christian civilization," the beliefs of the believing soul tend to be shaped by amoral desires, against the very evidence to which the believing soul appeals. This first distortion calls in turn for a second distortion to hide it, just as a crime often calls for a lie to keep it from being exposed. In the first distortion reality is misrepresented (relative to the believing soul's own standards). In the second that misrepresentation is itself misrepresented or disguised. Belief becomes the disguised fulfillment of a repressed wish.

This is the psychoanalytic path Freud takes to the Humean conclusion that systems of religious belief are all too often the "comfortable views" that "give rise" to immoral, even barbaric behavior when that behavior is "authorized by" or merely "compatible with" those beliefs (see above, chapter 4). Freud writes:

> It is doubtful whether men were in general happier at a time when religious doctrines held unrestricted sway; more moral they certainly were not. They have always known how to externalize the precepts of religion and thus to nullify their intentions. The priests, whose duty it was to ensure obedience to religion, met them halfway in this. God's kindness must lay a restraining hand on His justice. One sinned, and then one made a sacrifice or did penance and then one was free to sin once more. Russian introspectiveness has reached the pitch of concluding that sin is indispensable for the enjoyment of all the blessings of divine grace, so that, at bottom, sin is pleasing to God. It is no secret that the priests could only keep the masses submissive to religion by making such large concessions as these to the instinctual nature of man. Thus it was agreed: God alone is strong and good, man is weak and sinful. In every age immorality has found no less support in religion than morality has. (21:37-38)

11 The Paranoid Dr. Schreber as Victim

Freud's treatment of the relation of religion and morality is somewhat distinctive. To be sure, he shares with Marx and Nietzsche this claim that religion can often be seen serving immorality. But whereas Marx and Nietzsche tend to treat religion and morality as closely related species of the same genus, Freud treats them as generically different. Morality is based on introjection, the internalizing of social rules as mediated by parents and other "significant others," whereas religion is based on projection, the externalizing of representations grounded in desire.[1] Since projection is so basic to Freud's account of religious beliefs as illusions, since his primary account of projection is developed in the Schreber case study, and since the delusions of the paranoid Dr. Schreber happen to have a religious content, we turn from the general theory of distorted representation to the specifics of this famous case. Ironically, while illustrating the feature that most significantly distinguishes religion from morality for Freud, this 1911 case study illumines the partnership between religion and immorality as well as any text in the Freudian corpus.

Dr. Schreber, a distinguished jurist, was not a patient of Freud's. But he published an extensive account of his illness, which became the basis of Freud's interpretation.[2] Freud insists that the case is not merely of interest for the study of paranoia but also for the more general

1. Paul Ricoeur emphasizes this difference in *Freud and Philosophy: An Essay on Interpretation,* trans. Denis Savage (New Haven: Yale University Press, 1970), pp. 233, 236. For a good overview of such Freudian technical terms as *introjection* and *projection,* including references to the key texts in which they are developed, see J. Laplanche and J.-B. Pontalis, *The Language of Psychoanalysis,* trans. Donald Nicholson-Smith (New York: Norton, 1963).

2. Daniel Paul Schreber, *Memoirs of My Nervous Illness,* trans. Ida Macalpine and Richard A. Hunter (London: Dawson and Sons, 1955; reprinted with a new introduction by Samuel Weber, Cambridge: Harvard University Press, 1988; German original 1903).

understanding of the workings of the human mind, for "even mental structures so extraordinary as these and so remote from our common modes of thought are nevertheless derived from the most general and comprehensible of human impulses." Accordingly, the case is to be located "in the familiar complexes and motive forces of mental life" (12:18, 35). Just as Plato seeks to see the human soul writ large in the life of the city, so Freud hopes to find the workings of the "normal" psyche writ large in the mental processes of neurotic and psychotic patients. In the exotic details of the Schreber case he invites us to look for light on the quotidian piety of ordinary people.[3]

Schreber's paranoia comes in two stages, first a delusion of persecution and then a delusion of grandeur. In the former he sees himself as the victim of "soul murder" for the purpose of sexual abuse in the form of emasculation. At first his persecutor is his physician, Dr. Flechsig. But though soul murder and emasculation are contrary to the moral Order of Things, it turns out that God has yielded to Flechsig's influence and become his accomplice, or possibly the instigator of the plot (12:39, 19).[4] So, much of the verbal abuse with which Schreber replies to the threat of sexual abuse is directed against God rather than Flechsig (12:25-27).

The delusion of grandeur that constitutes the second stage makes use of God's presence on the scene. Now Schreber's emasculation enables him to become God's wife. In this role he becomes the Redeemer of the world by giving birth to a new race.

As Freud reads the reports of Dr. Weber, who treated Schreber, they suggest "that the motive force of this delusional complex was the patient's ambition to play the part of Redeemer, and that his *emasculation* was only entitled to be regarded as a means for achieving this end" (12:18).[5] Freud vigorously rejects this view. He acknowledges that this

---

3. The account here of the Schreber case is based on the more detailed analysis in my essay "Paranoia and Piety: Reflections on the Schreber Case," in *Psychoanalysis and Religion*, ed. Joseph H. Smith and Susan A. Handelman (Psychiatry and the Humanities, 11; Baltimore: Johns Hopkins University Press, 1990), pp. 117-35.

4. At this point we encounter Freud at his funniest, though he seems not to notice. On his view, Flechsig is a surrogate for Schreber's father, Daniel Gottlieb Moritz Schreber. In seeking to show how easily God could become the second surrogate for the elder Schreber, Freud tells us that after all the latter "was a *physician*" (Freud's emphasis) and indeed "a most eminent physician, and one who was no doubt highly respected by his patients. . . ." Recalling the euhemerism of the ancients, Freud writes, "Such a father as this was by no means unsuitable for transfiguration into a God in the affectionate [sic] memory of the son . . ." (12:51-52).

5. These reports are appended to Schreber's *Memoirs*, pp. 267-83, 315-27.

means-end relationship is the shape of the Redeemer delusion, but he sees this final product (manifest content) as the result of distortion designed to disguise the primacy of the idea of being transformed into a woman. One piece of evidence to which Freud points is Schreber's account of the time, shortly before the onset of the delusions of persecution and two full years before the Redeemer delusion emerged, when the idea occurred to him as he was waking one morning "that after all it really must be very nice to be a woman submitting to the act of copulation" (12:13).

The other evidence is the sequence of the delusions.

> For we learn that the idea of being transformed into a woman (that is, of being emasculated) was the primary delusion, that he began by regarding that act as a piece of persecution and a serious injury, and that it only became related to his playing the part of Redeemer in a secondary way. There can be no doubt, moreover, that originally he believed that the transformation was to be effected for the purpose of sexual abuse and not so as to serve higher designs. The position may be formulated by saying that a sexual delusion of persecution was later on converted in the patient's mind into a religious delusion of grandeur. (12:18)

The last sentence of this statement is doubly misleading. The delusion of persecution is as religious as it is sexual, at least as soon as God replaces Flechsig as primary persecutor. And the delusion of grandeur is as sexual as it is religious, for Schreber is to become a woman in order to be impregnated by God. Both stages are at once sexual and religious. The question concerns the relation of the two, and Freud's answer comes in three parts. In his rejection of Dr. Weber's analysis we have already seen the first of these. The cornerstone of Freud's interpretation is the primacy of homosexual libido in the latent text of Schreber's illness.

The second point is Schreber's rejection of this libido. Freud writes, "Before his illness Senatspräsident Schreber had been a man of strict morals: 'Few people', he declares, and I see no reason to doubt his assertion, 'can have been brought up upon such strict moral principles as I was, and few people, all through their lives, can have exercised (especially in sexual matters) a self-restraint conforming so closely to those principles as I may say of myself that I have done'" (12:31). Schreber constantly speaks of the moral Order of Things, and it is clear that at least at the outset he finds homosexuality to be contrary to this order. Freud is surely correct when he says that the idea "that after all it really must be very nice to be a woman submitting to the act of copulation" is "one which [Schreber] would have rejected with the greatest indignation if he had been fully conscious" (12:13).[6]

This is, of course, exactly what Schreber does in the persecution stage of his illness (12:33), which brings us to the third and decisive step in Freud's answer to the question about the relation of sexuality and religion in this case. Schreber's delusions, including their religious content, are defenses against his homosexual desire.[7] Freud claims that

> the exciting cause of the illness was the appearance in [Schreber] of a feminine (that is, a passive homosexual) wish-phantasy, which took as its object the figure of his physician. An intense resistance to this phantasy arose on the part of Schreber's personality, and the ensuing defensive struggle . . . took on, for reasons unknown to us, that of a delusion of persecution. The person he longed for now became his persecutor, and the content of his wish-phantasy became the content of his persecution. (12:47)

The mechanisms at work here are fairly obvious. The homosexual wish-fantasy, unacceptable because of Schreber's morality, is *projected* onto Dr. Flechsig (and eventually onto God). This permits him both a *denial* of this unwelcome desire and a corresponding and supportive *reversal* of affect. In place of "I love Flechsig," he says "I hate Flechsig (since he is persecuting me)" (12:63).

Two elements of distortion in the text of this delusion are strikingly similar to that in the text of Freud's dream about his uncle. First, if Freud is correct in seeing Flechsig as a surrogate for Schreber's father (or brother) (12:47, 50), then we have a disguise of the real subject matter similar to that in which the uncle took the place of the two rival colleagues. And in the reversal of affect, from loving Flechsig (= father or brother) to hating him, we have a censor's editing of the latent text like that in which the competitive hatred of his colleagues is disguised by the strong affection with which the uncle is viewed in the manifest text.

What is most important, however, is not the means but the end, not the mechanisms of defense but their function.[8] The goal is perfectly

---

6. Morton Schatzman has called our attention to more evidence in support of this claim than Freud was aware of. See *Soul Murder: Persecution in the Family* (New York: Random House, 1973), chapters 5-6.

7. On the concept of defense and defense mechanism, see Laplanche and Pontalis.

8. Ricoeur is surely right in suggesting that the Schreber case throws more light "on the function of projection than on its mechanism." *Freud and Philosophy,* p. 238 n. 18.

plain: The delusion of persecution renders Flechsig innocent of his homosexual wishes. Its function is to relieve Schreber of the anxiety he would experience (both as guilt and as fear of punishment)[9] were he to acknowledge the direction of his desire (which was possibly incestuous as well as homosexual). But whereas Freud's dreams provided a similar self-justification, Schreber's delusion goes one better. It allows him to *retain* the fantasy of playing the female role in copulation. Like parapraxes, dreams, and neurotic symptoms, this delusion is a compromise (15:66, 130; 16:301-59). Schreber must repudiate his fantasy, but in return for this he is able to retain it without anxiety. As long as he can give the appearance of being offended, he can remain innocently preoccupied with his fantasy. One is reminded of the minister who preaches so passionately about the evils of miniskirts or who waves pornographic magazines before his congregation in order to protest against "all that filth."

It may not seem to matter whether the persecutor is Flechsig or God, and indeed, God's primary importance in this whole affair is to make possible the transition to the second stage, where grandeur replaces persecution. But before turning our attention to that part of the story, we would do well to notice an important detail about God's role in the persecution stage. Schreber is not very clear about what he means by "soul murder," but he indicates that it is usually done "by the Devil, who entices a human being into selling his soul to him . . . yet it is difficult to see what the Devil has to do with a soul so caught, if one is not to assume that torturing a soul as an end in itself gave the Devil special pleasure."[10] The threatening Flechsig is a demonic character from the outset. Moreover, the God who replaces him is regularly described as the "posterior realms of God" or the "lower God," Ahriman by name (12:23-24, 44). But Ahriman is the Zoroastrian *devil*. So it is not surprising that Dr. Weber should describe Schreber, in summarizing his complaints, as "the plaything of devils" (12:14).

The question this raises in the present context is, of course, not that of metaphysical dualism or the existence of Satan. It is, rather, the question of the function of the demonic in the religious life-world. The function that comes to our attention here is that of the scapegoat, not the scapegoat of Leviticus 16, who is punished for the sins of the people, but the scapegoat who unites the following two dictionary definitions:

9. That guilt and the fear of punishment are to be sharply distinguished, though they are often conjoined in what we might call dread, as I have argued in chapter 4 of *God, Guilt, and Death* (Bloomington: Indiana University Press, 1984).

10. Schreber, *Memoirs*, p. 55. Cf. Freud, 12:38.

"3a: a person or thing bearing the blame for others . . . b: a person, group, race, or institution against whom is directed the irrational hostility and unrelieved aggression of others."[11] In Schreber's case it is clearly projection that unites a to b.

Nietzsche has taught us to notice the difference between the two kinds of scapegoat. Nobler than the holy God are the Greek gods, "those reflections of noble and autocratic men, in whom *the animal* in man felt deified and did *not* lacerate itself, did *not* rage against itself! For the longest time these Greeks used their gods precisely so as to ward off the 'bad conscience' . . . the very opposite of the use to which Christianity put its God." Meditating on Zeus's view of humankind as "wretched through folly," Nietzsche shouts at us: "Foolishness, *not* sin! Do you grasp that?" But even the foolishness must be misfortune, and so the Greeks say "He must have been deluded by a god." "In this way the gods served in those days to justify man to a certain extent even in his wickedness, they served as the originators of evil — in those days they took upon themselves, not the punishment but, what is *nobler*, the guilt."[12]

It is useful for the sacred to take on this demonic function. For when it does I remain blameless both in the wrong I may do (or wish to do) and in any punishment I may receive. Both the doing and the receiving are reduced to the category of misfortune, and I am immune from moral categories.[13] To the degree that I am able to project my own deeds and desires onto a deity, I carry out a teleological suspension of the ethical that frees me from all moral accountability. I may not live free from pain, but I can live free from guilt and shame. It isn't all bad to be a victim.

---

11. *Webster's Third New International Dictionary of the English Language Unabridged* (Springfield, MA: Merriam-Webster, 1981), s.v.

12. Friedrich Nietzsche, *Genealogy of Morals*, II, 23; cf. *Ecce Homo*, "Why I Am So Wise," 5, and *Thus Spoke Zarathustra* I, "On the Adder's Bite." E. R. Dodds gives a splendid example: Agamemnon does not deny the deed by which Achilles was wronged, only that it was his. " 'Not I,' he declared afterwards, 'not I was the cause of this act, but Zeus and my portion and the Erinys who walks in darkness: they it was who in the assembly put wild *atē* in my understanding, on that day when I arbitrarily took Achilles' prize from him. So what could I do? Deity will always have its way.' " *The Greeks and the Irrational* (Berkeley: University of California Press, 1971), p. 3.

13. Kierkegaard helps us understand the advantage of reducing punishment to misfortune: "Punishment is not the pain in and for itself; the same pain or suffering can happen to another merely as a vicissitude of life. Punishment is the conception that this particular suffering is punishment. When this conception is taken away, the punishment is really taken away as well." *Søren Kierkegaard's Journals and Papers*, vol. II, trans. Howard V. Hong and Edna H. Hong (Bloomington: Indiana University Press, 1970), p. 52.

12 The Paranoid Dr. Schreber as Redeemer

We are exploring the Schreber case in the light of Freud's observation about the historical frequency with which religion has been the partner of immorality. So far we have seen one process by which this can happen. We can call it the denial of responsibility.[1] When the juvenile gang in *West Side Story* explains to Officer Krupke that their delinquency is a "social disease," saying, in effect, "Don't blame us, blame our environment," they are employing this technique.

What the Schreber case calls to our attention is the possibility of blaming the sacred instead of the environment. Suppose, for example, I am a televangelist who is engaged in sexual conduct contrary to the standards I profess and preach. I am bound to feel guilty. This might lead to a change in my behavior, but I might also try to defend myself with a little help from projection. First I might find my Flechsig, another mortal onto whom I can transfer this evil. If there should happen to be another televangelist whose sexual misconduct I can expose and denounce, I may be able to avoid noticing, for a while, my own behavior, which has made me so eager and happy to discover his sins. The fact that there is a basis in fact for my projection does not lessen its projective function for me. But suppose he or his friends return the favor and *I* am publicly exposed. Can I avoid the blame and the discipline that my church imposes on me? Yes, and easily. I say the devil made me do it and return to my ministry as quickly as possible.

Here we are dealing with actual behavior rather than fantasy, as

1. See Gresham M. Sykes and David Matza, "Techniques of Neutralization: A Theory of Delinquency," reprinted from *The American Sociological Review* 22 (1957), pp. 664-70, in *Guilt: Man and Society*, ed. Roger W. Smith (Garden City, NY: Doubleday, 1971).

with Schreber. (Freud, of course, finds this difference minor as far as the need to defend oneself against guilt is concerned.) More importantly, we are dealing with perfectly "sane" behavior rather than with anything certifiably psychotic. But do we not see here the point of Freud's claim that psychotic and "normal" behavior are not so different? Is not projection the visibly operative defense mechanism in both cases? Do not the two demonologies function in quite the same way? And does the sanity of one case make it any less sick? Whenever the sacred becomes the scapegoat who takes the blame (as distinct from the punishment) for human behavior, whether as God or as Satan, religion becomes the enemy of ethics and the partner of immorality.

We may or may not agree with the sexual standards of Schreber and our televangelist. That is not the point. What is at issue is what they do with their own best moral judgments: They do not obey them. Nor do they provide reasons to revise them. They simply find a way to exempt themselves from them. Instead of serving God, they make God their servant. Instead of resisting the devil, they use the devil to resist the truth about their own immorality.

"The devil made me do it" is not always, however, a very satisfactory strategy. I can use it to justify something I have already done, perhaps, but what if I want to continue doing the same thing? We have already noted in the Schreber case the high price of retaining homosexual fantasies, pretending or convincing oneself that they are not welcome. He can enjoy them only by simultaneously suffering from them.

This brings us to the real import of the move from Flechsig to God. This move is made not so much to perfect the delusion of persecution as to transcend its limitations in the delusion of grandeur. As both Freud and Schreber clearly see, it opens the path to a superior strategy, a compromise formation with a more favorable cost-benefit ratio. The replacement of Flechsig by God

> seems at first as though it were a sign of aggravation of the conflict, an intensification of the unbearable persecution, but it soon becomes evident that it was preparing the way for the second change, and, with it, the solution of the conflict. It was impossible for Schreber to become reconciled to playing the part of a female prostitute towards his physician; but the task of providing God himself with the voluptuous sensations that he required called up no such resistance on the part of his ego. Emasculation was no longer a disgrace; it became "consonant with the Order of Things," it took its place in a great cosmic chain of events, and was instrumental in the

re-creation of humanity after its extinction. (12:48; for Schreber's own account, see 19-20)

There are three advantages to Schreber's new self-deception. First, his homosexual wish-fantasy becomes morally acceptable and need no longer be repudiated. The initiative remains with God, but now, since it is God who requires this teleological suspension of the ethical, Schreber can accept it in good conscience. Schreber writes:

> I shall show later on that emasculation for quite another purpose — a purpose *in consonance with the Order of Things* — is within the bounds of possibility, and, indeed, that it may quite probably afford the solution of the conflict. . . . On the other hand, God demands a *constant state of enjoyment*, such as would be in keeping with the conditions of existence imposed upon souls by the Order of Things; and it is my duty [remember Frederic and Mabel, chapter 3 above] to provide Him with this . . . [Freud's ellipsis] in the shape of the greatest possible generation of spiritual voluptuousness. And if, in this process, a little sensual pleasure falls to my share, I feel justified in accepting it as some slight compensation for the inordinate measure of suffering and privation that has been mine for so many past years. (12:20, 34; cf. 20-21)[2]

Schreber actually develops this "slight compensation" into an unconstrained identification of heavenly bliss with voluptuousness so that, in Freud's summary, "the state of heavenly bliss is to be understood as being in its essence an intensified continuation of sensual pleasure upon earth!" (12:30).

The second strength of this second defense strategy is that bringing the desire "to be a woman submitting to the act of copulation" into consonance with the Order of Things makes possible reconciliation with God and Father. The homosexual desire remains projected onto God, but since it is now acceptable it ceases to be the basis for war against God. Whereas before he and God exchanged mockery and scorn, now Schreber is the recipient of "direct inspiration from God, just as we are taught that the Prophets were" (12:16).

---

2. Dr. Weber underscores the rather obvious self-deception in all of this: "It is not to be supposed that he *wishes* to be transformed into a woman; it is rather a question of a 'must' based upon the Order of Things, which there is no possibility of his evading, much as he would personally prefer to remain in his own honourable and masculine station in life" (12:17).

Freud calls attention to the link between these two strengths. Prior to the mission as Redeemer, Schreber "had been inclined to sexual asceticism and had been a doubter in regard to God; while after it he was a believer in God and a devotee of voluptuousness" (12:32). Actually, during the first stage of delusion Schreber was more an outspoken enemy of God than a doubter, but the point does not change. As God's wife he is able for the first time to say yes both to his sexuality and to his father. It is no wonder that he speaks of finding "the solution of the conflict" (12:20).

And there is yet a third advantage. Freud accepts the "popular distinction between ego-instincts and a sexual instinct" (12:74); and he calls attention to the way Schreber's "ego found compensation in his megalomania, while his feminine wishful phantasy made its way through and became acceptable" (12:48). Schreber thinks that "God does not have any regular communication with human souls" and that it is "only in exceptional instances that He would enter into relations with particular, highly gifted persons . . ." (12:22-23). Thus, in Dr. Weber's summary, Schreber finds himself to be "the most remarkable human being who has ever lived upon earth" (12:17).

In his delusion of becoming God's wife Schreber wins (1) moral legitimacy for his homosexual desires, (2) freedom to love his father rather than hate him, and (3) world-historical status as a Redeemer of cosmic importance. This solution is so clearly superior to the persecution compromise formation that it may seem puzzling to refer to it as a compromise formation at all. But there remains a cost for the benefits just listed. Schreber is not free to act out his sexual desires. The consummation of his marriage to God is postponed to an indefinite future. For the present he is free only to fantasize about it (constantly and innocently). Most importantly, since the world in which all these benefits accrue is indeed a fantasy world, Schreber pays the price of losing touch with reality (as socially defined). In the transition from persecution to grandeur Schreber remains a psychotic personality.

We are exploring the potential of religion for legitimizing immoral behavior in the world of ordinary people in the light of its capacity for justifying immoral fantasies in the world of psychotics. It would appear not only that the second stage of Schreber's illness is a better solution to his problem but also that it points as well to a better, more efficient way for "sane" people to justify their immorality religiously.

Suppose, for example, that we want to wage war against those who pose a threat to us, real or imagined, but find that the most effective

actions we can take are those we ourselves label "state sponsored terrorism" when directed against us or our friends. We might abandon
those actions. But then again we might turn to religion, not to justify
terrorism in general, but to exempt ourselves from our own (loud)
moral repudiation of terrorism. In this context "The devil made me do
it" is not a very promising line of defense. More to the point would be
a demonizing of our rivals as "the Great Satan" or "the Evil Empire"
or "godless communism" (as if capitalism were a version of theism).
The Schreber case shows us the psychology of holy war.

According to Dr. Weber's summary, Schreber came to accept the
sufferings of his persecutional stage by coming to view them as "all on
behalf of a holy purpose" (12:13-14), or, as it is translated in the *Collected
Papers*, a "sacred cause."[3] Holy war is a sacred cause not entirely unlike
Schreber's. Against the background of demonizing the enemy, it ele-
vates the agent to the role of God's specially chosen instrument, projects
onto God the agent's megalomaniacal will to power, thereby transforming action in accordance with that will to power from atrocity to duty,
the very upholding of the Order of Things.

There are differences to be sure. (1) In holy war the ego-instincts
of aggression are dominant, and any sexual gratification (e.g., rape) that
may be involved is secondary or symbolic. (2) In war the ego-instincts
involved are collective or tribal rather than individual. (3) The gratification of those instincts in war takes place in the real world as well as
in the fantasy of political rhetoric. (4) In holy war one may be called
upon to suffer on behalf of the sacred cause, but it is primarily others
who are called on to do the suffering: While the rhetoric of holy war is
the willingness to die, its reality is the willingness to kill. As John
Howard Yoder has remarked, "The real temptation of good people like
us is not the crude and the crass and the carnal, as those traits were
defined in popular puritanism . . . but that of *egocentric altruism;* of being
oneself the incarnation of a good and righteous cause for which others
may rightly be made to suffer."[4]

Thus from the Crusades to the Holocaust, Jews have been made
to suffer for the sake of Christian heroism or Aryan supremacy. Under
such slogans as the "white man's burden," "manifest destiny," and the
struggle against "atheistic Communism," dark-skinned peoples have

3. Sigmund Freud, *Three Case Studies*, ed. Philip Rieff (New York: Collier,
1963), p. 109.

4. John Howard Yoder, "What Would You Do If," *Journal of Religious Ethics*
2/1 (Fall 1974), pp. 82-83, quoted in Stanley Hauerwas, *The Peaceable Kingdom: A
Primer in Christian Ethics* (Notre Dame: University of Notre Dame Press, 1983), p. 131.

been subordinated to colonial and neo-colonial domination. We are reminded of Freud's own comments on "pious America" as "God's own Country" (21:19). In ironic reversals by which the persecuted become the persecutors, South African blacks and Palestinians are made to suffer today for the cause of Afrikaner culture and the Jewish state, respectively.[5] There are the many varieties of Islamic Jihad, which bring to mind Hiroshima and Nagasaki (not to mention the current superpower willingness to sacrifice millions of civilians on the altar of national security).[6] The list goes on and on.

No wonder Bob Dylan writes, "If God's on our side, we'll start the next war."[7] For in each of these cases, many, if not all, of those willing to make others into nothing but means to their own tribal ends have justified their behavior as that which is required by a sacred cause. In fact, they have followed the Schreber recipe to a T. They have come to see themselves first as threatened by a demonic enemy and then as the specially chosen vehicles of a divine purpose that suspends normal morality and justifies whatever they feel inclined to do. The question is why, if Schreber is plainly paranoid, these other cases are not also seen as paradigms of psychosis.

5. Against the background of these two tragic cases, Nicholas Wolterstorff poses some probing questions about nationalism in *Until Justice and Peace Embrace* (Grand Rapids: Eerdmans, 1983), chapter 5.

6. A passionate analysis of the idolatrous character of this willingness is to be found in Dale Aukerman, *Darkening Valley: A Biblical Perspective on Nuclear War* (New York: Seabury, 1981), especially Part II.

7. As sung by Joan Baez in "Joan Baez: The First Ten Years," two-record set from Vanguard, VSD 6560/1.

13 The Atheist Dr. Freud as
Theologian of Original Sin

The masters of the school of suspicion are the great secular theologians of original sin. Whether they give prominence to nature (Freud, Nietzsche) or to nurture (Marx), to instinct or to institutions, they vividly portray the deep divergence between human behavior and the moral ideals of Judeo-Christian theism. What is more, they show how deeply entrenched are human cruelty, greed, and the other manifestations of that unlimited self-assertion that, under the name of pride, has been seen by theologians as the heart of all human darkness, the one original sin. In doing this they accomplish what few theologians even attempt: (1) They bring to light the workings of what theologians call sin in the full concreteness of everyday life, and (2) they show how even religious life gets drawn into the service of the sin whose enemy it is supposed to be.

Freud is fully conscious that he plays this role and loves to highlight the agreement between psychoanalysis and religion that we are all miserable sinners (13:72; 9:123).[1] This feature of Freud's thought comes to the foreground as we turn from his analysis of religious beliefs (construed as the analogues of dreams) to his analysis of religious practices (construed as the analogues of neurotic symptoms).[2] For from

1. Norman O. Brown sees it as the task of psychoanalysis to be "the science of original sin." It is "equipped to study the mystery of the human heart, and must recognize religion to be the heart of the mystery." *Life Against Death* (Middletown, CT: Wesleyan University Press, 1959), pp. 13-14.

2. Ricoeur calls attention to this double structure of Freud's theory of religion in *Freud and Philosophy: An Essay in Interpretation*, trans. Denis Savage (New Haven: Yale University Press, 1970), pp. 231-36. Since Freud's clinical work on neuroses preceded his theory of dreams, and since his first essay on religion developed the parallel between religious and neurotic ceremonials rather than between religious

his earliest essay on religion, "Obsessive Actions and Religious Practices" (1907),[3] where he first introduces the crucial concept of "an unconscious sense of guilt" (9:123),[4] he treats religious behavior, both
ritual and moral, as a set of defenses against such guilt and the anxiety
that can scarcely be distinguished from it. In order to understand fully
Freud's critique of religious rites and righteousness, we need to have
before us his own understanding of human sinfulness.

Freud views our innermost self as a "positive Hell" (15:143).
Although " 'little children do not like it' when there is talk of the inborn
human inclination to 'badness,' to aggressiveness and destructiveness,
and so to cruelty as well," it is better "that the truth should be told by
psychologists rather than that the task should be left to cynics" (21:120;
15:206). That each of us is "a savage beast to whom consideration
towards his own kind is something alien" is a truth toward which we
will "bow humbly" if we reflect on the atrocities stretching from the
invasions of the Huns and the Mongols, through the Crusades, and
right up to "the horrors of the recent World War" (21:112). Freud insists
that

> men are not gentle creatures who want to be loved, and who at the
> most can defend themselves if they are attacked; they are, on the
> contrary, creatures among whose instinctual endowments is to be
> reckoned a powerful share of aggressiveness. As a result, their
> neighbour is for them not only a potential helper or sexual object,
> but also someone who tempts them to satisfy their aggressiveness
> on him, to exploit his capacity for work without compensation, to
> use him sexually without his consent, to seize his possessions, to

---

doctrines and dreams, it might seem that we are working backwards. But it makes
sense to look at Freud's account of religious beliefs first, as we have, (1) since for
Freud himself, *"The interpretation of dreams is the royal road to a knowledge of the
unconscious activities of the mind"* (5:608; his italics), (2) since in his most comprehensive presentation of psychoanalysis, *Introductory Lectures on Psychoanalysis,* he presents his theory of dreams first, and only then his theory of neurotic symptoms, and
(3) since *The Future of an Illusion* is his most widely known discussion of religion.

3. Important elements of the theory that comes to light in this essay are
already found in the 1896 essay "Further Remarks on the Neuro-Psychoses of
Defense." These include (1) the claim that religious anxiety is at work in some
obsessional practices, (2) the description of obsessive practices as "ceremonials,"
and (3) the description of these burdensome ceremonials as *"penitential measures"*
(3:171-74). But the analogy between neurotic and religious ceremonials does not
become the thematic focus of attention until the 1907 essay.

4. This concept plays an important role in *The Ego and the Id,* especially at
the end of the second and the beginning of the fifth chapter.

humiliate him, to cause him pain, to torture and to kill him. *Homo homini lupus*. Who, in the face of all his experience of life and of history, will have the courage to dispute this assertion? (21:111)

If we continue to downplay "the evil in the constitution of human beings," Freud has more questions for us.

But do your own experiences justify your [resistance]? I will not discuss how you may appear to yourselves; but have you found so much benevolence among your superiors and competitors, so much chivalry among your enemies and so little envy in your social surroundings that you feel it your duty to protest against egoistic evil having a share in human nature? Are you not aware of how uncontrolled and untrustworthy the average person is in everything to do with sexual life? Or do you not know that all the transgressions and excesses of which we dream at night are daily committed in real life by waking men? What does psychoanalysis do here but confirm Plato's old saying that the good are those who are content to dream of what the others, the bad, really do? (15:146)

It is important to notice this distinction between overt behavior and inner disposition, for like the theologian, Freud locates original sin in our inmost self. What theologians call the heart, he calls the id. This "cauldron full of seething excitations . . . knows no judgments of value: no good and evil, no morality" (22:73-74). Against psychological environmentalists like Rousseau, Marx, and Skinner, who would argue that the "primary mutual hostility of human beings" is due to bad social institutions such as private property, Freud insists that it is instinctual and for that reason an "indestructible feature of human nature" (21:112-14; cf. 120-22).

We can be confident that Freud did not develop this unflattering account of human nature from a sympathetic reading of Paul's Epistle to the Romans, Augustine's *Confessions*,[5] or Calvin's *Institutes*. Nor, when with reference to the id he writes that "we are 'lived' by unknown and uncontrollable forces," does this come from a careful study of Luther's *Bondage of the Will*. Where does it come from? Most prominently from his interpretation of dreams.

The Interpretation of Dreams is the record, as it were, of Freud's

---

5. In his insistence that aggression "already shows itself in the nursery" (21:113), however, Freud sounds a lot like Augustine in accounting for why we think of infants as innocent. Compare 15:210-11 with *Confessions* I, 6-7. See also the discussion of infantile evil with the "Rat Man" (10:185-86).

conversion to a secular theology of original sin. From the dreams of his patients, but especially from his own, he was led to the conclusion that "dreams are completely egoistical" and that "no dream is prompted by motives other than egoistic ones" (4:322-23; 5:440; cf. 4:270n.2). The appearance of altruism in a dream is just that, appearance, the product of a distorting censorship seeking to block the return of the repressed (4:267). The wishes that "are censored and given a distorted expression in dreams, are first and foremost manifestations of an unbridled and ruthless egoism" (15:142). Freud's dreams, in particular, are the expression of a "thirst for grandeur" that amounts to a "pathological ambition" and an "absurd megalomania" (4:192, 215-18).

The dreams about Irma's injection and the uncle with a yellow beard, discussed above in chapter 7, are good examples of what Freud has in mind. He calls our attention, in the first instance, not only to his desire to justify himself in the matter at hand, but also to his willingness to avenge himself on Irma, Dr. M., and especially Otto in the process (4:115-19). In the second case he is "uneasy over the light-heartedness with which I had degraded two of my respected colleagues in order to keep open my own path to a professorship." The reference is to the "well-designed slander" by which in his dream he had reduced R. and N., respectively, to a simpleton and a criminal (4:139-41).

Censorship, the coin whose two sides are repression and resistance, is evoked by the presence within us, in desire if not in act, of what is "reprehensible" and "repulsive" (15:142). Just as daydreams are undisguised fulfillments of "ambitious and erotic wishes which are well known to us" (15:130), so adult dreams have to distort two types of immoral impulse, erotic and non-erotic. On the one hand, there are "the demands of sexual desire," including those that "contradict all the requirements of moral restraint." Here we are dealing with a "desire for pleasure," known as libido, that "chooses its objects without inhibition, and by preference, indeed, the forbidden ones: not only other men's wives, but above all incestuous objects." On the other hand, "hatred, too, rages without restraint. Wishes for revenge and death directed against those who are nearest and dearest in waking life, against the dreamer's parents, brothers and sisters, husband or wife, and his own children, are nothing unusual. These censored wishes appear to rise up out of a positive Hell; after they have been interpreted when we are awake, no censorship of them seems to us too severe" (15:142-43; cf. 203-9).

If the religiously sanctioned moral standards before which humans appear as "miserable sinners" have both an ascetic and an altruistic component, the "unbridled and ruthless egoism" to which Freud points has both an erotic and an aggressive dimension, though the two are not always easy to separate. In spite of his reputation for being preoccupied with sex, Freud's "Confessions" are a powerfully concrete expression of the Augustinian understanding of sin as essentially pride. In fact, Freud's secular theology (like that of Thomas Hobbes) belongs to the anti-Platonic tradition that stretches from Augustine to Kierkegaard and Niebuhr in making pride more fundamental than lust. In *The Interpretation of Dreams* this is partly due to his understandable reluctance to go into too much detail about the sexual meaning of his own dreams, with the result that he comes across as a megalomaniac rather than a sex maniac. But by the time we get to the final chapter of *Civilization and Its Discontents* the primacy given to the problem of aggression and the impossibility of altruism is no longer accidental. Instead, these issues are seen as defining the most basic human task.

As we have regularly noticed, the Freudian self is not only utterly egocentric. It is also dishonest about its egocentricity, primarily to itself. Because we are conscience as well as concupiscence, superego as well as id, we do not approve of ourselves. We are guilty and ashamed of the darkness in our heart, or we would be if it were allowed to come fully to light. That is where censorship comes in. Repression and its correlate, resistance, have as their task to spare us the pain of seeing ourselves as we really are. In Augustinian language, it was "you Lord . . . who took me from behind my own back, which was where I had put myself during the time when I did not want to be observed by myself, and you set me in front of my own face so that I could see how foul a sight I was — crooked, filthy, spotted, and ulcerous . . . forcing me to look into my own face, so that I might see my sin and hate it. I did know it, but I pretended that I did not. I had been pushing the whole idea away from me and forgetting it."[6]

So it is that we end up self-deceived, not just about the degree

6. *The Confessions of St. Augustine*, trans. Rex Warner (New York: New American Library, 1963), VIII, 7. In the Pine-Coffin translation we read that Augustine "had turned a blind eye" on himself (*Confessions*, trans. R. S. Pine-Coffin [Baltimore: Penguin Books, 1961]). Freud says that in therapy "what happens is that the patient, who has hitherto turned his eyes away in terror from his own pathological productions, begins to attend to them and obtains a clearer and more detailed view of them" (10:223). In another place he writes, "The fact is that you must catch your thief before you can hang him, and that it requires some expenditure of labour to get securely hold of the pathological structures at the destruction of which the treatment is aimed" (10:124).

to which wish fulfillment shapes our beliefs, but about the character of our deepest self. Just as political censorship drives the opposition underground, so repression and resistance combine to produce an unconscious sense of guilt. For censorship is powerless either to make us good or to exterminate guilt. All it can do is drive guilt underground, helping us not to notice what would be all too painful to our self-esteem if we looked it (ourselves) in the face. In Freud's view, religious behavior must be understood as an attempt to deal with this situation.

It may seem strange for Freud to portray the believing soul as having an *unconscious* sense of guilt. Has he not himself called our attention to the believer's confession of being a "miserable sinner"? Yes, indeed. But he reminds us of the believer's awareness of being a "miserable sinner" in the paragraph immediately following the one that introduces the notion of an unconscious sense of guilt (9:123), and he has provided a conceptual framework in which there is no conflict between the two. Given his account of repression, our *conscious* sense of sin is likely to be quantitative, comparative, and occasional, in short, manageable. It will make sense for us to weigh our good deeds against our bad deeds, and to preserve our self-esteem by finding others whose evil is greater than ours, quantitatively and qualitatively, which is to say that their sins are either more frequent than ours or of a more serious sort, or both. Thus respectable citizens will abhor bank robbery, while bank robbers will abhor self-righteous hypocrisy. We will be conscious of (at least some of) our sins. But the sin of which they are the expression, the fundamental project of self-assertion, erotic and otherwise, without constraint, and the guilt that corresponds to this sin, we are likely to censor before looking at ourselves in the mirror.

The result of all this, as Freud sees it, is that the religious activities designed to deal with a guilt which is only partially and superficially allowed to see the light of day will themselves take place in a kind of spiritual black market, only partially and superficially available to consciousness. We will need to apply a hermeneutics of suspicion to religious behavior as well as to religious belief.

14 *Ceremonial as Defense*

Freud begins his first attempt to psychoanalyze religion with these words:

> I am certainly not the first person to have been struck by the resemblance between what are called obsessive actions in sufferers from nervous affections and the observances by means of which believers give expression to their piety. The term 'ceremonial', which has been applied to some of these obsessive actions, is evidence of this. The resemblance, however, seems to me to be more than a superficial one, so that an insight into the origin of neurotic ceremonial may embolden us to draw inferences by analogy about the psychological processes of religious life. (9:117)

The strength of this analogy in Freud's mind is due, as we shall see, to its multifaceted character. There are at least four points on which he finds religious and neurotic ceremonial to be alike. One of two significant *differences* he sees is that neurotic ceremonials have a "private nature as opposed to the public and communal character of religious observances," making the former "a travesty, half comic and half tragic, of a private religion." Thus Freud's central (hypo)thesis is that

> one might venture to regard obsessional neurosis as a pathological counterpart to the formation of a religion, and to describe that neurosis as an individual religiosity and religion as a universal obsessional neurosis. The most essential similarity would reside in the underlying renunciation of the activation of instincts that are constitutionally present; and the [other] chief difference would lie in the nature of those instincts, which in the neurosis are exclusively sexual in their origin, while in religion they spring from egoistic sources. (9:119, 126-27)

This analogy of sexual and egoistic instincts becomes absolutely basic to Freud's thought. It is repeated in his most important writings on religion and culture, *Totem and Taboo* (1913, 13:73), *The Future of an Illusion* (1927, 21:43-44), *Civilization and Its Discontents* (1930, 21:81-85), and *Moses and Monotheism* (1939, 23:55, 58, 80-81).[1] The distinction between the two forms of instinct could be misleading. In the *Interpretation of Dreams* we have seen Freud insist on the fundamental self-centeredness of the instinctive life that comes to (disguised) expression in dreams, and we have seen him distinguish two modes of this egoistic preoccupation with satisfying one's own desires without constraint. Sometimes what is repressed and then returns in dreams is sexual desire, but often it is desire of another sort, ambitious, aggressive, megalomaniacal. From a moral point of view sexual desire is no less self-centered than ambitious-aggressive desire. If Freud sometimes distinguishes the latter from the former as egoistic instinct, he does so because the goal of ambition and aggression is self-esteem rather than bodily pleasure.[2] To use language that he will develop later, one set of instincts has its home in the id, the other in the ego. But both know only how to "look out for number one." The distinction between erotic and egoistic instincts in no way parallels the familiar distinction between altruism and egoism.

Yet the distinction between them is important for Freud's analogy between neurotic and religious practices. Freud eventually formulates their relation this way: "When an instinctual trend undergoes repression, its libidinal elements are turned into symptoms, and its aggressive components into a sense of guilt" (21:139). Since the instinctual renunciation underlying neurosis is primarily sexual, while the instincts whose repression leads to religion are "from egoistic sources," we can expect the unconscious sense of guilt that motivates neurosis to play an even larger role in religion.

Because this concept of unconscious guilt is so central to the analogy between neurosis and religion, we have devoted the previous chapter to exploring Freud's secular theology of original sin. We have seen his claim both that (a) from a moral point of view we are rotten to the core, even if we present a more acceptable appearance, and that

---

1. In *Moses and Monotheism* Freud speaks as if the idea dates from *Totem and Taboo*. But see the last footnote to the Schreber case (12:82), where he rightly refers back to the 1907 essay.

2. Freud regularly distinguishes the erotic from the egoistic instincts in just this sense in *Introductory Lectures on Psychoanalysis* (see 15:98, 130, 142-43). But he is emphatic that the sexual instincts "are at bottom self-interested" (16:345; cf. 417-18).

(b) the believing soul, just by virtue of taking the moral point of view seriously, is likely to have an overload of guilt, more than can be acknowledged without too much pain. The result is the repression of at least a significant dimension of that guilt and the desires of the heart to which it is a response; in other words, the result is an unconscious sense of guilt.

We need now to turn to Freud's developing theory of obsessional neurosis as a strategy for dealing with unconscious guilt. This will be the key to understanding the similarities that Freud sees between neurotic and religious ceremonials, in spite of the two key differences already noted between them. The paper of 1907 draws on several important papers written during the 1890s, including "The Neuro-Psychoses of Defense" (1894), "Obsessions and Phobias: Their Psychical Mechanism and Their Aetiology" (1895), and "Further Remarks on the Neuro-Psychoses of Defense" (1896).

Freud views obsessional neurosis as one of several measures designed to defend the self against an "incompatible" or "unacceptable" idea of a sexual nature.[3] The primary component of this complex idea is a person's memory of a sexual trauma from infancy or childhood. Associated with this is an affective component, itself complex, including anxiety over the (not entirely unwelcome) possibility of repetition of the experience, over guilt or shame, and over fear of punishment.

The desire to forget the experience proves impossible to fulfill. So symptoms arise "through the psychical mechanism of (unconscious) *defense* — that is, in an attempt to repress an incompatible idea which [has] come into distressing opposition to the patient's ego" (3:162). In this way "the ego succeeds in freeing itself from the contradiction," but only at the price of carrying along with it like a parasite the symptom that has developed. As a "mnemic symbol" the symptom indicates that

3. Frankly I prefer the translation from *The Collected Papers of Sigmund Freud* (though it appears to be based on a misprint: see 3:51n.4) where in the three essays under consideration the threatening idea is interchangeably described as "intolerable" and "unbearable." These terms suggest the moral aspect of the problem. The use of "incompatible" in the *Standard Edition* has one advantage, however. By pointing to the logical aspect of the situation it relates what Freud is doing here to cognitive dissonance theory as developed by Leon Festinger in *A Theory of Cognitive Dissonance* (Stanford: Stanford University Press, 1957). This link might help some readers, whose background in American experimental psychology makes it hard for them to take Freud seriously, to overcome that bias long enough to explore the possibility that the clinical and experimental contexts are not completely incompatible.

"the memory-trace of the repressed idea has, after all, not been dissolved" (3:49).

In obsessional neurosis the symptom defends against an intolerable idea by separating the affect from this idea and then reattaching the affect, the "liberated anxiety," to a symbolically suitable substitute that is sufficiently different to be bearable (3:51-54). The affect *"which has become free, attaches itself to other ideas which are not in themselves incompatible; and, thanks to this 'false connection,' those ideas turn into obsessional ideas"* (3:52, Freud's italics), and the same thing happens with practices that arise from the substitute ideas. Because the substitute ideas become obsessional, *"the emotional state, as such, is always justified"*; in relation to the substitute idea it may appear quite irrational, but in relation to the original idea from which it derives, it is fully comprehensible (3:75, Freud's italics; cf. 54).

Later, in discussing the obsessional neurosis of the "Rat Man," Freud would refer to the *"mésalliance"* between the patient's self-reproach and its apparent source and put these words in the therapist's mouth: "No. The affect is justified. The sense of guilt is not in itself open to further criticism. But it belongs to another content, which is unknown *(unconscious)*. . . . The known ideational content has only got into its actual position owing to a false connection . . . much as our police, when they cannot catch the right murderer, arrest a wrong one instead" (10:175-76; cf. 187-89, 196-98).

Consider the hand washing compulsion of Lady Macbeth. The idea that is incompatible with the ego is the memory of adultery and murder. The painful affect, appropriately linked to the idea of a polluted soul, is transferred to the bearable idea of dirty hands, resulting in an abnormal concern for clean hands. The compulsion seems irrational only as long as we fail to see that it is not really about dirt but about adultery and murder. "The washing was symbolic, designed to replace by physical purity the moral purity which she regretted having lost" (3:79).[4]

Another example is the bedtime ritual of an eleven-year-old boy. He could not go to sleep until he had (1) recited the day's activities to his mother in detail, (2) removed all trash from the carpet, (3) pushed the bed against the wall and placed three chairs in front of it, (4) arranged the pillows in a certain way, (5) kicked both legs out several times, and (6) then turned on his side. In therapy Freud came to the following interpretation:

4. Freud is actually speaking of one of his patients, a woman with a dirt phobia and a hand washing compulsion whom he describes as "the case of Lady Macbeth." Her case involved only adultery, not murder as well (3:79).

Years before, a servant-girl who put the nice-looking boy to bed had taken the opportunity of lying down on him and abusing him sexually. When, later on, this memory was aroused in him by a recent experience, it manifested itself in his consciousness in a compulsion to perform the ceremonial I have described above. The meaning of the ceremonial was easy to guess and was established point by point by psycho-analysis. The chairs were placed in front of the bed and the bed pushed against the wall in order that nobody else should be able to get at the bed; the pillows were arranged in a particular way so that they should be differently arranged from how they were on that evening; the movements of his legs were to kick away the person who was lying on him; sleeping on his side was because in the scene he had been lying on his back; his circumstantial confession to his mother was because, in obedience to a prohibition by his seductress, he had been silent to his mother about this and other sexual experiences; and, finally, the reason for his keeping his bedroom floor clean was that neglect to do so had been the chief reproach that he had so far had to hear from his mother. (3:172n.1)

Freud sees two regular features in the substitutions that give birth to obsessional neurosis. First, something past is replaced by something present. Second, something sexual is replaced by "something analogous to it that is not sexual" (3:170). Thus in place of "I committed adultery and murder then" we have "my hands are dirty now," and in place of "I allowed the servant-girl to seduce me and hid this from my mother" we have "I have allowed my floor to get dirty and have not told my mother all that happened today."

The key to these displacements[5] is the self-reproach that is always a key ingredient in the original idea, against which the symptoms are a defense (3:169-71). The point is to eliminate or at least mitigate the tension, the incompatibility between self-reproach and self-esteem. Thus, as we have just seen, Lady Macbeth seeks to replace the intolerable moral stain with a tolerable physical stain.[6] It is guilt that makes the intolerable idea intolerable.

Because of this intimate link to guilt and the "burdensome"

---

5. Displacement is, of course, one of the basic techniques of dream work, the process of translating the latent content of a dream into a content sufficiently disguised to get past the censorship and become manifest. See chapter VI of *The Interpretation of Dreams*. For a particularly clear example of displacement in a case of obsessional neurosis, see 10:196-98. Cf. also 10:241.

6. See above, p. 70 n. 13.

nature of the resulting ceremonials, Freud calls them "*penitential* measures" (3:173).[7] Penance, the usual name for a penitential act, is defined as "an act of self-abasement, mortification, or devotion either voluntarily performed to show sorrow or repentance for sin or imposed as a punishment for sin by a church official."[8] The obsessive ceremonials Freud is considering are penitential in both senses. As a symbolic undoing or repudiation of the forbidden act(s) they express sorrow or *repentance,* and as a burdensome imposition on one's time and peace of mind they represent a self-imposed *punishment.* In the former capacity they are a defense against the anxiety associated with the ongoing temptation to repeat the forbidden act(s), while in the latter capacity they are a defense against both the fear of punishment and the guilt that gives rise to that fear. In the ceremonial I say to myself and anyone else concerned: (1) "I'm sorry and I'll never do it again," (2) "You don't need to punish me; I'm already punishing myself," and (3) "Because I've already been punished, I don't need to feel guilty."[9] The ceremonial provides triple protection: against anxiety, against fear, and against guilt.

7. In his *Introductory Lectures on Psychoanalysis,* Freud describes obsessional ceremonials as composed of actions whose performance brings "no enjoyment" and which, while harmless enough in themselves, become "extremely tedious and almost insoluble tasks" (16:258-59).

8. *Webster's Third New International Dictionary of the English Language Unabridged* (Springfield, MA: Merriam-Webster, 1981), s.v.

9. In speaking of the relation between "self-inflicted penance" and the deeply implanted sense "that guilt demands punishment," Kierkegaard speaks of the "happiness of childhood to be spanked" and explains this from what "makes the child's life so easy," namely "that so often 'quits' can be called and a new beginning is so frequently made." Punishment is more tolerable than recollection of guilt (*Concluding Unscientific Postscript,* 2 vols., trans. Howard V. Hong and Edna H. Hong [Princeton: Princeton University Press, 1992], 1:550-51).

My students have an instinctive understanding of what Freud and Kierkegaard are driving at. When asked whether anything in their own experience confirms Socrates' claim in the *Gorgias* that if we have done wrong it is better (and therefore we should prefer) to be punished than to go unpunished, they regularly say, Yes, when I did wrong I felt guilty about it, but after I had been punished, my guilty conscience went away. In giving this response they are clearly not parroting Socrates, who says nothing at all about guilt feelings and their removal. For the reverse case, which might be called the sadness of childhood in not getting spanked, see my *God, Guilt, and Death* (Bloomington: Indiana University Press, 1984), pp. 74-75.

15 Ceremonial as Compromise

In the examples of Lady Macbeth and the eleven-year-old boy we can easily see how with the help of displacement a ceremonial can serve a defensive function, seeking to salvage self-esteem in the face of well-founded self-reproach. With an eye to the future I repudiate forbidden desire, and with an eye to the past I punish myself for having had the desire (and perhaps for having acted on it or for having enjoyed being acted upon). Since such an act can only be described as a "penitential" measure or an act of penance, a link between neurotic ceremonials and religious life begins to emerge.

But there is one aspect of Freud's theory of obsessional neurosis, crucial for the analogy with religious practices, on which these examples shed no light at all. Freud insists that obsessions represent a "*compromise* between the repressed ideas and the repressing ones" (3:170; cf. 172). In other words, the ceremonial is a symbolic reenactment as well as a symbolic repudiation of forbidden desire (and action).

The path toward seeing ceremonials as compromise formations has two simple steps. The first is recognition of ceremonials as embodying the (disguised and distorted) wish-fulfilling function already familiar from dreams. One of the two obsessive ceremonials around which Freud develops his theory of the meaning of neurotic symptoms in *Introductory Lectures on Psychoanalysis* exhibits just such a function (16:261-63). Interestingly enough, he first presented it in "Obsessive Actions and Religious Practices" (9:121). A woman's compulsive act, repeated many times a day, consisted of going into a particular room, arranging the tablecloth on the table there in a certain way, standing beside the table, calling the maid, and then sending her away with or without a task.

In therapy the following interpretation emerged. On the night of her wedding to an older man, he had proved impotent. To avoid feeling ashamed before the maid, when she discovered no blood on the sheets, he had poured red ink on them (though not in the proper place). When we discover that the tablecloth used in the ceremonial was itself stained and that the woman always stood beside it in such a way that the maid could not help but see the stain, the meaning of the ceremonial becomes clear. Playing the role of her husband, she was reenacting her wedding night, but "she was not simply repeating the scene, she was continuing and at the same time correcting it; she was putting it right . . . correcting . . . his impotence. So the obsessional action was saying: 'No, it's not true. He had no need to feel ashamed in front of the housemaid; he was not impotent.' It represented this wish, in the manner of a dream, as fulfilled in a present-day action" (16:263; cf. 298-300).

The second step in recognizing ceremonials as compromise formations is simply the realization that this wish-fulfilling function and the wish-denying, defensive, penitential function we have already observed can coexist in the same rite. The ceremonial that perhaps best exhibits this is the other one Freud chooses for the exposition of his theory of neurosis in *Introductory Lectures on Psychoanalysis*. As with the eleven-year-old boy, this is another nighttime ritual, now of a nineteen-year-old woman. Due to her extreme conscientiousness about doing it right and the necessity of repeating various elements until she was fully satisfied, it would often take as long as two hours before she, and, as it turns out, her parents, could get to sleep.

The rite had seven elements: (1) The clock in her room was stopped and all watches were removed. (2) Flowerpots and vases were placed on the writing table so that they could not fall and break during the night. (3) The door between her bedroom and her parents' was set half open. (4) The pillow on her bed was placed so that it would not touch the wooden bedstead. (5) A smaller pillow was placed to lie in a diamond shape on the larger pillow. (6) The young woman had to lie so that her head was exactly along the vertical axis of the diamond. And (7) the eiderdown had to be shaken so that its bottom end would be very thick when laid on the bed, but this lump had then to be smoothed out (16:265).

On interpretation this ritual turns out to be more complicated than the similar one of the eleven-year-old boy. But the interpretation began in exactly the same way. Freud and the patient became convinced in therapy that the timepieces, flowerpots, and vases were symbols of female sexuality and that the first two steps of the ceremony were a symbolic denial of (some) sexual desire (16:267, 300). But the fifth and sixth steps turned out to be the symbolic fulfillment of incestuous wishes toward her father. She thus combined in a single ceremony the self-denial of the boy's bedtime ritual with the wish fulfillment of the other woman's tablecloth ritual.

There is perhaps another way in which this young woman's obsession is a compromise formation. Simply as a tedious task it is a striking example of the self-punishment function of ceremonial as defense. Like similar rites, it is possible only "at the cost of great sacrifice" (16:264). But, as already noted, it keeps the young woman's parents as well as herself from getting to bed, and keeping them apart can only be satisfying to her. This is clear from the interpretation of the third and fourth parts of the rite. These steps turn out to be the symbolic continuation of a childhood practice of keeping her parents apart at night by keeping the door to their room open, by arranging to lie in bed between them, and even by arranging to change places with her mother, sleeping beside her father with the mother in the daughter's bed. The Oedipal significance of all this links steps three and four of the rite quite clearly to the incestuous wish fulfillment meaning of steps five and six.[1] By keeping herself awake she punishes herself for the forbidden desire that she simultaneously satisfies (in part) by keeping her parents awake.

Thus "the rules laid down by the ceremonial reproduced the patient's sexual wishes at one point positively and at another negatively — in part they represented them, but in part they served as a defense against them" (16:269). Symptoms thus aimed at both fulfilling "sexual satisfaction" and "fending it off" must be seen as "the products of a compromise and arise from the mutual interference between currents; they represent not only the repressed but also the repressing force which had a share in their origin" (16:301). Symptoms presuppose inner conflict. "The two forces which have fallen out meet once again in the symptom and are reconciled, as it were, by the compromise of the symptom. . . . It is for that reason, too, that the symptom is so resistant: *it is supported from both sides*. . . . The opposition which has been raised against [libidinal desire] in the ego . . . compels it to choose a form of expression which can *at the same time* become an expression of the

---

1. The final, seventh, step is interpreted as a symbolic pregnancy, which is annulled. Freud relates this to the woman's long-standing fear that "her parents' intercourse would result in another child and so present her with a competitor" (16:268). Competitor for what? No doubt her parents' attention and affection. But in the light of the rest of the rite we can hardly avoid thinking of another child not just as a competitor but as *another* competitor, in addition to her mother, for possession of her father.

opposition itself. Thus the symptom emerges as a many-times-distorted derivative of the unconscious libidinal wish-fulfillment, *an ingeniously chosen piece of ambiguity with two meanings in complete mutual contradiction"* (16:358-60, emphasis added).

The key to this semantic ambiguity of symptoms is the affective and volitional ambivalence from which they arise. While we are able to recognize the tension between opposing feelings and conflicting desires, and thus experience cognitive dissonance, we are frequently unable to keep such battling birds from building their nests in our hair. In his own self-analysis, Freud had discovered a powerful hatred of his father quite unpeacefully coexisting with respectful love. Needless to say, repression had rendered the hatred unconscious.[2]

Freud notes that in obsessional neurosis the two meanings that are the ambiguous expression of ambivalent feeling or desire are often separated so that the rite "consists in two actions, one after the other, which cancel each other out" (16:301). Good examples of such "diphasic" rites are found in one of Freud's two extensive studies of obsessional neurosis, the famous case of the "Rat Man."[3]

---

2. Ernest Jones, *The Life and Work of Sigmund Freud,* one-volume edition by Lionel Trilling and Stephen Marcus (Garden City, NY: Doubleday, 1963), chapters 13-14.

Augustine's classic account of volitional ambivalence is worth citing here. He wonders why he wants to change his life, but nothing happens, why he prays "Make me chaste and continent, but not yet" (*The Confessions of St. Augustine,* trans. Rex Warner [New York: New American Library, 1963], VIII, 7).

> The mind gives an order to the body, and the order is obeyed immediately: the mind gives an order to itself, and there is resistance. . . . The mind orders the mind to will; it is the same mind, yet it does not obey. What can be the explanation of such an absurdity? The mind, I say, orders itself to will: it would not give the order, unless it willed it, yet it does not obey the order. The fact is that it does not will the thing entirely; consequently it does not give the order entirely. The force of the order is in the force of the will, and disobedience to the order results from insufficiency of the will. . . . But it is not entire in itself when it gives the order, and therefore its order is not obeyed. . . . So it is not an absurdity partly to will and partly not to will; it is rather a sickness of the soul which is weighed down with habit so that it cannot rise up in its entirety, lifted aloft by truth. So the reason there are two wills in us is because one of them is not entire, and one has what the other lacks. (VIII, 9)

3. The other is the "Wolf Man" case. Because of their complexity, I will not comment on the central symptoms of the "Rat Man's" case, the compulsive idea of the rat punishment and the compulsion to make an impossible repayment. Freud's interpretation makes clear their compromise function when combined, the first being an insult expressing (unconscious) hostility toward the young man's father and

Like Freud himself, this young man was deeply ambivalent toward his father, combining a conscious love and respect with a repressed and thus unconscious hatred. Freud knew how love and hatred are dialectically linked and how in a case like this "love has not succeeded in extinguishing the hatred but only in driving it down into the unconscious. . . . In such circumstances the conscious love attains as a rule, by way of reaction, an especially high degree of intensity, so as to be strong enough for the perpetual task of keeping its opponent under repression." It is even possible to say that "precisely such intense love" is the "necessary precondition of the repressed hatred" (10:239, 180).

This ambivalence is the key to one of the young man's ceremonials, in which he would study late into the night, would go to the door to lead his (dead) father in for a ghostly visit, and then would take out his penis and look at it in the mirror. Since his idleness during the father's lifetime had been a source of conflict, his hard work was an expression of respect and obedience. But the other act in this rite can only be taken as an act of defiance. "Thus, in a single unintelligible obsessional act, he gave expression to the two sides of his relation with his father, just as he did subsequently with regard to his lady by means of his obsessional act with the stone" (10:204).

This latter reference is to the young man's other deep ambivalence, for he discovered in therapy that he also harbored hostile feelings and fantasies of revenge toward the woman he loved (10:194-95). On the day of her departure from a visit with him he felt *"obliged"* to remove a stone from the road lest her carriage should "come to grief against this stone." But then the idea struck him as absurd and he felt *"obliged"* to replace the stone in the middle of the road (10:190). Freud writes, "A battle between love and hate was raging in the lover's breast, and the object of both these feelings was one and the same person. The battle was represented in a plastic form by his compulsive and symbolic act of removing the stone from the road along which she was to drive, and then of undoing this deed of love by replacing the stone where it had lain, so that her carriage might come to grief against it and she herself be hurt." The second act, that of replacing the stone, was itself compulsive. It was not simply the rejection of a pathological act but was itself part of that act. "Compulsive acts like this, in two successive stages, of which the second neutralizes the first, are a typical occurrence

---

ladylove, the second being the self-inflicted punishment by which he seeks to atone for this (10:217-19).

in obsessional neuroses" (10:191-92). Taken together, the two stages express an ambiguity grounded in ambivalence.

The person presiding at such a ceremonial does not, of course, understand what is going on but rather "puts forward a set of secondary motives to account for [the actions] — *rationalizes* them, in short" (10:192).[4] In the present case the act that needs to be given a phony justification, since its real motivation and meaning are unconscious, is the second act. The professed (manifest) reason for replacing the rock is the absurdity of removing it in the first place, but the real (latent) reason is the hostility felt toward the lady friend.

In a similar fashion, the young woman whose bedtime ritual we have considered rationalized the first two stages of her ceremonial by giving "as a *pretext* for her nightly precautions that she needed quiet in order to sleep and must exclude every source of noise," namely timepieces and vases that might fall (16:265).

It is just this feature that gives force to the final theme (at least for our purposes) of Freud's account of obsessive ceremonials, their similarity to behavior under hypnosis. In making this comparison, Freud refers to the umbrella experiments he had witnessed when he worked with Bernheim (16:277; cf. 4:147-48). When a man was told under hypnosis that upon awaking he would open an umbrella and carry it around in the room, the result was threefold. He did it, he did not know why he did it, and he made up a reason, namely that he wanted to see if the umbrella was okay. It was only "slowly and with difficulty" that he was able to see that the reason he had given "was not the real reason."[5]

---

4. Freud here refers to Ernest Jones's introduction of the concept of rationalization into psychoanalytic (and, eventually, everyday) vocabulary. See Jones, "Rationalization in Every-Day Life," in *An Outline of Psychoanalysis,* ed. J. J. Van Teslaar (New York: Boni and Liveright, 1924), pp. 98-107. Without intending to, Freud illustrates his own idea in "On the History of the Psycho-Analytic Movement," a sharp polemic against his two ungrateful "sons," Jung and Adler: "It was not surprising that they should be able to justify [their] rejection of my ideas on intellectual grounds though it was actually affective in origin. . . . In Falstaff's words, reasons are 'as plenty as blackberries' " (14:24). Not much later he raises the question of his own motives in writing against Jung and Adler. "It is no easy or enviable task to write the history of these two secessions, partly because I am without any strong personal motive for doing so — I had not expected gratitude nor am I revengeful to any effective degree. . . . I have no choice in the matter, however; only indolence or cowardice could lead one to keep silence" (14:49). It appears that the doctor protests too much. For a similar disclaimer in his analysis of Dora's hysteria, see the Prefatory Remarks to that case study, 7:7-8; cf. 48-49.

5. I am supplementing the brief accounts Freud gives with a fuller account

Like the hypnotized person, the obsessive neurotic performs actions without knowing why. The meaning is not understood because the motive is unconscious. Of course, it is not the likeness of hypnotized to compulsive behavior that primarily interests us. It is rather Freud's suggestion that religious practices are like the latter (and thereby like the former) that concerns us. We are now in a position more fully to comprehend his initial statement of that claim in "Obsessive Actions and Religious Practices."

---

found in Paul Roazen, *Freud: Political and Social Thought* (New York: Random House, 1968), pp. 48-49; cf. 69 on rationalization.

16 *They Know Not What They Do*

Freud's central claim about religious practices is that they resemble neurotic ceremonials. In chapter 14, where we first encountered this thesis, we noted two important qualifications he appends to this analogy. One concerns the public and communal dimension religious practices often have; the other concerns the nature of the instinctual renunciation involved, primarily erotic in the case of neurosis and primarily egoistic in the case of religion. But we have saved for now to explore, against the background of what we have learned of his theory of obsessional neurosis, the four similarities that make the analogy so powerful in Freud's mind, in spite of those two differences.

The first of the four similarities is the compulsive character of both neurotic and religious acts, which expresses itself both in the conscientiousness with which they are carried out and, more importantly, in the anxiety that accompanies any deviation, neglect, or interruption in their performance (9:118-19). Perhaps we should think here of the baseball player who cannot step into the batter's box without crossing himself, or of the student who cannot begin a meal in the cafeteria without bowing her head to give thanks (even if the average time for such prayers, according to one informal student experiment, is only six seconds), or of the faithful parishioner for whom interruption of a pattern of regular church attendance is accompanied by strong feelings of disorientation. Naturally these phenomena presuppose religious formation in a guilt-oriented piety. Those who grow up in a church whose liturgy includes Words of Assurance but no Prayer of Confession may know nothing of such experiences.

Second, there is the isolation of both kinds of acts from other activities, making them relatively easy to conceal, since they "leave [the performer's] social behaviour unaffected" (9:119). The separation of the sacred from the secular, of Sunday from the rest of the week, is a familiar feature of religion in our pluralistic, secular society.[1] Perhaps we should think here of the Wall Street broker who was asked, in the midst of breaking news stories about a variety of investment scandals, how his Christian faith made a difference in his work. His reply: "I don't allow any cussing in this office." Given such a minimal effect on his vocational life, his religious activities would indeed be easy to conceal from his Wall Street associates and hard for them to detect. The two parts of his life are quite disconnected.

Third, both kinds of acts are symbolically meaningful, even in their details (9:119-20). Though at first this might be more obvious for religious practices than for obsessive actions, we have seen that the latter are richly meaningful, even if that meaning is not immediately evident. It is even the case that the depth of meaning in obsessive actions might not be obviously reflected in religious practices. It is the task of the final similarity to redress this imbalance.

So fourth, at the heart of the analogy we are exploring is the claim that religious practices are also more meaningful than they seem, that they are the bearers of hidden as well as of overt and obvious meaning. If both neurotic and religious ceremonials are meaningful, it is also the case, in Freud's view, that those who perform a given act in either case do so "without understanding its meaning — or at any rate its chief meaning" (9:122). It is here that the analogy between ceremonials and hypnotic behavior comes to the fore with its concept of agents who know not what they do.

Freud's first attempt to say what it means to perform a religious rite without understanding its meaning is far too weak either to be very interesting or to be adequate to the theory that inspires it. He calls on us to "remember that as a rule the ordinary pious individual, too, performs a ceremonial without concerning himself with its significance, although priests and scientific investigators may be familiar with the — mostly symbolic — meaning of the ritual" (9:122). One hardly needs psychoanalysis to notice that people cross themselves, say prayers, sing hymns, recite creeds, and even participate in sacraments without paying much attention to what they are doing. Their minds, as we say, are in other places. In such cases the meaning that is not understood is not

---

1. On the privatization of piety in the modern world, see Karl Marx, "On the Jewish Question," in *Karl Marx: Selected Writings*, ed. David McLellan (Oxford: Oxford University Press, 1977). Cf. Peter Berger, *The Sacred Canopy: Elements of a Sociological Theory of Religion* (Garden City, NY: Doubleday, 1967), chapters 5-7.

unconscious but preconscious, readily available by simply directing our attention to it.

A theory of religious practices is interestingly Freudian only if it hooks up to the unconscious. In the second formulation of its central thesis, Freud's theory does just this. Right after mentioning the "*unconscious* motives and ideas" expressed in neurotic ceremonials, he writes, "In all believers, however, the motives which impel them to religious practices are unknown to them or are represented in consciousness by others which are advanced in their place" (9:122-23). In this claim that the account of a religious practice given by a believing soul will be a rationalization we have both the explicit linkage of meaning and motive so crucial to Freud's theory of dreams and neurotic symptoms, and the distortion of the meanings that spring from repressed (unconscious) motives that gives that theory its bite.

That this fourth component of the analogy between neurotic and religious rituals is the most important is clear from the fact that only at this point does Freud find it necessary and helpful to summarize his theory of obsessive neurosis. To help the reader understand the misunderstanding with which the believing soul acts, Freud introduces such concepts as renunciation, repression, an unconscious sense of guilt, defense, displacement, and compromise into his essay (9:123-27).

By now we can tell Freud's story for him. The believing soul is more of a miserable sinner than it can let itself know and thus is burdened by unconscious as well as conscious guilt. As acts of symbolic renunciation religious practices are symbolic defenses against the temptation stemming from repressed evil impulses and symbolic protection against anticipated punishment. At the same time "a ceremonial represents the sum of the conditions subject to which something that is not yet absolutely forbidden is permitted, just as the Church's marriage ceremony signifies for the believer a sanctioning of sexual enjoyment which would otherwise be sinful. . . . [Like neurotic symptoms, rituals are] a compromise between the warring forces of the mind. They thus always reproduce something of the pleasure which they are designed to prevent; they serve the repressed instinct no less than the agencies which are repressing it" (9:124-25). Due to displacement, both sides of the compromise remain unconscious. The believing soul knows not what it does (9:123-26).

Given his theory of obsessional neurosis, this is what Freud's analogy calls for. But at this point he encounters a difficulty. "The character of compromise which obsessive actions possess . . . is the character least easily detected in corresponding religious observances.

Yet here, too, one is reminded of this feature of neuroses when one remembers how commonly all the acts which religion forbids — the expressions of the instincts it has suppressed — are committed precisely in the name of, and ostensibly for the sake of, religion" (9:126). The example he gives relates to the religious requirement for the individual "to sacrifice his instinctual pleasure to the Deity: 'Vengeance is mine, saith the Lord.' In the development of the ancient religions one seems to discern that many things which mankind had renounced as 'iniquities' had been surrendered to the Deity and were still permitted in his name" (9:127).

Evoking Hume, Freud reminds us of the religious legitimation of violence in such phenomena as holy wars and religiously rationalized enthusiasm for capital punishment.[2] He calls attention to an important feature of such phenomena, their character as scapegoat rituals.[3] With the least amount of imagination we will be led to think as well of less lethal forms of power practiced in the name of religion, including colonial, racial, and gender domination, and of the "blaming the victim" rationalizations that are appended to the "this is God's will" legitimations of such power monopolies.[4] No doubt all of the following are true with respect to such practices: (1) They happen all too frequently. (2) They involve the self-deception of justifying self-interest by disguising it. (3) There is indeed an element of compromise, inasmuch as there is a price to be paid for such permissions. (As with all other commodities, prices fluctuate. Sometimes, but not always, what one wants can be purchased at sale prices.)

2. There is no explicit mention of Hume here, but Freud does know Hume's *Natural History of Religion* (see chapter 4 above), and refers to it in *Totem and Taboo* (13:77).

3. We have encountered scapegoating in the Schreber case (chapter 11 above). In this case, however, the scapegoat is called on to take both the guilt and the punishment of those who practice "sacred" violence. Punishment is, of course, a repudiation of a certain evil, which means, as Paul Roazen notes, that we can punish others to relieve our own guilt. But he also notes the compromise character of scapegoat rituals such that "in punishing the offender there is an opportunity of vicariously committing the very crime that is to be punished" (Roazen, *Freud: Political and Social Thought* [New York: Random House, 1968], pp. 138-40). Hence the toleration of crimes committed against criminals by police and in prisons and the temptation to practice terrorism on terrorists. Roazen summarizes, "Just as Freud could see how useful criminality could be, how society might even foster disobedience, so he could see the pleasure of vengeance beneath our upright moralism" (p. 157).

4. For the sociological development of this concept, see William Ryan, *Blaming the Victim* (New York: Random House, 1976).

The problem is this: As important as it may be to see the ritual character of a holy war or an execution, neither act is the kind of ordinary religious practice Freud has led us to believe he has been discussing. He needs to show us how quotidian liturgical and devotional practices can be understood as disguised compromises. That is the task to which he turns in *Totem and Taboo*. But before we turn to that text, a brief digression into action theory can help us get a bit clearer about what it is Freud will be trying to illustrate more concretely.

He tells us that the believing soul engages in religious practices without understanding their meaning, without, for example, awareness of the motives which give to the rite its wish-fulfilling character. As the title of this chapter indicates, one way to express this feature, which Freud sees in common among actions under hypnosis, obsessive ceremonials, and religious practices, is to say that the "agent" does not know what he or she is doing.

We know what we are doing when we can correctly identify the action we perform. What distinguishes an action from a mere motion, and is thus essential to the former's identity, is intention. If by means of ropes my arm is raised over my head and by means of electronic stimulus my hand is formed into a fist, we have motion but not action. If, however, I clench my fist and raise it over my head, we have an action. But what action? If I am wearing a zebra shirt in the middle of a football game, the action can easily be identified as "signaling fourth down." If, by contrast, I am an Olympic athlete receiving a medal, my action may well be taken as "making a symbolic political protest." No doubt these descriptions are not sufficiently specific to preclude all doubt or uncertainty, but they do serve to indicate how two different intentions make the same motion into two different actions.

But suppose I am the Olympic athlete. Contextual clues make it a pretty safe bet that no one will think I am trying to signal fourth down. But even when my action is correctly identified as raising the Black Power salute, might it not still be one of several different actions that have yet to be adequately identified? Here we can distinguish *what* I do from *why* I do it, and we can speak of the motive as the clue to the Why just as we spoke of the intention as the clue to the What. (I make no claim that we normally distinguish intention from motive in this way, only that it is useful to do so in this context.) Suppose the reason I give the Black Power salute at the Olympics is to win a bet. Then my action might well be described as frivolous and irresponsible. Suppose I do it to cause my mother embarrassment and pain. Then it might well be described as cruel. Suppose I do it out of sincere and thoughtful political commitment. Then it might well be described as courageous (or foolish, but not frivolous). We could go on indefinitely, but the point is clear. Different motives, like different intentions, constitute different actions. That we have several different actions here is clear, not only from the fact that we evaluate them differently, but also from the fact that in evaluating them we describe them, and thus identify them differently.

We can now distinguish two senses in which it would be possible to act without knowing what we do. If we are unaware of our *intention* we will not know what action we are performing (and it might even be questioned whether we are acting at all). Perhaps the only way, and surely the easiest way, to be unaware of our intention is to be distracted. We might be, for example, reciting the Lord's Prayer mechanically while thinking of matters academic, athletic, financial, sexual, or whatever. In forgetfulness of the intention to address God, we might be said not to know what we are doing. But this is surely true, if at all, in a very weak sense. For if anyone should interrupt us and ask what we are doing, we would have no difficulty in telling them that we are saying the Lord's Prayer. We would get a similar weak sense of ignorance if through inattention we were unaware of the motive underlying our intention. Again, if someone were to ask what we were doing, we could easily answer, for example, "I'm winning a bet by pretending to make a political protest."

But we get a much stronger sense of ignorance if we are unaware of our *motive* through repression. I might really be motivated by hostility toward my mother. But the idea that I would do this as an act of cruelty toward her is one my self-esteem cannot face, and so I rationalize my behavior by persuading myself that it is an act of political commitment and courage. In this case the sense in which I know not what I do is both stricter and more interesting than before. When the decisive motivation is unconscious through repression rather than preconscious through inattention, I cannot say what action I am performing, even if a question brings my full attention to the matter at hand. Only by breaking through the resistance that protects the original repression will I be able to identify my action correctly.

I cannot identify my action as an action if I do not know the intention that it expresses, and I cannot identify it as the action it is if I do not know the motive that it expresses.[5] It should be clear by now

---

5. It is in reflection on the notion of expression that Wayne Proudfoot links our ability to identify actions with our ability to explain them. "The identification

that when Freud speaks about not knowing the meaning of an action he means the same thing that has just been expressed in terms of not knowing the proper identity of the action. The weak and strong senses of not being able to identify my action correspond to the weak and strong senses Freud gives in "Obsessive Actions and Religious Practices" to not knowing the motive and thus the meaning of my action. Just to the degree that this account is seen to fit ordinary religious practices, the pious can be said to know not what they do.

---

of linguistic or other behavior as expressive assumes an explanation of that behavior. Were I to overhear someone engaging in invective and angry expressions, I would initially take that as evidence of his anger. If I then noticed that I had wandered onto a stage and had overheard an actor rehearsing his lines, I would discount his words and gestures as evidence of what he was feeling." I would also switch from a moral to an aesthetic appraisal of his behavior, corresponding to my reidentification of his action. Only when I properly identify the motive can I properly identify the action. Proudfoot continues with an example relevant to our reflection. "If the setting were a ceremonial one in which a pastor were leading his congregation in the recitation of the Apostles' Creed, one would be less likely to accept those words as a direct expression of [their] beliefs . . . than one would in another context. That is because an alternative explanation is available. The conventions governing the service dictate that those words are to be said at that time and in that place." In short, the operative motive may be conformity rather than piety. *Religious Experience* (Berkeley: University of California Press, 1985), p. 37.

17 Of Savages and Salieri

Freud's article "Obsessive Actions and Religious Practices" serves as a program statement for the more extensive study of religion he was to undertake in *Totem and Taboo: Some Points of Agreement between the Mental Lives of Savages and Neurotics* (1913; see 9:116 in relation to 19:206). Naturally it is obsessional neurosis he has in mind, while his "savages" are members of tribal societies whose totemistic practices had been extensively studied by Frazer and others. If we are now too aware of the savagery of "civilized" societies to call members of preliterate tribal societies "savages" and too aware of the cultural complexity of such societies to call their religions "primitive," this is less a cause for self-congratulation than a reminder that we can count on no comfortable assurance that we are really quite different from the members of such societies. In any case, Freud's working hypothesis is that the subjects of his psychoanalytic ethnology, like the patients of psychoanalytic therapy, are more similar to than different from Freud himself and us his readers.

His point of departure in *Totem and Taboo* is the incredibly strong and broadly defined incest taboos found in tribal societies (chapter 1) and the deep ambivalence on which they rest (chapter 2), their strength and severity corresponding to the (repressed) desire to do precisely what they prohibit. "They must therefore have an ambivalent attitude towards their taboos. In their unconscious there is nothing they would like more than to violate them, but they are afraid to do so; they are afraid precisely because they would like to, and the fear is stronger than the desire. The desire is unconscious, however, in every individual member of the tribe just as it is in neurotics" (13:31).

Rites associated with these taboos have a defensive character; their purpose is to ward off the punishment that would surely (and rightly) follow any violation.

If the violation of a taboo can be made good by atonement or expiation, which involve the renunciation of some possession or some freedom, this proves that obedience to the taboo injunction meant in itself the renunciation of something desirable. [Hence the ambivalence.] Emancipation from one renunciation is made up for by the imposition of another one elsewhere. This leads us to conclude that atonement is a more fundamental factor than purification in the ceremonials of taboo. (13:34)

We are immediately in the world of penance as self-punishment, previously encountered in obsessive ceremonials.[1]

One example Freud gives concerns rites relating to slain enemies. The desire to kill the enemy is obvious enough, but Freud finds that his "savages [are] in possession of a living commandment: 'Thou shalt not kill,' a violation of which would not go unpunished" (13:39). In short, out of the ambivalence comes a taboo, and out of the taboo comes a ceremonial, or rather a variety of them.

These observances fall easily into four groups. They demand (1) the appeasement of the slain enemy, (2) restrictions upon the slayer, (3) acts of expiation and purification by him and (4) certain ceremonial observances. . . . The conclusion that we must draw from all these observances is that the impulses which they express towards the enemy are not solely hostile ones. They are also manifestations of remorse, of admiration for the enemy, and of a bad conscience for having killed him. (13:36-39; cf. 51-67 for similar rites relating to the dead in general)

But ambivalence is not yet compromise, and Freud has not forgotten that ceremonials go beyond defense to compromise, that they embody wish fulfillment as well as renunciation. Speaking of the obsessive acts that are his heuristic clue, he reminds us that "from one point of view they are evidences of remorse, efforts at expiation, and so on, while on the other hand they are at the same time substitutive acts to compensate the instinct for what had been prohibited" (13:30). His first example of this relates to the incest taboos whose strictness he

1. On the basis of *Totem and Taboo*, Theodor Reik continues a psychoanalytic ethnography in *Ritual: Psychoanalytic Studies*, trans. Douglas Byran (New York: International Universities Press, 1976). Its first study, "Couvade and the Psychogenesis of the Fear of Retaliation," focuses entirely on these features of renunciation and self-punishment as a defense against the consequences of forbidden desire.

has emphasized. "It must strike us as all the more puzzling to hear that these same savages practice *sacred orgies*, in which precisely these forbidden degrees of kinship seek sexual intercourse" (13:11, emphasis added). That rites of atonement and rites of transgression coexist as separate acts that cancel each other out, comprising together a ceremonial compromise, will come as no surprise to those who understand the neurotic who removes the stone from the road and then replaces it (see above, chapter 15).

But the compromise can be embodied in a single rite.[2] Freud illustrates this with rites surrounding sacred kingship.[3] "The king or chief arouses envy on account of his privileges; everyone, perhaps, would like to be a king" (13:33). This results in "excessive solicitude. . . . It appears wherever, in addition to a predominant feeling of affection, there is also a contrary, but unconscious, current of hostility. . . . The hostility is then shouted down, as it were, by an excessive intensification of the affection, which is expressed as solicitude and becomes compulsive, because it might otherwise be inadequate to perform its task of keeping the unconscious contrary current of feeling under repression. . . . We shall realize that alongside of the veneration, and indeed idolization, felt towards [privileged persons], there is in the unconscious an opposing current of intense hostility" (13:49). This strictly parallels the situation among Freud's patients, where "the original *wish* that the loved person may die is replaced by a *fear* that he may die. So that when the neurosis appears to be so tenderly altruistic, it is merely *compensating* for an underlying contrary attitude of brutal egoism" (13:72). In the tribal situation, this hostile egoism finds its expression in the rites surrounding sacred kingship.

Quoting from Frazer, Freud describes, as an example, the Timmes people from Sierra Leone, "who elect their king [and] reserve to themselves the right of beating him on the eve of his coronation; and they avail themselves of this constitutional privilege with such hearty goodwill that sometimes the unhappy monarch does not long survive

---

2. Theodor Reik's extensive study "The Puberty Rites of Savages," in *Ritual* (see previous note), traces the link between psychic ambivalence and ritual compromise for both the fathers and sons involved.

3. For a masterful study of sacred kingship in ancient Egypt and Mesopotamia, see Henri Frankfort, *Kingship and the Gods: A Study of Ancient Near Eastern Religion as the Integration of Society and Nature* (Chicago: University of Chicago Press, 1948). My own analysis is in chapter 10 of *God, Guilt, and Death* (Bloomington: Indiana University Press, 1984).

his elevation to the throne." To which Freud adds, "Even in glaring instances like this, however, the hostility is not admitted as such, but masquerades as a ceremonial" (13:49).[4]

Somewhat more subtle are the elaborate protection rituals surrounding sacred rulers like the Mikado of ancient Japan. "It must strike us as self-contradictory that persons of such unlimited power should need to be protected so carefully from the threat of danger; but that is not the only contradiction. . . . For these peoples also think it necessary to keep a watch on their king to see that he makes a proper use of his powers." He then quotes Frazer again on the proper use of kingly power. In such societies the sovereign

> exists only for his subjects; his life is only valuable so long as he discharges the duties of his position by ordering the course of nature for his people's benefit. So soon as he fails to do so, the care, the devotion, the religious homage which they had hitherto lavished on him cease and are changed into hatred and contempt; he is dismissed ignominiously, and may be thankful if he escapes with his life. Worshipped as a god one day, he is killed as a criminal the next. (13:43-44)

The journey from Palm Sunday to Good Friday is short indeed.

But sacred kings experience the ambiguity of honor not only when they are deposed. "A king of this sort lives hedged in by a ceremonious etiquette, a network of prohibitions and observances, of which the intention is not to contribute to his dignity, much less to his comfort, but to restrain him from conduct which, by disturbing the harmony of nature, might involve himself, his people, and the universe in one common catastrophe" (13:44).

Here is the finest coup d'état one could imagine, for the effectiveness of the rebellion consists precisely in its being unacknowledged and unnoticed. Such a king is "hedged in" by rites which "restrain" him and "annihilate his freedom," even though they purport to "contribute to his dignity" (13:44). I am reminded of the Mother's Day celebrations of my childhood, in which the restriction of women to one particular role in society was reinforced and legitimized by rites of veneration in which Mother was placed on a pedestal as Queen for a Day. I am also reminded of the relation between the press (tabloid and serious) and both English royalty and the American presidency. (It

---

4. For a somewhat similar ritual on the Babylonian Day of Atonement, see *God, Guilt, and Death*, pp. 203-8.

would be interesting to trace the correlation between the rise of the imperial presidency and the ritual revenge wreaked by the fourth estate in the United States, resulting in the now more or less permanent war between the White House and its press corps.)[5]

Freud's summary is succinct:

> The obsessional act is *ostensibly* a protection against the prohibited act; but *actually*, in our view, it is a repetition of it. The "ostensibly" applies to the *conscious* part of the mind, and the "actually" to the *unconscious* part. In exactly the same way, the ceremonial taboo of kings is *ostensibly* the highest honour and protection for them, while *actually* it is a punishment for their exaltation, a revenge taken on them by their subjects. (13:50-51)

If we remember that kingship is one of the central symbols of Judeo-Christian monotheism, we will realize that Freud is not primarily interested in Sierra Leone, Japan, Mother's Day, or press constraints on royal and quasi-royal figures. He is inviting us to recognize ourselves in the "savages" he describes, suggesting that there is a profound ambiguity in the rites by which the God of the Bible is worshipped. This is not to say that there is no genuine love expressed in them, but only that, especially where that love is unusually intense, it may very well be the mask behind which our envy of God's privilege and power and our revenge against his authority come to expression.

We would like to say, "But surely, we have no rites in which our sacred king is beaten, nearly to death." Freud makes us not so sure. We do have a rite, the Eucharist, that commemorates (some would say, reenacts) the cruel torture and execution of one who was mocked as a king by Roman soldiers, labeled "King of the Jews" by Pontius Pilate, and hailed as Christ the King by his followers. Of course, Jesus was not originally crucified by those who acknowledged his sovereignty, and there is no doubt that his death holds a very important place in the New Testament. But there is a piety that focuses so heavily on the blood of Jesus — it comes in both Protestant and Catholic versions — that the life of Jesus, his resurrection, and his coming again in glory are effectively reduced to the status of footnotes. Are this piety and the rites

---

5. Similar treatment is the fate of the other gods and heroes of American culture, superstar athletes and entertainers. Cf. Jürgen Habermas's comment that in ritual the primal powers "are hallowed and outsmarted at the same time." *The Philosophical Discourse of Modernity*, trans. Frederick Lawrence (Cambridge: MIT Press, 1987), p. 108.

that enact it a compromise formation, one that says, in effect, We will acknowledge Jesus to be Christ the King, but like the tribal subjects of Sierra Leone, we will see to it that he pays dearly for his elevation?

Although the eucharistic liturgy of my own denomination speaks of the "holy Supper" as "a feast of remembrance, of communion, and of hope" and devotes a careful paragraph to the meaning of each of these three dimensions of meaning,[6] I have yet to participate in a celebration of this rite that focused on either communion or hope. The inscription on the communion table always reads "In remembrance of me," never "Until he comes" (1 Cor. 11:23-26). And, although the paragraph on remembrance speaks of the life, resurrection, and ascension of Jesus as well as of his death, the focus is always, not just on remembrance, but specifically on the crucifixion. Is there something going on in this central Christian ceremonial that we do not notice?

Freud's other example may come even closer to home. In this case envy of the sacred king expresses itself not as ritual revenge but in rites that "annihilate his freedom" while purporting to "contribute to his dignity." In short, the strategy is to domesticate the divine power, to co-opt and control it for one's own purposes. When Freud first speaks of envy against persons of privilege he mentions the frequent taboo against touching them, since touching "is the first step towards obtaining any control over, or attempting to make use of, a person or object" (13:33-34). Then, in chapter 3 of *Totem and Taboo*, he describes the worldview of the rites he is describing. Its science is animism and its technology is magic (13:75-79). When we combine the goal of magic, which is control of the world, with the magical character of ceremonials (13:78, 87), we see that what is at issue in this combination of theory and practice is omnipotence and the human attempt to exercise control over whatever sacred powers might exist. Throughout the entire discussion it is power rather than pleasure that is at issue, confirming once again Freud's "Augustinian" priority of pride over lust among the deadly sins.

No doubt one of the ways in which the faithful annihilate God's freedom while purporting to contribute to the divine dignity is through the liturgical equivalent of the demand for orthodoxy.[7] By insisting that God be worshipped precisely through the rites that we practice and

---

6. *The Liturgy of the Reformed Church in America together with the Psalter Selected and Arranged for Responsive Reading*, ed. Gerrit T. Vander Lugt (New York: Board of Education of the Reformed Church in America, 1968), p. 65.

7. See my article "Orthodoxy and Inattention," *Reformed Journal* 30/1 (January 1980), pp. 13-15.

that these be interpreted only as we interpret them, we transform the covenant formula, "I will be your God, and you will be my people,"[8] into a vehicle for making God our personal property. (This can happen at the national as well as at the denominational level. Thus, Iran, Israel, and the United States represent Islamic, Jewish, and Christian versions of what might be called possessive monotheism, at least in the practices of some of their most devoutly religious citizens.) We thus become the definition of the good and the saved, making those who differ from us into the wicked and the lost. If we are among those who preside over the sacramental rites of our faith, we become the dispensers or withholders of divine favor.

In the rites by which we effect this elevation of ourselves into an elect elite, we are conscious of the desire to honor and glorify God but manage not to notice how once again we tempt Satan to ask, "Do they serve God for naught?" To the precise degree that our worship makes us into the possessors and purveyors of the sacred power, we know not what we do.

Freud's claim, it will be remembered, is that the believing soul is unaware of the meaning of its ritual act, "or at any rate of its *chief* meaning" (9:122, emphasis added). Ricoeur asks how this "forgetfulness of meaning in religious observances pertain[s] to the essence of religion," and whether this situation belongs to "the underlying intention of religion" or is rather "the result of its degradation and regression," but it is a bit misleading to suggest that Freud does not himself raise such questions.[9] The issue is not whether Freud thinks this "amnesia" (13:30) belongs to the essence of religion, but how we might find whether this is true of our own piety. Perhaps the patience of Job and the honesty of Salieri (see above, chapter 1) can be helpful to us here. If we can identify the bargains we have tried to make with God in the form of ceremonial compromises (and here our trio of atheists can be very helpful just by virtue of their hostility), we can put to ourselves the question faced by Job and by Salieri: If the god of bargains refuses to bargain and the god of possessive monotheism refuses to be possessed, what happens to my faith?

8. For biblical references and commentary on them, see *God, Guilt, and Death,* pp. 232-33, including n. 57.

9. Paul Ricoeur, *Freud and Philosophy: An Essay on Interpretation,* trans. Denis Savage (New Haven: Yale University Press, 1970), pp. 232-33. Freud gives a somewhat more modest evaluation of the role of psychoanalysis vis-à-vis religion at 13:100.

18 Of Obedience and Sacrifice

The prophets of ancient Israel were perhaps the first "masters of suspicion." On behalf of Yahweh they were as hostile to the religion practiced in their society as Marx, Nietzsche, and Freud were to those of theirs. The king was often their target. In the first such confrontation between prophet and king over the nature of true religion, Samuel angrily announces Yahweh's rejection of Saul as king and of the sacrifices he and the people planned to offer to Yahweh from the forbidden spoils of war they had kept:

> Behold, to obey is better than sacrifice,
>   and to hearken than the fat of rams.
> For rebellion is as the sin of divination,
>   and stubbornness is as iniquity and idolatry.
>
> (1 Sam. 15:22b-23a)

According to Samuel's hermeneutics of suspicion, the sacrifices are not motivated by an obedient heart but by a stubborn rebelliousness that renders them acts of divination and idolatry, forbidden commerce with false deities, the very opposite of what they purport to be.

Freud's critique of religious practices should be taken seriously by those who practice religion just because he helps us see some of the many ways in which our practices reprise Saul's sacrifice. What we have yet to see is how the Freudian account applies to ethical as well as liturgical practices, to righteousness as well as ritual. In other words, obedience is as ambiguous as sacrifice, as Jesus' critique of the Pharisees will show (see below, chapters 42 and 43).

The ceremonies we have looked at in the previous chapter, those growing out of taboos surrounding slain enemies and sacred kings, nicely exhibit Freud's thesis about the compromise character of religious rituals. But they are somewhat peripheral in *Totem and Taboo*. At its center is the totemic sacrifice that is itself the center of totemism as a religion. Ironically, it is in Freud's analysis of this sacrifice in chapter four of *Totem and Taboo* that the ambiguity of obedience comes to light.

But he has been preparing the way for this from the very beginning. He divides moral consciousness into conscience, the voice that says "Don't do it," and guilt, the voice that says "You did it" (13:67-68). In the preface of *Totem and Taboo* and repeatedly thereafter he emphasizes the similarity between tribal taboos, neurotic taboos, and the categorical imperative that underlies moral conscience and guilt. All three involve the presence of a powerful prohibition for which its possessor can assign no motive or reason (13:x, 21-22, 26, 28, 30-31, 68-69).

Freud appears to be a moral Kantian who distinguishes the unconditional and categorical character of moral obligation from the instrumental, utilitarian, and hypothetical character of non-moral imperatives. The latter have the form, If you want x, do y, or, in the case of prohibitions, refrain from doing y. The motive or reason for taking a hypothetical prohibition seriously can always be named: "Because I want x." But in the case of a taboo or a categorical prohibition, I simply know that I must not do something, though I cannot justify this in terms of instrumental rationality. Freud concludes: "Taboo conscience is probably the earliest form in which the phenomenon of conscience is met with" (13:67).

Another anticipation of the ethical significance of the critique of ceremonials is found in a passage cited previously: "If the violation of a taboo can be made good by atonement or expiation, which involve the renunciation of some possession or some freedom, this proves that obedience to the taboo injunction meant in itself the renunciation of something desirable. Emancipation from one renunciation is made up for by the imposition of another one elsewhere" (13:34). It is clear that renunciation is the key and that it can take two forms. The renunciation of "some possession" typically takes place in sacrifice and offering, while the renunciation of "some freedom" typically takes place in ethical obedience. Thus Saul sought to make up for his self-declared emancipation from obedience by the self-imposition of sacrifice. Debts in one currency can be paid in the other.

Presumably it could work the other way as well. The ethical renunciation of "some freedom" might be the bargain I try to strike with God, the price I am willing to pay for the privilege of not renouncing "some possession" or perhaps "some other freedom." If my besetting sin is greed, for example, I might adopt a work ethic whose worldly asceticism places severe restrictions on my leisure time and sexual practices, a price I am willing to pay for pursuing greed without guilt.

Totemism involves such a renunciation of "some freedom." To see its ambiguity we need to begin with the sacrificial meal central to totemism. It involves the corporate killing of the totem, the tribe's sacred animal, an act strictly forbidden at all times to individuals. Through his own therapy with "little Hans" and from similar cases reported by Wulff and Ferenczi, Freud has no doubt that the totem animal is a symbolic substitute for the father (13:126-32), and just to make sure we do not overlook the import of his analysis for biblical monotheism, he reminds us that "at bottom God is nothing other than an exalted father" (13:147-48; cf. 153-55). The rite is thus a symbolical satisfaction of the hostility normally directed at persons of power and privilege.

Freud thinks the rite expresses historical memory as well. He accepts the Darwinian hypothesis and writes that humans "originally lived in comparatively small groups or hordes within which the jealousy of the oldest and strongest male [the father] prevented sexual promiscuity" (13:125). The "great event" that gave birth to civilization (13:145, 152) occurred when the sons ganged up on the father and killed him.

> Cannibal savages as they were, it goes without saying that they devoured their victim as well as killing him. The violent primal father had doubtless been the feared and envied model of each one of the company of brothers: and in the act of devouring him they accomplished their identification with him, and each one of them acquired a portion of his strength. The totem meal, which is perhaps mankind's earliest festival, would thus be a repetition and a commemoration of this memorable and criminal deed. (13:142)

I do not know where one would look to find someone who takes this historical hypothesis seriously. But surely Roazen is right in saying that, just as social contract fictions can be theoretically illuminating, so in Freud's case, "his argument can be reconstructed as a psychological theory, entirely apart from the problem of the actual occurrence of a primal deed."[1] And Ricoeur is wise to treat this account as myth rather

---

1. Paul Roazen, *Freud: Political and Social Thought* (New York: Random House, 1968), p. 136. Roazen continues, "One could, if one wanted to throw stones, have a field day with Freud's Lamarckianism; but since we are interested in Freud for what he has to say about human psychology, we will focus on how he extends our understanding of people."

than history.[2] For the question concerns the meaning of the rite, and its psychological origin is a more reliable clue to that than its historical origin.[3]

If we are to understand totemism as a compromise formation rooted in ambivalence toward the father, we need to look, not for a primordial historical event, but for the renunciation that expresses the love that coexists with hatred of the father and defends against guilt and fear of punishment vis-à-vis the symbolic parricide. Freud finds this renunciation in "the two principal ordinances of totemism, the two taboo prohibitions which constitute its core — not to kill the totem and not to have sexual relations with a woman of the same totem," the renunciation of "the two crimes of Oedipus, who killed his father and married his mother" (13:132). Through this "deferred obedience," the sons expressed remorse and "revoked their deed by forbidding the killing of the totem, the substitute for their father; and they renounced its fruits by resigning their claim to the women who had now been set free. They thus created out of their filial sense of guilt the two fundamental taboos of totemism" (13:143).

Without denying that this "deferred obedience" (13:143, 145) expresses genuine love, Freud presents it primarily as a strategy of guilt management (13:144-45). As such it is part of a compromise formation.

> Totemic religion not only comprised expressions of remorse and attempts at atonement [in the form of ethical obedience], it also served as a remembrance of the triumph over the father. Satisfaction over that triumph led to the institution of the memorial festival of the totem meal, in which the restrictions of deferred obedience no longer held. Thus it became a duty to repeat the crime of parricide again and again in the sacrifice of the totem animal. . . . We shall not be surprised to find that the element of filial rebelliousness also emerges, in the *later* products of religion, often in the strangest disguises and transformations. (13:145)

2. Paul Ricoeur, *Freud and Philosophy: An Essay on Interpretation*, trans. Denis Savage (New Haven: Yale University Press, 1970), pp. 207-8.

3. It is ironical that Freud should have insisted on the historicity of the primal patricide while coming to hold that the childhood seductions his patients regularly reported were only imaginary. While it is hard to know even what would count as evidence to support such a claim, we now have abundant evidence that the sexual abuse of children is a frequent occurrence, which is not to say that it might not also be fantasized. For the view that Freud himself suppressed evidence that the seductions were real events, see Jeffrey Moussaieff Masson, *Freud: The Assault on Truth: Freud's Suppression of the Seduction Theory* (New York: Farrar, Straus and Giroux, 1984).

Freud has just presented one of the basic disguises, morality as the indulgence by which I purchase the right to guilt-free rebellion. When we remember that the act of parricide is repeated again and again, that it has now become a duty, and that "these same savages practice sacred orgies, in which precisely these forbidden degrees of kinship seek sexual intercourse" (13:11; cf. 152), we realize that the believing soul is back to its favorite pastime, striking a deal with the god of bargains. The renunciation expressed in the commandments "Thou shalt not kill" and "Thou shalt not commit incest" is but the penance portion of this compromise formation.

Freud speaks of this renunciation as a "reconciliation with their father . . . a covenant with their father, in which he promised them everything that a childish imagination may expect from a father — protection, care and indulgence — while on their side they undertook to respect his life, that is to say, not to repeat the deed which had brought destruction on their real father" (13:144). Perhaps we should call it, by analogy with the Half-Way Covenant of seventeenth-century New England Puritanism, a "One-Way Covenant," a negotiation carried out in the absence of one of the parties. For when we realize that deferred obedience is the condition under which rebellion can continue to be celebrated, that the sons are not abandoning symbolic murder and real incest but only restricting them to totemism's high holy days, we might wonder whether this is a covenant the living father would have accepted. Roazen's talk of renunciation and self-punishment as bribery in the service of guilt management is probably closer to what Freud is pointing to than Freud's own talk of covenant and reconciliation.[4] In this diphasic compromise rebellion is cancelled out by repentance, which in turn is cancelled out by repeated rebellion.

As totemism is replaced by polytheism and monotheism, sacrifice takes on a different meaning. Once the remembrance of rebellion, it becomes the renunciation of some possession. This is what makes it possible for Saul to be the opposite of the totemic sons. While he offers sacrifice as a bribe to pay for his lack of obedience, they offer obedience as a bribe to permit the repetition of the sacrifice. But this difference is superficial. What is essential is the ambiguous role of religious renunciation, whether ritual or moral. For to the very degree that renunciation is in the service of rebellion, manifest piety is latent impiety. Once again, we know not what we do.

4. Roazen, p. 141.

19 *Willful Renunciation and the One-Way Covenant*

Several years ago a chance comment by a student of mine led me to a fuller understanding of what Freud is driving at. We were preparing for a unit on crime and punishment in a course on social ethics. I had asked the students to develop their own theory of punishment by reflecting on their own experience of being punished as children. One student spoke of "the punishments that I asked for." The context made it sound as if this did not refer to the behavior that was to be punished, as when one says to a misbehaving child "You're asking for it," but rather to some kind of request subsequent to misbehavior. When she came in to discuss her paper, I asked about this and heard a most remarkable story.

From the time she was five until she was ten she had been a very rebellious and disobedient child. Her parents did not put up with this, and the result was a lot of spankings, on the average once or twice a week by her estimate. These were normally given by her mother with the help of a flyswatter. She hated these punishments and always put up whatever physical resistance she could, though she always lost the ensuing wrestling match. On occasions when her behavior was judged to be unusually bad, her mother applied the flyswatter to her bare bottom. Since these spankings decidedly hurt more than the normal ones, which were themselves by no means merely symbolic, they were both the most hated and the most vigorously resisted.

From time to time an act of disobedience would go undetected, one the girl knew would be punished if it were discovered. On those occasions she would initiate a conversation whose *conscious* purpose was that she be found out and punished. Without ever coming right out and saying what she had done, she gave her parents enough information to figure it out. The result was always the same. The deed was

discovered, and she was punished. In fact, on these occasions she always got that most dreaded of spankings, the one on her bare bottom.
This is what she meant when she spoke of "the punishments that I
asked for."

No doubt we are dealing with a compromise formation. The girl
does not abandon her wayward ways but continues to earn a spanking
or two each week. Her punishments represent "the sum of the conditions
subject to which something that is not yet absolutely forbidden is permitted" (9:124-25; see p. 98 above), namely her misbehavior. Like her
nineteen-year-old colleague, she is indeed able to maintain her defiance
only "at the cost of great sacrifice" (16:264; see pp. 90-91 above), her
painful punishments. But this is obviously a price she is willing to pay for
a long time. Indeed, she takes the initiative to see to it that her account is
paid up. A guilty conscience is more painful than a sore bottom.

There is a peculiar twist to the story, however. Punishment is the
conscious purpose of the (indirect) confessions the girl describes. But a
number of factors suggest that it is also the unconscious purpose of the
deed itself to be discovered. We are reminded of Freud's claim that an
unconscious sense of guilt "can turn people into criminals. . . . In many
criminals, especially youthful ones, it is possible to detect a very powerful sense of guilt which existed before the crime, and is therefore not
its result but its motive. It is as if it was a relief to be able to fasten this
unconscious sense of guilt on to something real and immediate" (19:52;
cf. 14:332-33). As Roazen puts it, "In Raskolnikov, in *Crime and Punishment*, a man [first] acts out his irrational guilt by attaching it to an
external crime, in this instance a murder, and [only] then proceeds
slowly to give himself away to the public authorities."[1]

One indication that our five- to ten-year-old is a young Raskolnikov is found in God's role in this strange story. At the heart of her
theology lies the belief that God feels good about us when we are
punished. She says she got this idea from what she was told in Sunday
school, though she is aware that this is not what they taught her. The
remarkable thing is the categorical character of her doctrine. It is not
that if we have sinned, God thinks we should be punished. It is simply
that God feels better about us when we are punished. It is as if her own
self-esteem, here linked overtly to divine approval, calls for punishment
not specifically attached to determinate misdeeds. She seems to feel the
kind of guilt commensurate with Freud's theology of original sin.

---

1. Paul Roazen, *Freud: Political and Social Thought* (New York: Random House,
1968), p. 142.

A second factor suggests that the need for punishment precedes the act that merits it. She says that after making her indirect confessions once or twice, she got very good at it. She found out what worked and got to be very efficient at giving herself away. She would open the conversation with the comment, "It's been a while since I've been spanked." Once she had her mother thinking about the flyswatter, it was relatively easy to get her first to suspect and then to confirm that she ought to use it. But the significant clue is the "It's been a while" portion of her opening line. It is as if she had an open-ended need for punishment that was satisfied in the normal course of events by her habitual naughtiness and its normal consequence. But from time to time the system would break down, and when it had been too long since she had been punished, the situation became unbearable. She then did something whose unconscious purpose was the same as the conscious purpose of the subsequent quasi-confession, to be found out and punished.

Another peculiar feature of the situation tends to confirm this reading. Since the young woman insisted that the purpose of her quasi-confession was fully conscious, I asked her why she didn't just come right out and say "I did such and such" or even "I did such and such and deserve to be punished." Without hesitation she replied that she was afraid that she might appear too repentant and her mother would either not punish her at all or would give her only the normal instead of the most dreaded spanking. In short, her conscious purpose was not just to be punished but to receive the maximum punishment. And she *always* succeeded. How is that possible unless the conscious purpose of the confessional stage had already been the unconscious purpose of the criminal stage, unless the deed had already been designed to be serious enough to merit a punishment that would make up for the fact that "It's been a while"?

The final clue is perhaps the decisive one. When the girl was ten, her parents finally decided to quit playing the game and announced that there would be no more spankings. The almost immediate result was "a complete change of personality" in the girl. She became an obedient and cooperative child. In the present context I would be the last to suggest that her new obedience was free of ambiguity. We have just seen, in the case of the totemic brothers, how obedience can play the same role in one compromise formation that penance plays in another. Whether this is what happened in this girl's case we have no way of knowing.

I have found this story exceptionally helpful in teaching *Totem and Taboo* for two reasons. First, it makes dramatically clear that the meaning of a renunciation cannot be determined by its severity.[2] Great or small, it may be an expression of the purity of heart that wills one thing and expresses itself without reservation in such selfless words as these:

> Our Father who art in heaven,
> Hallowed be *thy* name.
> *Thy* kingdom come,
> *Thy* will be done.

But just as easily, great or small, ritual or ethical, a religious renunciation may be in the service of "the dear self" and "some secret impulse of self-love" (see above, chapter 3) that leaves us able to pray such words without willing them entirely (see above, p. 92 n. 2). It may be an expression of impurity of heart even more than of purity.

The story is also helpful because of the way it highlights the one-way character of a One-Way Covenant. (Lawyers might want to speak here of an unconscionable contract, one so patently unfair as to be legally invalid even if agreed to by the victimized party.) From the parents' point of view the purpose of the punishments was to change the girl's behavior and basic attitude. But from her point of view their purpose was to preserve her behavior and attitude. She said, in effect, "You may spank me as often and as hard as you like. That is the price I am willing to pay to be able to continue my disobedient behavior and rebellious attitude without guilt." This is not a covenant to which her parents would ever have agreed, and it took them a long time to discover that they had been snookered into being party to it. (Perhaps the girl was a useful scapegoat for them and punishing her helped to relieve their guilt.) But once they recognized her One-Way Covenant for what it was and made it clear that they would no longer be a party to it, it collapsed.

In a religious context the hermeneutics of suspicion has a double task to perform. On the one hand it must expose the piety of compromise formations and One-Way Covenants for what it is, while on the other it must make it clear that God cannot be snookered into accepting the bribes offered by such pseudo-piety. We only deceive

---

2. This throws interesting light on the suggestion by Dean Kelly that conservative churches grow because of their "strictness" as "high-demand" communities. See *Why Conservative Churches Are Growing* (2nd ed.; San Francisco: Harper and Row, 1977; reprinted, Macon, GA: Mercer University Press, 1986).

ourselves in thinking that God has been playing along with us all the time. While Freud hopes that the hermeneutics of suspicion will lead to the collapse of religion, prophetic consciousness hopes that it will lead to the collapse of irreligion posing as religion, creating a space wherein true faith might flourish.[3]

3. Paul Ricoeur develops this difference as the dialectic of religion and faith at the conclusion of *Freud and Philosophy: An Essay on Interpretation,* trans. Denis Savage (New Haven: Yale University Press, 1970), and in the final section of *The Conflict of Interpretations,* ed. Don Ihde (Evanston: Northwestern University Press, 1974).

III Marx and the Critique of Religion as Ideology

20 Feuerbach's Bourgeois Atheism

Religion is, according to Marxian atheism, "the opium of the people" (SW 64; OR 42).[1] This verdict is as central to Marx's view of religion as it is familiar. The degree to which we understand it will be the degree to which we understand his critique. But the meaning of the metaphor is not self-evident, especially in a time when it is possible to speak of the recreational use of drugs. For Marx, religion and opium are painkillers[2] that are not only addictive but even worse, since they treat symptoms rather than diseases. While there may be medically hopeless situations in which narcotics play a useful role, religion invariably distracts attention from a social disease that *can* be treated and cured.[3] Rather than a desperate response to genuine hopelessness, it is the diabolical creation of *unnecessary* hopelessness concerning the human social order.

The essay in which Marx calls religion the opium of the people

1. Citations from Marx and Engels in the text use the following abbreviations:

CA   Karl Marx, *Capital*, vol. 1, trans. Samuel Moore and Edward Aveling (New York: International Publishers, 1967).

LT   David McLellan, *Karl Marx: His Life and Thought* (New York: Harper and Row, 1973).

OR   Karl Marx and Friedrich Engels, *On Religion* (New York: Schocken Books, 1964; reprinted Atlanta: Scholars, 1982; introduction by Reinhold Niebuhr).

PS   *Writings of the Young Marx on Philosophy and Society*, ed. L. D. Easton and K. H. Guddat (Garden City, NY: Doubleday, 1967).

SW   *Karl Marx: Selected Writings*, ed. David McLellan (Oxford: Oxford University Press, 1977). Quotations from this volume appear by permission of Oxford University Press.

2. See above, p. 39 n. 1.

3. At least in the aftermath of the Industrial Revolution.

begins with these words: "As far as Germany is concerned, the criticism of religion is complete, and the criticism of religion is the presupposition of all criticism. . . . The foundation of irreligious criticism is this: man makes religion, religion does not make man" (SW 63). These last words are a paraphrase of Ludwig Feuerbach's statement: "Man first unconsciously and involuntarily creates God in his own image, and after this God consciously and voluntarily creates man in his own image" (EC 118).[4]

Marx's atheism is built on Feuerbach's, and it is indeed to Feuerbach that Marx refers when he says that in Germany the criticism of religion is complete. But this is a strange statement, since it stands at the beginning of seven paragraphs (about a page and a half in the German edition) in which the thesis is that any critique of the type offered by Feuerbach is radically and essentially incomplete.[5] In the following year Marx would call Feuerbach and the other intellectual terrorists known as "Young Hegelians" sheep in wolves' clothing (SW 160), implying that their atheism was more the product of bourgeois Christendom than its enemy. This stance of the youthful Marx becomes a permanent part of his own critique of religion. Still, since Marx incorporates Feuerbach into his own quite different atheism, we must begin with Feuerbach's version.

In 1842 Feuerbach published a brief essay entitled "Preliminary Theses on the Reform of Philosophy"[6] that had an enormous impact on the young Marx. Its opening words are, "The secret of *theology* is *anthropology* . . ." (FB 153). This claim succinctly summarizes Feuerbach's earlier and most famous book, *The Essence of Christianity*. This idea that what seems to be said about God is actually about humankind is implicit in the notion that we first create God in our own image before we are created in God's image.

4. Citations from Feuerbach will use the following abbreviations:
EC *The Essence of Christianity*, trans. George Eliot (New York: Harper and Brothers, 1957).
EF *The Essence of Faith According to Luther*, trans. Melvin Cherno (New York: Harper and Row, 1967).
ER *Lectures on the Essence of Religion*, trans. Ralph Manheim (New York: Harper and Row, 1967).
FB *The Fiery Brook: Selected Writings of Ludwig Feuerbach*, trans. Zawar Hanfi (Garden City, NY: Doubleday, 1972).
5. The opium metaphor occurs in the fourth of these paragraphs.
6. The words "theses" and "reform" may very well be intended to suggest that Feuerbach will be for philosophy what Luther was for theology.

Feuerbach speaks of projection in this context. "Man cannot get beyond his true nature. He may indeed by means of the imagination conceive individuals of another so-called higher kind, but . . . the positive final predicates which he gives to these other individuals are always determinations or qualities drawn from his own nature — qualities in which he in truth only images and projects himself" (EC 11). For Feuerbach the mystery of religion is simply this: "Man . . . projects his being into objectivity, and then again makes himself an object of this projected image of himself thus converted into a subject" (EC 29f.).

This theory of projection, like Freud's, is a theory of false consciousness. Cognitively speaking, we know not what we do.[7] But only a moment's reflection will reveal a major difference from Freud. As we learned from the case of the hapless Dr. Schreber, Freudian projection is a mechanism for getting rid of some affect, such as lust or hostility, that we cannot acknowledge without shame. For Feuerbach, by contrast, in religion we project only "that which is worthy of adoration" (EC 12). "What man praises and approves, that is God to him. . . . Religion is a *judgment*. The most essential condition in religion — in the idea of the divine being — is accordingly the discrimination of the praiseworthy from the blameworthy, of the perfect from the imperfect" (EC 97).

I want to suggest that there are three layers of meaning in Feuerbach's theory of religion as projective false consciousness. There are Hegelian[8] and Freudian layers that, while quite distinct, are both clearly visible. Then there is a Marxian layer that is only hinted at and never quite in focus. It is by making this last layer fully explicit that Marx radicalizes the Feuerbachian critique of religion.

There are two themes in the Hegelian stratum of *The Essence of Christianity*. The first is found in the thesis that "God is the idea of the species as an individual" (EC 153). Feuerbach repeatedly insists that while the perfections we represent to ourselves as divine are really human, they belong not to the individual but to the species. While it would be not merely vain but ludicrous for the individual to view his or her perfections or excellences as infinite, this does not apply to the species. To say, for example, that there is no greater beauty than human beauty is quite different from saying that there is no beauty greater than

---

7. Thus, while God is represented as consciously and voluntarily creating humankind, the first creation, that of God in our image, is represented as unconscious and involuntary.

8. No need to panic. What follows does not presuppose any prior familiarity with Hegel on the part of the reader.

mine (EC 6-7). "The divine being is nothing else than the human being, or, rather, the human nature purified, freed from the limits of the individual man, made objective — i.e., contemplated and revered as another, a distinct being" (EC 14; cf. 35, 42).

This motif in Feuerbach continues the Hegelian strategy of affirming the religious sense of transcendence but reinterpreting it as the transcendence of the human spirit in some collective sense to the religious consciousness of the individual.[9] What distinguishes Feuerbach from Hegel on this point is that he neither presents himself as a Christian philosopher nor seeks to deny that his theory is atheistic in the usual sense of the word.

The other Hegelian theme in *The Essence of Christianity* concerns the relation of consciousness to self-consciousness.[10] Because in religion the human subject is aware of its own true nature, of its own spirit (Hegel) or species (Feuerbach), "consciousness of the object and self-consciousness coincide. . . . Consciousness of God is self-consciousness, knowledge of God is self-knowledge" (EC 12; cf. 1f.). But it belongs to the religious stage of experience that the believing soul does not know this (having unconsciously and involuntarily created God in the image of his or her own species) and takes God to be something quite beyond everything human. Thus

> when religion — consciousness of God — is designated as the self-consciousness of man, this is not to be understood as affirming that the religious man is directly aware of this identity; for, on the contrary, ignorance of it is fundamental to the peculiar nature of religion. To preclude this misconception, it is better to say, religion is man's earliest and also indirect form of self-knowledge. Hence, religion everywhere precedes philosophy, as in the history of the race, so also in that of the individual. Man first of all sees his nature as if *out of* himself, before he finds it in himself. . . . Religion is the childlike condition of humanity. . . . Hence the historical progress of religion consists in this: that what by an earlier religion was regarded as objective is now recognized as subjective. . . . And it is our task to show that the antithesis of divine and human is alto-

9. I have developed this aspect of Hegel's thought in chapter 7 of *History and Truth in Hegel's Phenomenology* (Atlantic Highlands, NJ: Humanities Press, 1979 and 1990), suggesting that Durkheim's theory in *The Elementary Forms of the Religious Life* is a helpful guide to reading Hegel.

10. Hegel and Feuerbach are sufficiently Cartesian and Kantian to retain the belief that the problem of knowledge can be solved only if the object of knowledge and its subject turn out somehow to be the same.

gether illusory, that it is nothing else than the antithesis between the human nature in general and the human individual. (EC 13f.)

Religion is false consciousness, or, to use a term of which Feuerbach is as fond as Freud, it is an illusion (EC xxxviii-xl, 13, 16, 127). And yet, in this Hegelian dimension of the text, religion is as natural as childhood. As a necessary stage in the path of self-discovery, it is nothing to be ashamed of, even if it is something to grow out of. The transition from (theistic) religion to (atheistic) philosophy is simply the developmental discovery of the projective character of religious knowledge, the realization that consciousness is self-consciousness, that God is humankind. This discovery is not entirely unlike the discovery of the true ontological status of Santa Claus, who turns out to be but the personification of the human spirit of giving.

I have already mentioned that, while for Freud projection is a means for dealing with what cannot be acknowledged without shame, for Feuerbach we project in religion what is *best* about humankind. In spite of this important difference, Feuerbach's understanding of religion also contains a Freudian stratum. It is when Feuerbach moves from the language of illusion (unrecognized projection) to the language of dream that it begins to appear. "Religion is a dream, in which our own conceptions and emotions appear to us as separate existences, beings out of ourselves" (EC 204). At first it looks as if this is merely another way of generating the comfortable Hegelian thesis that this is the natural course of human development, phylogenetically and ontogenetically: "And so in revelation man goes out of himself, in order, by a circuitous path, to return to himself!" (EC 207).

But between these two texts a disruptive idea emerges, that of wish fulfillment. "A fact, I repeat, is a conception about the truth of which there is no doubt, because it is no object of theory, but of feeling, which desires that what it wishes, what it believes, should be true. . . . A fact is every wish that projects itself on reality" (EC 205-6). Earlier Feuerbach gives an even more fully explicitly "Freudian" reading of dreams as wish-fulfilling illusions: "The fundamental dogmas of Christianity are realized wishes of the heart. . . . Religion [is] the dream of waking consciousness: dreaming is the key to the mysteries of religion" (EC 140f.).

The Hegelian and Freudian strata in Feuerbach's text are joined by the agreement that religion is projective, illusory, false consciousness. But if we ask why all this occurs, we get two quite different answers. According to the first, projection is the path providence has ordained to bring us to maturity. According to the second, projection is the unrealistic attempt to compensate for unfulfilled desires. What was incipient self-knowledge for the Hegelian Feuerbach becomes wishful thinking for the Freudian Feuerbach.[11]

This would not be so bad if the desires and wishes were simply for something to adore, to approve, and to admire. But in the Freudian stratum of the text Feuerbach portrays those desires as utterly egoistic and crassly utilitarian.

The earliest hint that religious projection may be in the service of desires that need to be hidden does not arise in connection with religion in general. It comes, rather, in relation to extreme journeys along the *via negativa* that culminate in "the proposition that God is unknowable or undefinable" (EC 14f.). One who says this "denies God practically by his conduct, — the world has possession of all his thoughts and inclinations, — but he does not deny him theoretically, he does not attack his existence; he lets that rest. *But this existence does not affect or incommode him.* . . . The *alleged* religious horror of limiting God by positive predicates is only the *irreligious wish* to know nothing more of God, *to banish God from the mind*" (EC 15, emphasis added). Here we are in the Freudian world of the God who is only seemingly stern, the world of "self-flattering wishes," in which the believing soul "drops what is disagreeable in a fact, and holds fast alone what is agreeable" (EC 136f.).

Beginning with chapter 10 of *The Essence of Christianity*, on the doctrines of providence and creation *ex nihilo*, Feuerbach applies this analysis to positive affirmations about God and to belief in immortality as well. Thus in the doctrine of creation man "makes Nature the abject vassal of his selfish interest, of his practical egoism," and the doctrines of special providence and miracles only extend this process (EC 113). The will of God is but the thinly disguised will to power of human finitude fully given over "to utilism [*utilismus*], to egoism" (EC 115-17). This is where we read that we first create God in our own image before we are created in God's image (EC 118). Our creative act may be unconscious, but it is anything but disinterested. In the chapter on prayer we read, "God is the Love that satisfied our wishes, our emotional wants; he is himself the realized wish of the heart" (EC 121). As this

---

11. Robert Tucker has suggested that for Feuerbach metaphysics turns out to be "esoteric psychology, or more accurately psychopathology." *Philosophy and Myth in Karl Marx* (2nd ed., New York: Cambridge University Press, 1972), p. 85. If the first description fits the Hegelian stratum, the second identifies the Freudian stratum quite succinctly.

analysis goes on and on, Feuerbach constantly emphasizes the egoism at the heart of worship, the instrumental character of religious belief. Then, as if he has failed to make the point clearly enough in *The Essence of Christianity* (1841), he devotes another essay to it, *The Essence of Faith According to Luther* (1844).[12]

But this is the Freudian Feuerbach and not yet Marx.

12. A hint of the argument there can be found in the following sentences: "But the object of faith is the inviolable holiness of self-love. Love is the heart which beats for others, but faith is the heart which only beats for itself. . . . Over love stands faith; that is, over the lover of others stands love of oneself" (EF 100). Marx will give a distinctly social sense to this point, as the following summary nicely shows. With reference to the Christian ideal of love, Marx claims that "those who talk most about charity and love of one's neighbour, have more often than not used those fine words as a hypocritical excuse for perpetuating a social system whose law is the opposite of love: permanent violence against the worker and the perversion, by the very law of the régime, of all human feelings. . . ." Roger Garaudy, *Marxism in the Twentieth Century*, trans. René Hague (New York: Charles Scribner's Sons, 1970), p. 135.

21 Feuerbach's Radical Atheism

In search of the meaning of the Marxian claim that religion is "the opium of the people," we have turned to the theoretical roots of his atheism. The Freudian stratum in Feuerbach's text is closer to Marx than is the Hegelian stratum. For with Freud religious consciousness is, to use a Hegelian expression, essentially unhappy consciousness. The presence of religion is the sign of a deeply unacceptable situation. As Marx himself will shortly say, religion is "at the same time an expression of real suffering and a protest against real suffering" (SW 64).

Moreover, for this reason religion is instrumental. While religion in the Hegelian stratum is celebrative, in the Freudian stratum it is more nearly calculative. Human beings always want more power in the face of nature (and the death that is its final fact); and they always want freedom from guilt in the face of culture (EC 141).

The problem, from the Marxian perspective, is this "always." The Freudian Feuerbach simply identifies the "deeply unacceptable situation" mentioned above with the human condition. The universality of these needs renders them metaphysical rather than political, while their necessity renders them essential rather than historical. As Marx wrote to his friend Arnold Ruge, with reference to Feuerbach's "Preliminary Theses on the Reform of Philosophy," "I approve of Feuerbach's aphorisms, except for one point: he directs himself too much to nature and too little to politics."[1] By distracting attention from the political and historical dimensions of needs that come to expression in religion, Feuerbach provides the same kind of intellectual support for the current forms of social domination as is provided

1. Quoted in Schlomo Avineri, *The Social and Political Thought of Karl Marx* (Cambridge: Cambridge University Press, 1968), p. 10.

by the political economy that he ignores and the religion that he criticizes.

All three, Feuerbach, religion, and the political economy, foster an ahistorical perspective that treats present social structures as natural and inevitable. Questions about changing the world do not need to be answered because they are not even allowed to arise. It is with reference to Feuerbach that Marx complains, "The philosophers have only interpreted the world, in various ways; the point is to change it" (SW 158). Since Marxian suspicion evaluates theories in terms of their function rather than in terms of their content, the difference between religious (idealistic) interpretations of the world and antireligious (materialistic) interpretations of the world like Feuerbach's does not amount to much. Both bodies of belief serve to buttress the social status quo. This is what it means to speak of Feuerbach's atheism as "bourgeois."

It would appear, then, that the critique of religion is anything but complete with Feuerbach. Marx will seek to give the critique an active character; its goal will be to change behavior and not just belief, to change the world rather than just to reinterpret it. There are hints of such a move in Feuerbach's own text, though its political possibilities remain peripheral at best.

As we seek to move from Feuerbach's bourgeois atheism to the radical elements buried within it, we will find our attention decisively redirected from the first to the second mark of instrumental religion as analyzed by Hume (see pp. 27-28 above). The first, it will be recalled, is flattery. Like irony, flattery is a mode of speech whose apparent (professed) purpose is at odds with its real (operative) purpose. Purporting to be a mode of giving, it is in fact an attempt to get. Freud has deepened our understanding of the potential in religious beliefs and practices, liturgical and moral, for flattery, for hustling God while giving the appearance (to ourselves and others) of honoring him.

The second characteristic of what Hume calls idolatry or superstition is the manner in which it legitimizes cruel and barbaric social practices. If flattery corrupts love for God, here it is love for one's neighbor that gets short shrift. Like Hume, Marx has in mind institutional practices rather than the private practices of individuals, and his critique is directed at the way in which religion serves to legitimize these by authorizing them or simply by being compatible with them.

Our search for a radical stratum in Feuerbach can begin with the impoverishment motif. In theology, which denies the identity of the human and divine by making God transcendent, "the human, considered as such, is depreciated. . . . To enrich God, man must become poor; that God may be all, man must be nothing" (EC 26). This is what Feuerbach means when he says, "Religion is the disuniting of man from himself . . . a differencing of man with his own nature" (EC 33).

In texts like these human impoverishment is regarded as universal and metaphysical. It is the result of religious projection. We can only attribute perfections to God that we have first taken from ourselves. But what would this motif look like if the poverty were economic rather than metaphysical and if it were the cause and not the result of religious projection? At times this is just how Feuerbach writes. "Only he who has no earthly parents needs heavenly ones. . . . The triune God has a substantial meaning only where there is an abstraction from the substance of real life. The more empty life is, the fuller, the more concrete is God. The impoverishing of the real world and the enriching of God is one act. Only the poor man has a rich God. God springs out of the feeling of a want; what man is in need of . . . that is God" (EC 73). Here it would seem that the difference between rich and poor has not been swallowed up in the human condition. This begins to sound like Marx.

Another text from the Marxian stratum in Feuerbach concerns the religion of ancient Israel. "To the Jew . . . Jehovah himself was nothing else than the self-consciousness of Israel made objective. . . ."

> If we let fall the limits of nationality, we obtain — instead of the Israelite — *man*. As in Jehovah the Israelite personified his national existence, so in God the Christian personified his subjective human nature, freed from the limits of nationality. As Israel made the wants of his national existence the law of the world, as, under the dominance of these wants, he deified even his political vindictiveness; so the Christian made the requirements of human feeling the absolute powers and laws of the world. . . . The miracles of Christianity . . . have not the welfare of a nation for their object, but the welfare of man. (EC 120)

What is fascinating about this text is Feuerbach's flight from his own insight. Ancient Israel is by no means the proletariat, though the experience of slavery in Egypt had a formative influence on Hebrew religion. Still, Feuerbach sees Israel as a historically particular social group that creates its God in its own image, that is, in the service of its own desires. If this religion is to be understood, the sources of the "political vindictiveness" it expresses will have to be explored; the critique of religion will have to become social theory, for it will no longer be possible to appeal to timeless human nature.

Of course, Feuerbach does not do this. He is not Marx. Instead, he suggests that Christianity's superiority to Judaism consists in the fact that it better conforms to the ahistorical and apolitical character his own theory usually assumes. But it is too late. His account of Judaism has already let a Marxist cat out of the bag.

In later texts similar themes arise, only to be similarly abandoned. In the essay on Luther, for example, we read:

> If man were blessed . . . how could he imagine another being outside himself as a blessed being. . . . Only an imprisoned man considers a free man blessed. . . . But if I have what God has, nothing is lacking if God is lacking. . . . If . . . I am free, I am above all else free from God. The homage granted to God by a free person is at best only a protestation of courtesy, a gallantry, a compliment. Only in the needy, miserable, and deprived mouth does the word "God" have weight, earnestness, and meaning; but on the lips of religiously free men — on the politically free men's too, of course — the word "God" rings only of scorn. (EF 37-38)

Here poverty is economic rather than essential, and it is the cause of religion, not its result. Here the historical difference between political freedom and political domination plays a decisive role in the projection of the human onto the divine. But Feuerbach does not follow his argument as it leads from metaphysics to history.

Probably Feuerbach comes closest to Marx in a passage from his *Lectures on the Essence of Religion:*

> Those human desires that are not imaginary and fantastic are fulfilled in the course of history, of the future. Many desires which today remain mere desires will someday be fulfilled; innumerable things which the presumptuous champions of present-day religious dogmas and institutions, present-day social and political conditions, regard as impossible, will one day be reality. . . . We must therefore modify our goals and exchange divinity, in which only man's groundless and gratuitous desires are fulfilled, for the human race or human nature, religion for education, the hereafter in heaven for the hereafter on earth, that is, the *historical future,* the future of mankind. (ER 281)

Perhaps by the time Feuerbach wrote this he had read the opening paragraphs of Marx's "Towards a Critique of Hegel's *Philosophy of Right:* Introduction," and the teacher was learning from the student. In any case, it is time for us to turn to the text in which Marx seeks to formulate for himself the repressed but undeniably radical dimension of Feuerbach's atheism.

22 Marx's Radical Atheism

Our continued search for the meaning of the Marxian claim that religion is "the opium of the people" brings us to the text in which that phrase appears. Written in early 1844, it is one of the earliest of Marx's philosophical essays. While it is a key text of the "early" Marx, it represents a point of view presupposed by all of his subsequent writings. Marx apparently intended to revise and publish the detailed critique of Hegel's theory of the state, on which he had been working during much of 1843, but only this brief essay saw the light of day during his lifetime.[1] Its title, appropriately, is "Towards a Critique of Hegel's *Philosophy of Right:* Introduction."

I will give here the full text of each of Marx's seven opening paragraphs in turn, each followed by my comments.

[1] As far as Germany is concerned, the criticism of religion is essentially complete, and the criticism of religion is the presupposition of all criticism.

This refers above all to Feuerbach. But the second clause of the statement refutes the first. As the point of departure or presupposition for a larger totality of criticism, the criticism of religion could not possibly be complete in itself. Just as the beginning of a story gets its meaning from the ending, or, to be more precise, from the story as a

---

1. The full text of this critique, discovered in 1922 and published in 1927, can be found in *Karl Marx: Early Writings*, trans. Rodney Livingstone and Gregor Benton (New York: Random House, 1975), and, with an excellent introduction by Joseph O'Malley, in Karl Marx, *Critique of Hegel's "Philosophy of Right"* (Cambridge: Cambridge University Press, 1970). The translation in these pages is from SW.

whole, so the beginning of criticism does not stand by itself but requires the rest of criticism for its completion.[2]

Marx's biographer, David McLellan, writes of the Young Hegelians, the circle of intellectual radicals among whom Marx's intellectual development took a decisive turn:[3] "It was quite natural that [their] discussion should at first be theological: most members of the Hegelian school were interested in religion above all; and the attitude of the Prussian Government made politics an extremely dangerous subject for debate. Yet granted the Establishment of the Church in Germany and the close connection between religion and politics, it was inevitable that a movement of religious criticism would swiftly become secularized into one of political opposition" (LT 31).

Marx himself saw the move from religious critique to political critique as inevitable in the sense that it was required by the realities of the situation. Religion is essentially political. As he wrote to his friend Arnold Ruge, ". . . religion has no content of its own and lives not from heaven but from earth, and falls of itself with the dissolution of the inverted reality whose theory it is" (LT 58).[4]

But in another sense the move to political critique was anything but inevitable. Had not Feuerbach remained all but entirely unpolitical? And was not his atheism for the most part as bourgeois as the religion it attacked? Marx came to see it as his task to make the move to politics seem as inevitable as he believed it actually was. So when he says that in Germany the critique of religion is (in Feuerbach) "essentially complete,"

2. Like Hegel, Marx believes that the truth is the whole. This holism is diametrically opposed to foundationalism, which holds that the parts we begin with are meaningful and true in themselves and only externally related to the larger contexts to which they belong. For a sustained analysis of Hegelian holism, see Tom Rockmore, *Hegel's Circular Epistemology* (Bloomington: Indiana University Press, 1986).

3. Marx describes his "conversion" to Hegelianism in a famous letter to his father: "A curtain had fallen, my holy of holies was rent asunder, and new gods had to be installed. I left behind the idealism which, by the way, I had nourished with that of Kant and Fichte, and came to seek the idea in the real itself. If the gods had before dwelt above the earth, they had now become its centre" (SW 8). It was this abandonment of the romantic-idealistic separation of "is" and "ought" that Marx sought to work out among the Young Hegelians and especially in his struggle with Feuerbach.

4. Early in *Capital* Marx reaffirms this position: "The religious world is but the reflex of the real world. . . . The religious reflex of the real world can, in any case, only then finally vanish, when the practical relations of every-day life offer to man none but perfectly intelligible and reasonable relations with regard to his fellowmen and to Nature" (CA 79).

he does not mean that it has reached its goal. Rather, he means that it has gone as far as it can go while concerning itself merely with religion. As the "presupposition of all criticism" it must now go on to play its proper role, not as the completion but as the beginning of critique.

> [2] The profane existence of error is compromised as soon as its heavenly *oratio pro aris et focis* [prayer for hearth and home] is refuted. Man has found in the imaginary reality of heaven where he looked for a superman only the reflection of his own self. He will therefore no longer be inclined to find only the appearance of himself, the non-man, where he seeks and must seek his true reality.

And where would that be? Not in heaven but on earth. Not in eternity but in history. Not in self-consciousness but in social transformation. The second sentence of this paragraph is pure Feuerbach; the third seeks to give central importance to those hints of political radicality described in the previous chapter. To see through the projective character of religious consciousness must be not merely to lose faith in God but more importantly to lose faith in the ultimacy of the present human situation.

It is possible to read this as a metaphysical claim to the effect that faith in God necessarily and inevitably leads to faith in the ultimacy of the social status quo. Such a claim is fairly easy to refute, and it is therefore a temptation to any who wish to be done with Marx as quickly as possible to read him in this way. But he was a historical thinker more than a metaphysician, and his claim is both more interesting and more disturbing if taken as a historical claim, namely, that religion and social complacency are (in his historical present) and regularly have been (in the history of Europe), as a matter of historical fact, deeply linked.

Surely Marx is right that the disturbance of such religious faith will be politically disruptive. In spite of his Jewish roots, which were not very deep, he seems oblivious to the possibility that such a disturbance could itself be religiously motivated and to the historical fact that before there was Feuerbach there was Amos.

> [3] The foundation of irreligious criticism is this: man makes religion, religion does not make man. Religion is indeed the self-consciousness and self-awareness of man who either has not yet attained to himself or has already lost himself again. But man is no abstract being squatting outside the world. Man is the world of man, the state, society. This state, this society, produces religion's inverted attitude toward the world because they are an inverted world themselves.

Religion is the general theory of the world [note how Marx virtually quotes here from his own letter to Ruge cited above], its encyclopaedic compendium, its logic in popular form, its spiritual *point d'honneur,* its enthusiasm, its moral sanction, its solemn complement, its universal basis for consolation and justification. It is the imaginary realization of the human essence, because the human essence possesses no true reality. Thus, the struggle against religion is indirectly the struggle against the world whose spiritual aroma is religion.

The pattern is by now familiar. The first two sentences are pure Feuerbach. The remainder of the paragraph is a political reading of Feuerbach's atheism.

We can distinguish a number of crucial claims here: (a) Human deprivation is prior to religious projection. It is the cause and not merely the effect of the process of creating gods.

(b) This deprivation is not metaphysically universal and necessary but historically specific and contingent. It is the condition of human beings in *this* society, under *this* state that gives rise to *this* religion. The character of any given society is reflected in the religion that serves as its "encyclopaedic compendium," its "logic in popular form," and its "spiritual aroma."

(c) But religion does more than mirror the society in which it occurs. It also functions to legitimize it. As society's self-celebratory "enthusiasm" and its "universal basis for consolation and justification," it is above all else society's "moral sanction."

(d) When we see religion's role in justifying the social institutions that dehumanize its members, we see that "the struggle against religion is indirectly [but consciously] the struggle against the world whose spiritual aroma [i.e., deodorant] is religion." Thus the criticism of religion requires for its completion a criticism that is directly aimed at that world. This is the path from Feuerbach to the critique of social domination in *The Communist Manifesto* and *Capital.*

[4] Religious suffering is at the same time an expression of real suffering and a protest against real suffering. Religion is the sigh of the oppressed creature, the feeling of a heartless world, and the soul of soulless circumstances. It is the opium of the people.

Again several observations are in order: (a) Once more the relation of religion and society is twofold, and one of the relations is a mirroring one. Religious suffering expresses real, worldly suffering.

(b) But now the other function is protest rather than legitimation.

Religion has a socially disruptive possibility built into its mirroring, expressive character. Marx does little to explore the history of this dimension of religion,[5] with the result that his account of religion historically has a noticeable one-sidedness to it.[6] Marxian theory points powerfully to the role of religion in justifying slavery, segregation, and apartheid, but has little to say about the role of religion in abolitionist, civil-rights, and anti-apartheid movements. No doubt this is due in part to Marx's atheistic bias, but it is also due to the argument implicit in this paragraph, as follows.

(c) In spite of its protest character, religion is the opium of the people. How does protest become painkiller so quickly? Quite easily. If because of violent repression or political and economic hopelessness, protest cannot or does not take the form of social activism, its only alternative is escapism. We have only to think of the role played by drugs among the ghettoized underclass of our own society to see how a practice can be at once a protest and an escapist consolation. The next paragraph will express the unwillingness at the heart of Marxism to give up on social activism. But first a final point about religion as the opium of the people.

(d) From the setting of the opium metaphor in the context of suffering it is tempting to read "people" *(Volk)* as "masses." Religion is the opium of the oppressed, not needed by the power elites whose desires are served by the system. But the process of legitimizing domination is more complex than this, and Marx has already pointed to this complexity by calling religion not only the "consolation" offered to its victims by an "inverted world" but also that world's "moral sanction" and "justification." A social system that exploits its masses will get only minimal legitimation in their eyes from moral justifications to the effect that they are in their divinely appointed places in a divinely ordained hierarchy or that their suffering is the punishment for their sins (in this or a previous life). What they need is consolation, the hope that in a heavenly Beulah Land just over Jordan "all God's chillun got shoes."

If the masses need a painkiller to deal with the physical and emotional deprivations of poverty and powerlessness, their masters need a painkiller to assuage their guilty consciences. They will be able to enjoy their wealth, status, and power just to the degree that they can persuade themselves that God is in his heaven and all is right with the

---

5. Engels does more, as we shall see in what follows; but he stays within the limits of the analysis offered here by Marx.

6. Is religious history much less one-sided? Or has religion more frequently served to confirm than to challenge power and domination?

world (except for a few troublemakers here and there who are without
moral standing). Thus it is the ruling classes who benefit most from
moral arguments. Unless they can persuade themselves that their social
role is essential to some moral cosmos, they will experience a painful
cognitive dissonance between their belief that they are decent and their
perception that the price of their privileges is the poverty and powerlessness of others. By providing consolation for some and justification
for others, religion can function as the opium of *all* the people.[7]

> [5] The abolition of religion as the illusory happiness of the
> people is the demand for their real happiness. The demand to give
> up the illusions about their condition is a demand to give up a
> condition that requires illusions. The criticism of religion is therefore
> the germ of the criticism of the vale of tears whose halo is religion.

Here the Freudian-Feuerbachian language of illusion appears.
But now the task is to change the world, not just by making atheists
out of believers but by making it a place of real happiness. Just to the
degree that religion functions to legitimize various forms of social injustice, the Marxian analysis places the same demand upon believers.
For, as we have learned from our study of Freud, this kind of critique
discredits religion even if, contrary to Marxian assumptions, it should
turn out to be metaphysically correct. Even if there is a God, or better,
especially if there is a God like the one described in the Bible, when
religion functions as Marx describes, killing the pains of injustice rather
than challenging its right to exist, it deserves the diatribes he directs
against it. At least that is what the prophet Amos would have said.

> [6] Criticism has plucked the imaginary flowers from the chains
> not so that man may bear chains without any imagination or com-
> fort, but so that he may throw away the chains and pluck the living
> flowers. The criticism of religion disillusions man so that he may
> think, act, and fashion his own reality as a disillusioned man come
> to his senses; so that he may revolve around himself as his real sun.
> Religion is only the illusory sun which revolves around man as long
> as he does not revolve around himself.

After repeating his challenge to change the world, Marx adds a
non sequitur. Later in the same essay he writes, "The criticism of religion

---

7. Cognitive dissonance theory is the form experimental psychology gives
to the hermeneutics of suspicion. See above, p. 85 n. 3.

ends with the doctrine that man is the highest being for man, that is, with the categorical imperative to overthrow all circumstances in which man is humiliated, enslaved, abandoned, and despised" (SW 69). In both passages he implies that atheistic humanism is the only premise for a humane world, that only if humankind deifies itself will it have reason to oppose oppression. This does not follow from anything Marx has said, and it stands as a dogmatic assertion. But it also stands as a challenge deserving serious attention from people of faith. For in any historical context where religion supports exploitation by giving its active or passive support to unjust social structures, it gives to atheistic humanism a plausibility it does not deserve.[8]

> [7] It is therefore the task of history, now the truth is no longer in the beyond, to establish the truth of the here and now. The first task of philosophy, which is in the service of history, once the holy form of self-alienation has been discovered, is to discover self-alienation in its unholy forms. The criticism of heaven is thus transformed into the criticism of earth, the criticism of religion into the criticism of law, and the criticism of theology into the criticism of politics.

In other words, only with the transformation of Feuerbach into Marx can the criticism of religion that began with Feuerbach be considered complete.

---

8. For a critical examination of the humane potential of atheistic humanism, see Henri de Lubac, S.J., *The Drama of Atheist Humanism* (Cleveland: World Publishing Company, 1963).

23 *Religion and the Christian State*

Feuerbach is doubly important for understanding Marxian atheism. As a primary source of that atheism he helps us to see it as a version of the hermeneutics of suspicion; and, as an essentially ahistorical thinker, he helps us by means of contrast to focus attention on the social substance of Marxian suspicion. The latter has a Feuerbachian form, to be sure, but a content that introduces us to a very different world. We would be seriously misled by what we have said in the previous three chapters if we were to conclude that Marx can be accounted for by those occasional hints of radicality in Feuerbach. Marx did not become Marx just by reading Feuerbach.

While Feuerbach was writing *The Essence of Christianity*, Marx was writing his doctoral dissertation on Democritus and Epicurus. In its preface he declares his atheism:

> As long as a single drop of blood pulses in her world-conquering and totally free heart philosophy will continually shout at her opponents the cry of Epicurus, "The profane man is not the one who destroys the gods of the multitude but the one who foists the multitude's doctrines onto the gods." Philosophy makes no secret of it. The proclamation of Prometheus — "in a word, I detest all the Gods" — is her own profession, her own slogan against all the gods of heaven and earth who do not recognize man's self-consciousness as the highest divinity. . . . Prometheus is the foremost saint and martyr in the philosopher's calendar. (SW 12-13)[1]

---

1. Marx gives the quotations from Epicurus and Prometheus in Greek. I have given only the English translations provided in SW. For a slightly different rendering, see OR 14-15.

This Promethean atheism is a far cry from positivism. At its heart is not the epistemological claim of evidentialism but the moral claim of humanism. In other words, it does not deny God for lack of evidence; it detests the gods for their treatment of humans. A friend would shortly write, "For Marx, at any rate, the Christian religion is one of the most immoral there is" (LT 42). So it is not surprising that in an appendix to his dissertation, Marx writes, "What else does this mean except that *God exists for the man to whom the world is non-rational and who is therefore non-rational himself? In other words, non-rationality is God's existence*" (PS 66).

Marx first worked out these ideas as a journalist. From early 1842 to early 1843 he wrote an article for a journal edited by his friend Ruge, the *Deutsche Jahrbücher*, and a series of essays for a liberal (not radical) newspaper, the *Rheinische Zeitung*, whose editor he became in October 1842. Both of these periodicals were banned by the Prussian authorities, leading Marx to leave Germany for Paris. It is natural that these pieces were a sustained attack on the censorship policies of Kaiser Frederick William IV, but their ultimate target was the very idea of a Christian state that those policies sought to implement.

Marx wrote "Comments on the Latest Prussian Censorship Instruction" for the *Deutsche Jahrbücher*. The new guidelines to censors on interpreting the censorship law of 1819 purported to support greater freedom of the press, but Marx sought to show (1) that they entailed greater restriction, (2) that they were in overt opposition to the law they were meant to interpret, and (3) that they were internally incoherent. While the 1819 edict stated that the purpose of the censorship was "to control whatever opposes the *fundamental principles* of religion WITHOUT REGARD to the opinions and doctrines of *particular* religious groups and sects permitted in the state," the new instructions abandoned this rather deistic stance: "Nothing will be tolerated which opposes *Christian* religion in general or a *particular doctrine* in a *frivolous* and *hostile* manner" (PS 75).

The idea of religion in general, which Marx pillories here as an irreligious idea, was a common Enlightenment response to religious wars and persecutions. Its defense in 1819 was meant "to oppose the fanatical injection of religious convictions into politics and the ensuing *intellectual confusion*" (PS 76). But what, Marx asks, "does fanatical injection of religious convictions into politics mean? It means that specific religious convictions can determine the state and that the *particular nature of religion* can become *the norm of the state*," which sounds to him like a good description of the Prussia envisaged by the new instructions (PS 76-77).

On the face of it Marx is opposing political power in the service of religious zeal. But he is suspicious that something even more sinister is at work here, religious power in the service of political zeal.

> You should forbid that religion be drawn into politics — but you do not want to do that because you wish to base the state on faith rather than on free reason, with religion constituting for you the *general sanction of the positive*. Or you should permit the fanatical injection of religion into politics. Religion might be politically active in its own way, but you do not want that either. *For religion is to support secular matters without the latter's being subject to religion.* Once religion is drawn into politics, it becomes an insufferable, indeed an irreligious presumption to want to determine on secular grounds how religion has to operate within politics. If one allies himself with religion from religiosity, one must give religion the decisive voice in all matters. Or do you perhaps understand by religion the *cult of your own sovereignty and governmental wisdom?* (PS 77-78)[2]

Marx could scarcely be clearer. He sees Prussia as a "police state" (PS 91) that is seeking to deodorize itself with the "spiritual aroma" (see pp. 136-37 above, Marx's ¶3) of religion, to legitimize itself by making religion the sanction for its practices. Far from religious zeal being the operative motive, it is political power that here seduces religion into its own service with the perks that it can offer. The proof of this is that religion is allowed to say Yes but not No, for *"religion is to support secular matters without the latter's being subject to religion."* It is not surprising that when Marx returned to the subject of censorship a

---

2. I have omitted some of Marx's emphases in this citation, and added one of my own in order to highlight what I take to be the point of central interest for us. That Marx uses the term "positive" for historically particular de facto political practices and not just for those features of religious life that derive from "special revelation" is clear from "The Philosophical Manifesto of the Historical School of Law" (PS 96ff.). In the present context it is clear that the *"general sanction of the positive"* refers to the legitimation of social structures.

That it is the function of religion *"to support secular matters without the latter's being subject to religion"* was the view of Bismarck. He was eager to present his social legislation as "applied Christianity," but the churches were to have no part in it and its central aim was to strengthen the state. "The church . . . was not to advise on public affairs nor could the individual Christian apply Christian principles to his political activities . . . since the plan of God was unknown to man, there were no universal Christian principles which a statesman could apply to politics. . . . Bismark actually took the *raison d'état* as the guiding star of his policy." Hajo Holborn, *A History of Modern Germany* (Princeton: Princeton University Press, 1969), pp. 290, 150-51.

few months later, this time for the *Rheinische Zeitung,* he described religion as "in a more or less conscious manner, simply a sacred cloak to hide desires that are . . . very secular" (SW 17).[3]

By calling the result of this the *"cult of your own sovereignty and governmental wisdom,"* Marx identifies the actual god of this religion as the state. In other words, his atheism, like Elijah's prophecy, consists essentially of the charge of idolatry. The state is Ahab, its leading ladies Jezebel, and its clerics the priests of Baal. The only difference is that the latter profess to be the priests of Yahweh. We are dealing here with third commandment idolatry, with those who take the name of the Lord their God in vain. Christendom is Babylon. In plagiarizing from Elijah, Marx ends up sounding a lot like Kierkegaard.[4]

Marx continued his critique of the Christian state in an essay entitled "The Leading Article of No. 179 of *Kölnische Zeitung,"* responding to an essay that called for more rigorous censorship, especially in defense of Christianity. The Christian state, in the eyes of its apologists, is a police state because Christianity "is not so sure of victory that it can scorn the help of the police" (OR 25).

Once again Marx challenges the Christian state to take its profession seriously. "The truly religious state," he writes,

> is the theocratic state; the prince of such states must be either the God of religion, Jehovah himself, as in the Jewish state, God's representative, the Dalai Lama, as in Tibet, or finally, as Görres correctly demands of Christian states in his last work, they must all submit to a church which is an "infallible church." For if, as in Protestantism, there is no supreme head of the church, the domination of religion is nothing but the religion of domination, the cult of the will of the government. (OR 36)

Marx nearly quotes himself and makes the same point as he did earlier. Religion is not allowed to be an independent variable or to place any serious constraints on social policy (any more than the very pious wife

---

3. This essay appeared in the *Rheinische Zeitung* before the earlier essay was published, in Switzerland, as it turned out, due to problems with the censor. This view of religion as a sacred mask for secular interests is Marx's first published verdict on religion.

4. For an account of Kierkegaard's philosophy as a prophetic critique of Christendom long before the famous essays published as *The Attack Upon Christendom,* see my *Kierkegaard's Critique of Reason and Society* (Macon, GA: Mercer University Press, 1987). There is no better example of the hermeneutics of suspicion in the service of faith than Kierkegaard's writings.

of the Godfather is allowed to have a say in his "business"). Its task is to sacralize current power arrangements, thereby becoming instrumental religion, or, in Marx's more colorful language, "the religion of domination, the cult of the will of the government."

The *ad hominem* character of Marx's argument is just as clear when he writes: "When in the Holy Alliance at first a quasi-religious alliance of states was to be formed and religion was to be the state motto of Europe, *the Pope* showed profound sense and perfect consistence in refusing to join it, for in his view the universal Christian link between nations was the Church and not diplomacy, not a worldly alliance of states" (OR 35-36). Marx is no friend of the papal view, but in appealing to it he poses a sharp question to the politicians of his day and ours: Why do you talk about religion so much and allow it to shape your policies so little?

The writer to whom Marx is responding had argued that religion "is the foundation of the state, as it is the most necessary condition for every social association not aimed merely at attaining some ulterior aim. . . . In its crudest form as *childish fetishism* it raises man to a certain extent above sensuous appetites. . . ." Marx sees this as letting the cat out of the bag. "Fetishism is so far from raising man *above* the appetites that it is on the contrary 'the *religion of sensuous appetites.*' The fantasy of the appetites tricks the fetish worshipper into believing that an 'inanimate object' will give up its natural character to gratify his desires. The crude appetite of the fetish worshipper therefore smashes the fetish when the latter ceases to be its most devoted servant" (OR 22).[5] It seems that Marx knows all about Salieri (see above, chapter 1). The clear implication is that the orthodox Protestantism that prevails in Prussia differs from "*childish fetishism*" more in appearance than in reality. It is still a matter of gratifying human desires.

Finally, the editor of the *Kölnische Zeitung* writes that for nations of the highest historical importance "the prime of national life coincides with the highest development of their sense of religion, and the decline of their greatness and power coincides with the decline of their religious culture" (OR 22-23). This seems to be an admission that the writer holds the irreligious view that religion is to be valued as a means to empire. Marx overlooks this point in order to make two others. The first, of little interest in the present context, is the claim that Greece and Rome

---

5. The Freudian character of this passage is patent. Cf. especially the third chapter of *Totem and Taboo*, entitled "Animism, Magic and the Omnipotence of Thought."

reached their zenith against the background of a secular culture. The second, of more interest here, is the claim that the real religion of the Greeks and Romans was "the cult of 'their nationality,' of their 'state.' It was not the downfall of the old religions that brought the downfall of the old states, but the downfall of the old states that brought the downfall of the old religions" (OR 23). In other words, the state was the independent variable and, as such, the true object of veneration in the cultus. Therefore, the appeal to high antiquity is as embarrassing to its pious author as the appeal to "primitive" fetishism. For in Marx's analysis, the true God of the Christian state is the state.[6]

6. In addition to formulating his views on religion during this journalistic period, Marx also first formulated historical and sociological themes that would be central to his work. The historical theme is the realization that the French Revolution had been a bourgeois revolution and that in its aftermath the middle class had become the ancien régime. "It is a fact that the class possessing nothing today *demands* to share in the wealth of the middle class — a fact clearly evident in the streets of Manchester, Paris, and Lyons . . ." (PS 133). The sociological theme emerges in an essay devoted to the economic plight of the Moselle vintagers. "In the investigation of *political* conditions one is too easily tempted to overlook *the objective nature of the relationships* and to explain everything from the *will* of the persons acting. There are *relationships*, however, which determine the actions of private persons as well as those of individual authorities, and which are as independent as are the movements in breathing" (PS 144).

24 Religion and the Secular State

The *Rheinische Zeitung* published its last edition on March 31, 1843. Marx married Jenny Westphal in June, and they moved to Paris in October. Almost immediately he wrote the "Introduction" to his critique of Hegel's *Philosophy of Right* that we examined in chapter 22. Just prior to that move he wrote "On the Jewish Question," a response to two essays by Bruno Bauer on the question of Jewish emancipation.[1] This latter essay helps to fill out our picture of the developmental process leading to the opium metaphor of the "Introduction."

Bauer's essays were an attack on the Christian state, which he saw, according to Marx's summary, as "a regime of general enslavement" (SW 38). He argued that Jews should not seek equality with Christians in such a state but should realize that equal rights are possible only in a secular state, one without any established religion.[2] For Bauer "the political abolition of religion," that is, the separation of church and state, which Marx will call political emancipation, "is the equivalent of the abolition of all religion" (SW 42).

It is this assumption that Marx wishes to challenge. He points to North America, where political emancipation is complete. "Yet North America is the land of religiosity *par excellence*" (according to Toqueville and others), where "we find not only the existence of religion but a living existence full of freshness and strength . . ." (SW 43). With the separation of church and state religion does not disappear; it simply

---

1. Marx moved to Paris in order to publish a new journal, the *Deutsch-französische Jahrbücher,* with his friend Arnold Ruge. Both of these essays were published in 1844 in the first (and only) issue of the journal.

2. By education a child of the secular Enlightenment, Marx was by birth a Jew. His father had had to accept Christian baptism in order to continue practicing law. So for Marx as for Freud Christian racism was an all too palpable fact.

becomes a private matter. For this reason, Marx writes, "Political emancipation is not the completed and consistent form of religious emancipation because political emancipation is not the completed and consistent form of human emancipation" (SW 44).

Marx makes four observations about the private presence of religion in the secular state, where the public sphere has been secularized. First, in this condition "man liberates himself from an impediment," namely the requirement that one must belong to a particular religion in order to enjoy various civil and political rights, "by entering into opposition with himself . . ." due to the "separation of man into a public and private man" (SW 44, 47).

At this point Marx is drawing on his unpublished critique of Hegel's political theory (see above, p. 134 n. 1) to draw an analogy between privatized religion and private property. In that critique he argued that Hegel's division of the public domain into civil society, the capitalist marketplace of individual economic self-interest, and the state, the political domain where we experience community by seeking to articulate and institutionalize what Rousseau called the general will, left us with two incompatible identities.[3] In this schizophrenic condition we have a private, exclusive, self-seeking role to play and a public, communal, common-good seeking role to play at the same time. Toward the end of the same essay Marx extends this critique to the French and North American theories of human rights, which are divided into the rights of man, the private self, and the rights of the citizen, the public self. He complains bitterly that the latter has been reduced to a means to the former, that political life in the liberal state is viewed as a means to private economic goals (SW 51-57).

But earlier in the essay he introduces religion into the equation and argues that "the contradiction with his citizenship in which the adherent of a particular religion finds himself is only a part of the general secular contradiction between the political state and civil society" (SW 50-51).

Marx's second observation about the privatization of religion in the secular state is that "religion has [thus] become the spirit of civil

---

3. It is clear from this essay that Marx finds Hegel's theory an all too accurate description of the realities of the modern state, which is his ultimate target. What Hegel fails to see is the irreconcilability of the two spheres and their corresponding identities. Just as Marx attacks capitalism through a critique of the theories of the political economists, so he attacks the modern state through a critique of Hegel's philosophy of the state. In doing so he shows how seriously he takes the ideological buttresses of social domination, among which he includes religion.

society, the sphere of egoism, the *bellum omnium contra omnes* [the war of all against all]. Its essence is no longer in community but in difference." Marx continues by placing together these first two observations: Religion "has become the expression of the separation of man from his common essence, from himself and from other men" (SW 47).[4] So far the argument is that religion is oppressive in the Christian state and alienating in the secular state.

Marx's third observation is that the private sphere is by no means void of public influence. The state no longer maintains prerequisites of birth, class, education, profession, or property ownership for political participation. "Nevertheless the state still allows private property, education, and profession to have an effect in their own manner, that is as private property, as education, as profession, and make their particular natures felt. Far from abolishing these factual differences, its existence rests on them as a presupposition" (SW 45). Marx makes it clear that the same is true of religion, which is able to make its particular nature felt in the secular state.

The clear implication is that the role of religion as a legitimizer of social structures is not at all unique to the Christian state and is in no essential way diminished in the secular state as long as religion continues to flourish in private. To test this view, we can follow Marx's lead and ask about North America. Has the separation of church and state hindered religion from providing moral sanction for slavery, for other forms of racism directed against people of color (including native Americans) and Jews, for Manifest Destiny imperialism, for capitalism, for anti-Communist imperialism, and, in general, for militarism?

Marx's fourth observation regarding the privatization of religion is that religion continues to be a world of illusion, and that it does play a large role in its ongoing legitimizing capacity. At this point Marx pulls a sudden switch on us. He continues to relate religion to the modern dichotomy between the public realm (state) and the private (civil society). But whereas up to now religion was the spirit of civil society and the cultural analogue of private property, it now becomes the analogue of the state.

The crucial passage (SW 45-46) begins by reminding us that in the modern secular state we lead "a double life," as already described. But now Marx describes these two lives as "a heavenly one and an

---

4. These first two points correspond precisely to the third and fourth dimensions of alienated labor as developed in the "Economic and Philosophical Manuscripts" of 1844, first published in 1932. See SW 81-83.

earthly one." We understand this as a reference to the duality of the sacred and the secular, but he makes it clear that he also has in mind the worldly duality distinctive of modernity. "[Man] has a life both in the political community, where he is valued as a communal being, and in civil society where he is active as a private individual, treats other men as means, degrades himself to a means, and becomes the plaything of alien powers."

What can it mean to call the public realm our heavenly life as distinct from the private realm as our earthly life? The answer is immediate:

> The political state has just as spiritual an attitude to civil society as heaven has to earth. It stands in the same opposition to civil society and overcomes it in the same manner as religion overcomes the limitations of the profane world, that is, it must likewise recognize it, reinstate it, and let itself once more be dominated by it. Man in the reality that is nearest to him, civil society, is a profane being. Here where he counts for himself and others as a real individual, he is an inauthentic phenomenon. In the state, on the other hand, where man counts as a species-being, he is an *imaginary* participant in an *imaginary* sovereignty, he is robbed of his real life and filled with an *unreal* universality. (SW 46, emphasis added).[5]

Religion purports to be the overcoming of the world insofar as it is the scene of evil. According to the theory of the modern, liberal state, politics is the overcoming of the world insofar as it is the capitalistic marketplace where "looking out for number one" is the first commandment. Politics, as the attempt to enact the general will, is the cooperative, communal overcoming of the centrifugal forces of competition. But the theory corresponds to little or nothing in the real world, in Marx's view. His detailed comparison of Hegel's theory of the modern state (see above, p. 134 n. 1) with the world that he observed as a

---

5. SW and three other translations of this passage I have consulted translate *unwahre Erscheinung* as "illusory phenomenon." But Marx clearly does not mean that. He is contrasting the all too real, if pathetic, existence of people in civil society with the illusory life they think they have, but do not have, in the political and religious realms. So I have altered the translation to read "inauthentic phenomenon." In Hegelian usage, which Marx follows here, an *unwahr* story would be a lie or a fiction, but an *unwahr* phenomenon would be something quite real that does not live up to its billing, such as a car that does not start or a pen that does not write. What such a phenomenon lacks is not existence but existence in accord with its essence. It is more nearly fraud than fiction, inauthentic rather than illusory.

journalist was a major factor in his coming to this conclusion, which he never found reason to revise. He would agree entirely with the verdict of Alasdair MacIntyre that "modern politics cannot be a matter of genuine moral consensus. . . . *Modern politics is civil war carried on by other means.*"6 So, he says ironically, when politics overcomes the world "it must likewise recognize it, reinstate it, and let itself once more be dominated by it" (SW 46).

But this is what makes politics so "heavenly." For it is in the same way that religion overcomes the evil in the world, in theory but not in fact. Its sacred texts and its theologies are opposed to important features of the modern world. In one of his earlier polemics against the Christian state, Marx writes,

> Read Saint Augustine's *De Civitate Dei,* study the Fathers of the Church and the spirit of Christianity and then come back and tell us which is the "Christian State," the church or the state! Does not every minute of your practical life give the lie to your theory? Do you consider it wrong to appeal to the courts when you are cheated? But the apostle writes that that is wrong. Do you offer your right cheek when you are struck upon the left, or do you not institute proceedings for assault? Yet the Gospel forbids that. . . . Are you not furious at the slightest infringement of your personal liberty? But you have been told that the sufferings of this life are not to be compared with the bliss of the future, that suffering in patience and the bliss of hope are cardinal virtues. Are not most of your court proceedings and the majority of civil laws concerned with property? But you have been told that your treasure is not of this world. (OR 35)7

In these and other ways religion is the archetype of politics. For when religion overcomes the world it "recognize[s] it, reinstate[s] it, and let[s] itself once more be dominated by it," even to the degree of becoming its apologist and legitimizer. Marx's view recalls the couplets of Pope:

6. Alasdair MacIntyre, *After Virtue: A Study in Moral Theory* (Notre Dame: University of Notre Dame Press, 1981), p. 236, emphasis added. Richard John Neuhaus cites this passage repeatedly and tellingly in his critique of the secular state. But he seems to forget the tragic and bloody history that led to the expulsion of religion from the public square. See *The Naked Public Square: Religion and Democracy in America* (Grand Rapids: Eerdmans, 1984).

7. Cf. Marx's long footnote on Luther's view of usury as the will to power (CA 592-93).

Vice is a monster of so frightful mien,
As, to be hated, needs but to be seen;
Yet seen too oft, familiar with her face,
We first endure, then pity, then embrace.[8]

Marx is telling the story of the ways in which religion not only endures but eventually embraces evil. It is the same story told by Hume about how great crimes and barbarous practices are "compatible with" or even "authorized by" religion (see above, chapter 4).

The political analysis that accompanies Marx's critique of religion in the secular state is systemic (coming after his detailed study of Hegel's political philosophy) in comparison with the anecdotal accounts that accompany his critique of religion in the Christian state. Thus he adds to his earlier critique a concern about the way in which religion reinforces the split between the public and private identities of the self in modern society. But he subtracts nothing from the earlier account, and the main point remains the same: There is no essential difference between the Christian state and the secular state when it comes to the capacity of religion to be the ally of institutionalized evil.

The emphasis on the illusory character of religion's overcoming of the world enhances the force of the opium metaphor with which Marx will very shortly summarize his view of religion, or, more specifically, Christianity in the modern world. The paragraphs surrounding that metaphor are saturated with references to the "imaginary" (¶¶2, 3, 6; see pp. 136-37 and 139 above) and "illusory" (¶¶5, 6) character of religious comfort, happiness, and salvation. Like drugs and alcohol, he argues, Christianity provides "an illusory satisfaction to an authentic demand."[9]

The believing soul may be tempted to attempt a refutation of Marx by arguing that neither heaven nor fellowship with God here and now is an illusion. But that would be to miss the point by taking Marx to be a metaphysical rather than a historical thinker. Here we see once again that the hermeneutics of suspicion cannot be refuted by arguing for the truth of religious beliefs, for what suspicion attacks is the *function* of religious beliefs. Let them be ever so true, they discredit themselves morally (if not epistemologically) when they function in the service of evil, whether by enduring it or by embracing it.

8. Alexander Pope, *An Essay on Man,* Epistle II, lines 217-20.
9. This formulation is Roger Garaudy's in *Marxism in the Twentieth Century,* trans. René Hague (New York: Charles Scribner's Sons, 1970), p. 121.

When Marx accuses religion of being the Illusion of Overcoming the World, he is not asking whether God is real in some other world, be it future or inward and private, but whether God's presence in the public world of here and now is as an enemy or ally of injustice, oppression, and domination. If any religion says that that world can go to hell while it pursues some future or inward happiness,[10] Marx feels entitled to tell that religion to do the same, since in the world where children suffer it does the work of Satan.

A better refutation of Marx is the one described by Roger Garaudy: "To rebut the charge of being the 'opium of the people,' in which Marx and later Lenin summed up an irrefutable historical experience, is more than a matter of theory: it is a matter of political and social practice. And it is for Christians and their Church to give this practical proof."[11]

10. Something biblical religion can never do, though Christianity has often done so, having sold its soul to a platonizing Gnosticism.
11. Garaudy, p. 163.

25 Marxian Materialism

In search of the meaning of the Marxian claim that religion is "the opium of the people" we have looked closely at the text in which it occurs (see chapter 22 above) and explored its background both in Feuerbach (chapters 20-21) and in Marx's writings leading up to that text (chapters 23-24). The critique of religion at whose heart Marx introduces the opium metaphor is one that he would never abandon or revise. But he did reformulate it by incorporating it into his materialistic conception of history or, as it has come to be known, his historical materialism.

Although this theory of history has appropriately been identified as "the heart of the Marxist philosophy,"[1] we might ignore it on the grounds that it adds nothing to what Marx has already said about religion. But while that is true in an important sense, it is not true that it adds nothing to what we have already learned on the subject. For in his materialist conception of history Marx says it all again, but this time in other words; and who among us has not been in a situation where the sentence that began "In other words" was the sentence that brought us from perplexity to comprehension or from shallow understanding to deeper understanding? Since two of the "other words" that Marx uses here are integrally involved in almost every discussion of Marx and religion, it will be helpful for us to understand the distinctive meaning he gives to them.

The first of these is "materialism." By learning that Marxian materialism is not an answer to the question whether mind or matter is the basic stuff of the universe but to questions about the relation

1. By Louis Dupré in *The Philosophical Foundations of Marxism* (New York: Harcourt, Brace, and World, 1966), p. 146.

between economic, political, and intellectual factors in social structures and their transformations, we will be reminded that Marx is a historical rather than a metaphysical thinker. We will be able to recognize that, while Marx is indeed an atheist, there is no inherent incompatibility between historical materialism and Christian theism.

The other key term, also not discussed to this point, is "ideology." We often use this word to designate virtually any set of political beliefs, or, more generally, any set of evaluations orienting social behavior. Marx uses the term more precisely to identify certain characteristics that such beliefs and evaluations often have. Since the language of ideology is central to so many discussions of Marx's critique of religion, including his own discussion of it from 1845 on, adding his concept of ideology to our vocabulary will deepen our understanding of his critique.

Marx's stay in Paris was short. Early in 1845 Prussia asked that he be expelled from France, and France obliged. He moved with his family to Brussels, where, from September of that year until August of 1846, he worked with his newfound friend, Friedrich Engels, on the attempt to give a final and definitive statement of their differences with the Young Hegelians, especially (as it turned out) Feuerbach. The manuscript they produced is known as *The German Ideology*. It is at once the first attempt to formulate the materialist conception of history and the first attempt to give a precise and peculiarly Marxian meaning to the term "ideology."[2]

Not surprisingly, the preface to *The German Ideology* begins with a critique of Feuerbach and company that makes them sound at first like Marx himself. "Hitherto men have constantly made up for themselves false conceptions about themselves. . . . They, the creators, have bowed down before their creations. Let us liberate them from the chimeras, the ideas, dogmas, imaginary beings under the yoke of which they are pining away" (SW 159). Does not Marx himself wish to do this? Then why does he satirize the Young Hegelians, whom he identifies as holding these views, as the "philosophic heroes" who announce

---

2. This manuscript, like the "Economic and Philosophical Manuscripts" (Paris, 1844; see above, p. 134 n. 1), was not published until 1932. For Marx's later, cryptic comments on their inability to get it published, see SW 390. Engels's regular insistence that Marx had already worked out the materialist conception of history prior to their collaboration is supported by our own discovery of its key elements (as we shall see) in the writings we have already examined. For a summary of pre-Marxian uses of "ideology," see Leszek Kolakowski, *Main Currents of Marxism*, vol. 1: *The Founders*, trans. P. S. Falla (Oxford: Oxford University Press, 1978), pp. 153-54.

their critique "with the solemn consciousness of its cataclysmic danger-ousness and criminal ruthlessness"? And why does he state his goal as "uncloaking these sheep who take themselves and are taken for wolves" (SW 160)?

The first clue is already present in his summary of their pseudo-radical thought: "Let us revolt against the rule of thoughts. Let us teach men, says one, to exchange these imaginations for thoughts which correspond to the essence of man" (SW 159). We have already seen that Marx takes religious illusions to be symptoms, but not the disease; and if metaphysical error is not the disease, metaphysical truth can hardly be the cure.[3]

To drive home this point, Marx returns to satire: "Once upon a time a valiant fellow had the idea that men were drowned in water only because they were possessed with the idea of gravity. If they were to knock this notion out of their heads, say by stating it to be a super-stition, a religious concept, they would be sublimely proof against any danger from water. . . . This honest fellow was the type of the new revolutionary philosophers in Germany" (SW 160). In short, the prob-lem with the Young Hegelians is that they see "in the critique of religion a panacea for every human ailment."[4] As long as they only interpret the world differently (atheistically) without changing it (politically and economically), they are like the doctor who works hard to bring down a fever but who knows nothing, and therefore does nothing, about the plague that produces the fever.

Of course, Marx is not denying that "Hitherto men have con-stantly made up for themselves false conceptions about themselves." Historical materialism is a theory of (motivated and collective) self-deception. He does not for a moment challenge the view that religious ideas are superstitions, that the gods people worship are "chimeras" or "imaginary beings" that they have created for themselves. Moreover, he explicitly repeats his earlier claim that "the State . . . [is] an illusory communal life," and he speaks of "the illusory 'general' interest in the form of the State" (SW 169-70).

But the problem is not simply that religion offers an illusory comfort and politics an illusory community. False consciousness takes these realms to be autonomous and fails to see their derivative and

3. For Marx's rather pragmatic view of the relation between truth and practice, see Theses I and II, SW 156. Cf. Henri Lefebvre, *The Sociology of Marx*, trans. Norbert Guterman (New York: Random House, 1969), pp. 31-34.
4. Kolakowski, p. 156.

dependent character. It thereby misunderstands the entire historical process, since the "real basis of history has either been totally neglected or else considered as a minor matter."

> The exponents of this conception of history have consequently only been able to see in history the political actions of princes and States, religious and all sorts of theoretical struggles, and in particular in each historical epoch have had to share the illusion of that epoch. For instance, if an epoch imagines itself to be actuated by purely "political" or "religious" motives, although "religion" and "politics" are only forms of its true motives, the historian accepts this opinion. The "idea," the "conception" of the people in question about their real practice, is transformed into the sole determining, active force, which controls and determines their practice. (SW 173)

There is no mystery about what Marx takes the neglected "real basis of history" to be: "When the crude form in which the division of labour appears with the Indians and Egyptians calls forth the caste system in their State and religion, the historian believes that the caste system is the power which has produced this crude social form. While the French and the English at least hold by the political illusion . . . the Germans move in the realm of 'pure spirit,' and make religious illusion the driving force of history" (SW 173).

Thus the political illusion consists in the unreality of the community and general will, which is so prominent in political self-consciousness, *and* in the unrecognized reality of conflict among the classes generated by the division of labor. "It follows from this that all struggles within the State, the struggle between democracy, aristocracy, and monarchy, the struggle for the franchise, etc. etc. are merely the illusory forms in which the real struggles of the different classes are fought out among one another" (SW 169).

Similarly, the religious illusion consists in the unreality of the happiness it promises *and* in the unrecognized reality of the class interests at work in ethical-religious and metaphysical-religious ideas. "The ideas of the ruling class are in every epoch the ruling ideas,[5] i.e. the class which is the ruling material force of society is at the same time its ruling intellectual force. The class which has the means of material production at its disposal, has control at the same time over the means of mental production. . . . The ruling ideas are nothing more than the ideal expression of the dominant material relationships . . ." (SW 176).

5. Marx quotes this opening clause in *The Communist Manifesto* (SW 236).

A materialist approach to history recognizes these relationships and is able to set forth economic life "(i.e. civil society in its various states) as the basis of all history; and to show it in its action as State, to explain all the different theoretical products and forms of consciousness, religion, philosophy, ethics, etc., etc., and trace their origins and growth from that basis; by which means, of course, the whole thing can be depicted in its totality (and therefore, too, the reciprocal action of these various sides on one another)" (SW 172).[6]

To use a musical metaphor, we might say that the materialist theory of history develops a theme already introduced in "On the Jewish Question," namely the parallel between the political and religious illusions. Beyond that it places the intellectual, cognitive dimension of religion in the context of a larger theory about the status of ideas with social import. Marx now speaks not just about religion but about "the language of politics, laws, morality, religion, metaphysics, etc. of a people. . . . Morality, religion, metaphysics, all the rest of ideology and their corresponding forms of consciousness, thus no longer retain the semblance of independence" (SW 164).[7]

6. The longer and more frequently quoted summary of historical materialism that ends with the epigram, "Life is not determined by consciousness, but consciousness by life" (SW 164), also describes the derivation of both the state and religious, moral, and metaphysical ideas from economic life. The reference to reciprocity among the various elements indicates that the "economic determinism" implicit in historical materialism is not a simple, one-way street on which economic factors are causes and non-economic factors are effects, in spite of the "crude formulations" (Kolakowski, p. 157) that sometimes suggest that. Cf. Engels's letters to Bloch and Schmidt (OR 273-86) for the classical statement of the "dialectical" relation among the elements.

7. One important theoretical domain missing from these lists is the one against which the vast majority of Marx's theoretical effort is directed: political economy, or, as we call it today, simply economics. Thus *Capital: A Critique of Political Economy* attacks capitalism by attacking the theory that seeks to justify it. As we shall see in the next chapter, the derivative character of ideas does not, for Marx, render them impotent.

26 Religion as Ideology

The quotation with which the previous chapter concludes links the concept of ideology with that of "the semblance of independence." Ideas become ideology, a pejorative term in Marxian usage, when they are embedded in the Illusion of Autonomous Origin. The idea that our political, legal, economic, moral, religious, and metaphysical theories are deeply conditioned by the world into which they are born, in which they live, and from which they die, especially by the economic class struggles of that world, is expressed by Marx in a single word, "ideology." Thus ideology can be defined as "any interpretation of history which is based on a dialectic of ideas divorced from the social-economic realities in which those ideas originate."[1]

But this idea is not the only one that Marx builds into the concept of ideology, not even the most important. A more complete definition of ideology would read like this: "These ideas are in fact governed by laws of their own; they are characterized by the subject's unawareness of their origin in social conditions *and of the part they play in maintaining or altering those conditions.*"[2]

Up to the italics this definition spells out the Illusion of Autonomous Origin. But the section of italics refers us to the Illusion of Neutrality. The false consciousness that renders ideas ideological not only fails to notice their conditioned character; more importantly, it fails to notice their social impact. They may embody the Illusion of Overcoming the World (see above, chapter 24), but even if they do not

1. Louis Dupré, *The Philosophical Foundations of Marxism* (New York: Harcourt, Brace, and World, 1966), p. 146.
2. Leszek Kolakowski, *Main Currents of Marxism*, vol. 1: *The Founders*, trans. P. S. Falla (Oxford: Oxford University Press, 1978), p. 154, emphasis added.

overcome the world in the manner they allege, they are far from socially impotent. Ideas, including religious ideas, may be illusory and derivative, but they can also be very powerful. Not only do they mirror and express their social world; they can function to reinforce and maintain it.

Perhaps we can see this point best if we turn momentarily from the realm of ideas to the realm of political practices and institutions. We have seen that Marx thinks that politics (and not just political ideas) shares in the Illusion of Overcoming the World, since it professes an experience of community that it does not provide. Moreover, it also shares in the Illusion of Autonomous Origin, for its conditioning by the class structure of its world is often unnoticed, even vehemently denied. But in spite of this double illusion, politics is a power in the service of class interests. In *The Communist Manifesto* Marx writes that

> the bourgeoisie has at last, since the establishment of Modern Industry and of the world-market, conquered for itself, in the modern representative State, exclusive political sway. The executive of the modern State is but a committee for managing the common affairs of the whole bourgeoisie . . . your jurisprudence is but the will of your class made into a law for all, a will whose essential character and direction are determined by the economical conditions of existence of your class. . . . Political power, properly so called, is merely the organized power of one class for oppressing another. (SW 223, 234, 238; cf. 225-26)[3]

In short, vis-à-vis economic interests the state is neither impartial nor impotent. But if false consciousness fails to notice this fact, we have the Illusion of Neutrality. This illusion is especially attractive to those whose interests politics serves at the expense of the interests of others. For to the degree that it prevails the victims of political power will feel less resentful and the perpetrators of political power will feel less guilty. Here we have the same double effect as that produced by opium.

In this drama the lead role goes to the Illusion of Neutrality. The police state is inefficient. Politics can exercise its preferential power most easily when its true nature is not recognized. But this means that the Illusion of Autonomous Origin plays a crucial supporting role, for

---

3. Later, in his *Grundrisse*, Marx will write "that every form of production creates its own legal relations, forms of government, etc. . . . and that the right of the stronger continues to exist in other forms even under their 'government of law' " (SW 349).

it suggests the immaculate conception of politics vis-à-vis economic interests. At least as important a supporting role is played by the Illusion of Overcoming the World. By giving an honorific account of what politics is doing, for example, finding and institutionalizing the general will, it distracts attention from the ways in which political power serves special interests.

For example, by focusing considerable attention on the (undeniable) value of free elections, it is possible to distract attention from the ·role played by big money and cynical propaganda in determining the outcome of elections. Or, by focusing attention on the ideal of majority rule, it is possible to distract attention from the impact of the "majority's" decisions on two particular minorities, the one at the top of the economic totem pole and the one at the bottom.

Returning to the realm of ideas and theories, we find exactly the same structure. In chapter 24 we encountered Marx's account of religious ideas as embedded in the Illusion of Overcoming the World. In chapter 25 we met historical materialism and its account of the Illusion of Autonomous Origin. What we need to do now is fill out the picture by relating religious ideas to the Illusion of Neutrality, noting that the first two illusions remain in supporting roles, making possible the putative impartiality of religious ideas that is a prerequisite to their political and economic power. It is this triple illusion that makes it possible to define ideology as "the imaginary relationship of individuals to their real conditions of existence."[4]

Actually, Marx has already done this for us, but we did not note it at the time. When he was quoted in the last chapter as saying "The ideas of the ruling class are in every epoch the ruling ideas" (SW 176), the point was to reveal the "semblance of independence" (SW 164) of those ideas as just that, as mere semblance. But the passage obviously says more than that. The happy marriage of certain ideas to the ruling class makes them the ruling ideas. It gives them power, the power to make the "dominant material relationships" of the epoch, whose "ideal expression" they are, appear to be both natural and right, expressions of some "eternal law" (SW 176). To the degree that the ideas that serve the interests of the ruling class[5] can present themselves in theory as Truth or Nature or Eternal Law, the Illusion of Neutrality is maintained

4. Louis Althusser, "Ideology and the State," in *Lenin and Philosophy and Other Essays*, trans. Ben Brewster (New York: Monthly Review Press, 1971), p. 162.
5. Or classes. Marx's theory does not presuppose, as a close reading of this passage will show, that in every period a single class has uncontested economic hegemony. For Marx history is, after all, "the history of class struggles" (SW 222).

and the legitimizing power of the ideas in question is enhanced. The ruling ideas extend their rule beyond the realm of ideas.

When Marx repeats this linkage of ruling ideas to ruling class in *The Communist Manifesto* (SW 236), he emphasizes the same points: "Law, morality, religion are to [the proletarian] so many bourgeois prejudices, behind which lurk in ambush just as many bourgeois interests. . . . The selfish misconception that induces you to transform into eternal laws of nature and of reason the social forms springing from your present mode of production and form of property . . . you share with every ruling class that has preceded you" (SW 230, 234).

In summary, to speak of religion as ideology is to say the same thing as when one calls it the opium of the people. It is to invoke the distinction between the truth of ideas and the function of ideas that is at the heart of the hermeneutics of suspicion and that was basic to our study of Freud's critique of religion. For when we employ either the metaphor of opium or the concept of ideology, we identify not the content of religious ideas, and thereby their truth value,[6] but their role in making special interests seem like the common good.

It is tempting to speak of hypocrisy here, or even of cynicism, but Marx does not. For that would imply a fully conscious posing of private advantage as the general will. The language of self-deception is more appropriate, for in Marx's view the ruling class is the most vulnerable to the illusions that constitute ideological mystification. Just as the victims of oppressive social systems may recognize that opium is more an escape than a cure, so they may see through the rationalizations offered by the beneficiaries of those systems. For example, is it not true that the most devoted advocates of trickle-down theories have always been the rich rather than the poor?[7]

---

6. Marx's theory of ideology has given rise in the twentieth century to a discipline called the sociology of knowledge, "the study of ideas irrespective of whether they are true or false — for ideological mystification is not the same as error in the cognitive sense . . . the functional-genetic conditioning of thought is one thing and its scientific legitimacy another." Kolakowski, pp. 154-55. Marx's concept of mystification might well be summarized by the three illusions developed in this and the preceding chapters.

7. Richard Miller formulates this propensity of the powerful toward self-justifying beliefs in language that makes clear its linkage to Freudian rationalization theory and especially to cognitive dissonance theory (see above, p. 85 n. 3):

> In the following sense, the capacity for self-deception of an exploitive ruling class would be said by Marx to be practically infinite. The long-term non-moral interests of a typical member of such a class often sharply conflict with the moral principles which he puts forward without conscious hy-

According to Marx's analysis, when religion is an ally of injustice, wealth is a greater obstacle than poverty to recognizing that it plays that role. Could this be what Jesus meant when he said "it is easier for a camel to go through the eye of a needle than for someone who is rich to enter the kingdom of God" (Luke 18:25, NRSV)?

Addendum: Politics as Foundation and Superstructure

In 1859 Marx published *A Critique of Political Economy*. In its preface he refers back to his youthful journey of discovery, the journey we have been retracing, and gives a classical formulation of his historical materialism. It introduces the concept of superstructure in relation to foundation (or basis) for distinguishing the (relatively) dependent from the (relatively) independent variables in social structure and historical change.

He begins an oft-quoted passage by referring to the relations of production that develop in correspondence with the available productive forces, that is, with the current level of technology.

> The sum total of these relations of production constitutes the economic structure of society, the real foundation, on which rises a legal and political superstructure and to which correspond definite forms of social consciousness. The mode of production of material life conditions the social, political, and intellectual life process in general. It is not the consciousness of men that determines their being, but, on the contrary, their social being that determines their consciousness. (SW 389)

---

pocrisy; and when this conflict obtains, no reasoning from those moral principles can, in a typical case, dissuade an exploiter from doing what his nonmoral interests demand. It should also be noted that the emotional strain associated with the instances of self-deception most of us have encountered will typically be lacking in such cases.

How so? By virtue of beliefs that justify the actions that serve the nonmoral interests and "which the immense variety of ideological institutions operating in the interests of the ruling class promote, and which everyone in the social circle of a typical member of that class acknowledges." The self-deception in such a case "is not the sort . . . that imposes such strains as to make it preferable for a member of the exploitive ruling class to accept the objective fulfillment of his sense of justice." In other words, the task of ideology is to reduce cognitive dissonance. "Rawls and Marxism," in *Justice: Alternative Political Perspectives*, ed. James Sterba (Belmont, CA: Wadsworth, 1980), p. 90.

Marx then turns to the process of fundamental social change, which he views as triggered by changes in property relations. "With the change of the economic foundations the entire immense superstructure is more or less rapidly transformed." In such change we should carefully distinguish between the economic factors "and the legal, political, religious, aesthetic, or philosophic — in short, ideological forms in which men become conscious of this conflict and fight it out. Just as our opinion of an individual is not based on what he thinks of himself, so can we not judge of such a period of transformation by its own consciousness" (SW 389-90).

Much of this is by now familiar, but we should carefully note (1) that when Marx speaks here of the legal and political he is talking about practices and institutions, not just ideas and theories, and (2) that he nevertheless includes the legal and political within the superstructure and treats it as a form of ideology.

This way of speaking differs from his earlier pattern. In such texts as "Towards a Critique of Hegel's *Philosophy of Right*: Introduction" and the "Theses on Feuerbach," Marx distinguishes the earthly, secular world of state and society as the basis of the heavenly, religious world that is its imaginary solution. Whereas in the preface to his *Critique of Political Economy* the world of politics belongs to the superstructure and as such is the partner of religion, in these earlier texts politics belongs to the foundation or basis and as such is paired with civil society.

We need not assume that Marx has changed his mind, for there is no conflict between these two ways of speaking. By seeing the point of both of them we better understand Marx's view of the state; but beyond that, and more to the point in the present context, we also sharpen our understanding of his view of religion.

To treat politics along with economic practices as part of the basic or foundational dimension of society is to recognize it as part of the earthly world whose heavenly halo (or deodorant) religion often tries to be. It is political practices and structures, as well as economic practices and structures, that religion often serves to legitimize. The fact that the former are not nearly as independent variables as the latter does not really matter.

On the other hand, to treat politics along with religion as part of society's superstructure and to attribute to it an ideological role is to recognize that when religion puts its imprimatur on a set of political arrangements it is indirectly sanctioning the economic relations supported (or enforced) by them.

Perhaps the clearest statement of the intermediate position of politics comes from Engels in "Ludwig Feuerbach and the End of Classical German Philosophy." He writes, "The state presents itself to us as the first ideological power. Society creates for itself an organ for the safeguarding of its common interests against internal and external attacks. This organ is the state power. . . . But once the state has become an independent power vis-à-vis society, it produces forthwith a further ideology," which consists of legal theory, religion, and philosophy (OR 261-62; cf. 259-67).

The relation of religion to politics is complicated by the fact that politics both offers state power in support of particular economic institutions and seeks the seal of godliness for its own practices. In doing so it confesses that the pen is mightier than the sword, for it seeks to legitimize the violence that is its essence (the military and police power)[8] with ideas of a religious nature; and in making this confession it joins Marx in giving to religion an enormous responsibility for the political and economic shape of human life.

8. See Max Weber's definition of the state as "a human community that (successfully) claims the *monopoly of the legitimate use of physical force* within a given territory." "Politics as Vocation," in *From Max Weber: Essays in Sociology,* ed. H. H. Gerth and C. W. Mills (New York: Oxford University Press, 1946), p. 78.

27 Religion as Critique

A Harvard Law School professor writes:

> The extraordinary representation of the ideal in art, religion, and love has a two-faced significance for everyday life. On the one hand, it can offer the self temporary refuge. In this sense, the extraordinary is a mystification, the aroma that sweetens the air of the established order. Its very availability makes the absence of the ideal from everyday life seem tolerable and even necessary. . . . Nonetheless, the extraordinary also makes it possible to grasp the ideal, and to contrast it with one's ordinary experience of the world. In this sense, the extraordinary is the starting point for the critique and transformation of social life. It poses for men the task of actualizing in the world of commonplace things and situations what they have already encountered as a divine liberation from the everyday. Thus, the tools of mystification and of defiance are drawn from the same source.[1]

There is no reference to Marx here, but the text is virtually a paraphrase of passages that immediately precede Marx's introduction of the opium metaphor. It is there, for example, that he speaks of religion as the "spiritual aroma" of the world in this sense of deodorant (¶3 in the opening of Marx's "Towards a Critique of Hegel's *Philosophy of Right:* Introduction"); and it is there, more importantly, that he writes, "Religious suffering is at the same time an expression of real suffering and a protest against real suffering" (¶4; see above, pp. 136-37).

In our analysis of religion as opium and as ideology this notion

---

1. Roberto Mangabeira Unger, *Knowledge and Politics* (New York: The Free Press, 1984), p. 232.

of religion as protest, even of defiance, has been altogether invisible, just as it is altogether invisible in almost everything Marx says about religion. Yet it is there in Marx, and we cannot do justice to his theory of religion while completely ignoring it.

The first question we must ask is why Marx himself, having introduced this theme so explicitly, should himself have ignored it so completely thereafter. We can perhaps detect his answer in an 1847 newspaper reply to a certain Consistorial Councillor (Prussian bureaucrat) whose public defense of Prussia as a Christian state had included the following challenge: "If only those whose calling it is to develop the social principles of Christianity do so, the Communists will soon be put to silence" (OR 83).[2]

I quote Marx's scathing reply in full:

> The social principles of Christianity have now had eighteen hundred years to develop and need no further development by Prussian consistorial councillors.
>
> The social principles of Christianity justified the slavery of Antiquity, glorified the serfdom of the Middle Ages and equally know, when necessary, how to defend the oppression of the proletariat, although they make a pitiful face over it.
>
> The social principles of Christianity preach the necessity of a ruling and an oppressed class, and all they have for the latter is the pious wish the former will be charitable.
>
> The social principles of Christianity transfer the consistorial councillors' adjustment of all infamies to heaven and thus justify the further existence of those infamies on earth.
>
> The social principles of Christianity declare all vile acts of the oppressors against the oppressed to be either the just punishment of original sin and other sins or trials that the Lord in his infinite wisdom imposes on those redeemed.
>
> The social principles of Christianity preach cowardice, self-contempt, abasement, submission, dejection, in a word all the qualities of the *canaille* [rabble]; and the proletarian, not wishing to be treated as *canaille,* needs its courage, its self-feeling, its pride and its sense of independence more than its bread.
>
> The social principles of Christianity are sneakish and the proletariat is revolutionary.
>
> So much for the social principles of Christianity. (OR 83-84)

---

2. Here we encounter again the suggestion that the best refutation of Marx would take place in practice rather than in theory. See above, p. 153.

It would not be difficult to find voluminous verification of these charges throughout Christian history. To cite but a single example, in 1602 the city council of Hamburg invoked Lutheran theology to instruct its citizens that "even if magistrates were godless, tyrannical, and avaricious, subjects ought not rebel and disobey but should accept it as the Lord's punishment which the subjects deserved for their sins."[3]

It would also be easy to object that Marx's view, while not without foundation, is one-sided. Thinking of the role played by Christian faith in the abolition of slavery and the slave trade in the British Empire, in the abolitionist movement in the United States, in the civil rights movement a century later, in the anti-apartheid movement in South Africa, and in the resistance to neocolonial exploitation and violence in Latin America, we might well insist that there is a story about religion as critique that Marx has suppressed.

What might be more to the point (of learning from Marx) than either of these responses would be to ask why Marx's account, even if one-sided, is an all too accurate account of all too much of Christian history. To put the question more precisely, Why, in spite of the *utopian* content that gives it critical potential as protest and even defiance in the face of socially sanctioned suffering, has Christianity so often offered its *ideological* imprimatur to various forms of domination — political, economic, racial, gender-based, and so forth?

It is Karl Mannheim who has treated Utopia and Ideology as opposites, and a brief look at his theory will help us sharpen the focus of our question. His *Ideology and Utopia* seeks to build on Marx's theory of ideology by developing a more general sociology of knowledge, a theory of the social uses to which knowledge is put. He first directs our attention to ideas that we might call ideals, ideas that describe how the world ought to be, such as the biblical images of the Messianic shalom. Then he notes that such ideas can be put to two very different social uses. Sometimes they "take on a revolutionary function" and thus "pass over into conduct [and] tend to shatter, either partially or

---

3. Quoted by Hajo Holborn in *A History of Modern Germany 1648-1840* (New York: Alfred A. Knopf, 1964), p. 31. Holborn also describes the powerful impact during the seventeenth and eighteenth centuries of the theory of the Christian state developed in the writings of Veit Ludwig von Seckendorf, councillor to Duke Ernest the Pious of Saxony-Gotha. "In these writings princely absolutism and the division of classes appeared as a God-willed order" (p. 51).

wholly, the order of things prevailing at the time." In this transformative social role, Mannheim calls them Utopias.[4]

On the other hand, the very same ideas and images of a better world can be "effective in the realization and the maintenance of the existing order of things." This happens when the portrayal of the ideal serves to blind people to or distract them from the cruel realities of the present or when the ideal is constantly postponed to some indefinite future. In this case Mannheim calls the ideas in question Ideology, echoing Marx's usage.

Even those ideas that have utopian possibilities, or, better, *especially* those ideas, can serve ideological functions. Therefore, those who are interested in legitimizing the status quo have not always feared ideas with such potential. "Rather they have always aimed to control [them] . . . and thereby to render them socially impotent." For example, "As long as the clerically and feudally organized medieval order was able to locate its paradise outside of society, in some otherworldly sphere which transcended history and dulled its revolutionary edge, the idea of paradise was still an integral part of medieval society. Not until certain social groups embodied these wish-images into their actual conduct, and tried to realize them, did these ideologies become utopian" (Mannheim, pp. 192-93).[5]

In this way Mannheim reinforces the distinction we have drawn several times between the *content* of ideas and their *function*. The biblical concept of paradise or the Kingdom of God can serve to pacify serfs, slaves, landless peasants, the unemployed, and so forth, or it can lead them to insist on change, just as it can serve to assuage or rankle the consciences of those who benefit from various forms of economic inequality. When we pray, "Thy Kingdom come, Thy will be done in earth as it is in heaven," and then either endure or embrace the social structures that make a hell of earth, we put a true idea in the service of a false reality, and our theology becomes ideology.

Beyond this, however, Mannheim makes it necessary to distin-

---

4. Karl Mannheim, *Ideology and Utopia: An Introduction to the Sociology of Knowledge*, trans. Louis Wirth and Edward A. Shils (New York: Harcourt, Brace, and World, 1936), pp. 192-93. Subsequent references to this work are given in the text.

5. For two powerful studies of this possibility, see Norman Cohn, *The Pursuit of the Millennium: Revolutionary Messianism in Medieval and Reformation Europe and Its Bearing on Modern Totalitarian Movements* (New York: Harper and Row, 1961); Vittorio Lanternari, *The Religions of the Oppressed: A Study of Modern Messianic Cults*, trans. Lisa Sergio (New York: Alfred A. Knopf, 1963).

guish the *content* of our theology not only from its public, social *function* but also from its private, personal *intent*. This reinforces the earlier distinction between hypocrisy and self-deception, for conscious intent is no more reliable an index of the actual role played by ideas than is their content. "The idea of Christian brotherly love, for instance, in a society founded on serfdom remains an unrealizable and, in this sense, ideological idea, *even when the intended meaning is, in good faith, a motive in the conduct of the individual. To live consistently, in the light of Christian brotherly love, in a society which is not organized on the same principle is impossible*" (Mannheim, pp. 194-95, emphasis added). This historical point about feudalism raises an awkward question about contemporary society. Since the principle of capitalist society is possessive individualism rather than love of neighbor, can personal sincerity make Christian love anything more than a deodorant in North America today?

Or consider the southern governor who physically barred blacks from access to the state university and insisted that he had no hatred in his heart for blacks. We need not challenge the sincerity of this claim. For those with a biblical understanding of sin, it will be no surprise that personal affection for blacks can factually coexist with public practices which are demeaning and unjust toward them. And if the governor's theology tended to hide rather than expose this contradiction between his warm feelings and his cruel behavior toward blacks, it functions as an ideology in support of a racist status quo.

For the Latin American theologian José Míguez Bonino this means that the test of orthodoxy will have to be orthopraxy. When it comes to evaluating various theologies, "*The question, therefore, is not what is intended with words, but how do they operate. . . .* Very concretely, we cannot receive the theological interpretation coming from the rich world without suspecting it and, therefore, *asking what kind of praxis it supports, reflects, or legitimizes.*"[6]

These are reminders that our theology, however orthodox its content and however sincere our intent, has enormous potential for ideological usage and that we are quite skillful, personally and collectively, at managing not to notice facts about ourselves that conflict with our self-image and our professed values. For those who profess biblical faith, it should come as no surprise that "the heart is deceitful above all things, and desperately corrupt" (Jer. 17:9) or that we tend to think of ourselves "more highly than [we] ought to think" (Rom. 12:3).

This means that we must go beyond asking whether our beliefs

---

6. José Míguez Bonino, *Doing Theology in a Revolutionary Situation* (Philadelphia: Fortress Press, 1975), pp. 80 and 91, emphasis added.

are true and our conscious intentions respectable to asking the really hard questions. How does our theology function? What sort of relation does it establish between us and the poor and the powerless, including those racially and educationally different from ourselves, both in our own communities and throughout the world? What kind of institutions and social structures does it support? What injustice and suffering does it legitimize by tolerating it? Whose wars does it bless? Does it leave unchallenged the nationalism and consumerism that lie at the heart of so much of the world's suffering?

In asking these questions about our theology, we need to think of theology in the broadest sense. Theology is simply the reflective side of our faith, the way we express and explain our faith to ourselves and to others. It occurs in the massive tomes of Barth, Berkouwer, and Berkhof, and in the learned lectures of seminary professors. But it also occurs in every prayer. When we sing

> Jesus loves me! this I know,
> for the Bible tells me so
>
> > (Anna B. Warner)

we express a simple but beautiful and powerful theology. In view of the fact that children are the primary victims of poverty in this country and throughout the world, the question becomes whether that theology functions harmoniously in our lives with the simple, beautiful, and powerful theology of another song we may sing:

> Jesus loves the little children,
> All the children of the world.
> Red and yellow, black and white
> All are precious in his sight,
> Jesus loves the little children of the world.
>
> > (C. H. Woolston)

If our worship in the church and our service in the world are shaped only by the first theology while the second remains at the level of a sweet sentiment for children and idealists, our theology has become an ideology. In spite of the fact that its center is a profound biblical truth, the "praxis it supports, reflects, and legitimizes" will include systems of poverty and oppression rooted in racism. The critical potential of "all the children of the world" will have been neutralized; and, since the gods who are indifferent to the suffering produced by such systems — such deities as National Security and Economic Growth — are not the God of the Bible, our worship will have become idolatry.

28 Techniques of Neutralization

One of the reasons philosophical postmodernism is such a disturbing factor in current intellectual discourse is its keen awareness of Mannheim's point that content does not determine use. Thus Jacques Derrida is aware that "a project can always be kidnapped, so to speak, or exploited for different political and cultural purposes," and Michel Foucault says in an interview that "the 'best' theories do not constitute a very effective protection against disastrous political choices; certain great themes such as 'humanism' can be used to any end whatever. . . ."[1]

The implication of the preceding chapter is that Christianity can be "kidnapped" and "used to any end whatever." The historical record shows that this is no merely theoretical possibility. For example, one of the most depressing parts of the story of the Nazi regime in Germany was the ability of Christians to endure and even embrace its policies, including its anti-Semitism.

It is not surprising that Hitler would view the church as a means and the nation and party as the end. "With regard to the churches he remarked [in his first speech to the German parliament] that the national government saw in the two Christian denominations the most important factors for the preservation of German nationhood."[2] The Protestant churches were, in fact, "particularly open to the National Socialist onslaught."

1. Christopher Norris, *Derrida* (Cambridge: Harvard University Press, 1987), p. 195; *The Foucault Reader*, ed. Paul Rabinow (New York: Pantheon Books, 1984), p. 374. This theme is a recurring motif in one of the best studies of Foucault's work, Hubert L. Dreyfus and Paul Rabinow's *Michel Foucault: Beyond Structuralism and Hermeneutics* (Chicago: University of Chicago Press, 1983).

2. Hajo Holborn, *A History of Modern Germany 1840-1945* (Princeton: Princeton University Press, 1969), p. 728.

The deeper cause of the vulnerability of German Protestantism was the nationalistic and reactionary spirit that found a home in these churches. . . . The same ministers who during World War I had preached that the German military victories were proof that the German cause was favored by heaven now declared that the defeat was only one of the tribulations inflicted by the divine will and that the Germans, if they readopted the heroic qualities of the past, would be able to break the chains that their enemies had imposed and achieve historic greatness. In the early 1920's groups of ministers and laymen appeared who advocated that Christianity be purged of its Judaic heritage. They declared Jesus Christ to have been a Nordic man. . . .[3]

In spite of resistance to these ideas "the racist Christian ideas found an amazingly large mass following. . . . The churches happily welcomed the Hitler government."[4]

In retrospect Karl Jaspers speaks of the "unconditionality of a blind nationalism" that expressed itself in "the complete self-identification with army and state, in spite of all evil," made possible "by a misinterpretation of the Biblical warning: 'Let every soul be subject unto the higher powers.' . . ."[5]

Our task at this point, it seems to me, is not

1. to congratulate ourselves on agreeing with Jaspers that Romans 13 does not teach complicity with Hitler, or
2. to deny the historical reality of the kidnapping of Christian ideas by the Nazis and the complicity of Christian persons and institutions with the Third Reich and with other historical manifestations of evil, or
3. to insist that history has other, more pleasant stories to tell.

Our task is rather to seek to understand how this kind of misinterpretation can come to be seen as gospel truth and how this kind of evil can be "endured" by sincere Christians as "compatible with" their faith or "embraced" and "authorized" by it.[6] How does the Bible,

---

3. Holborn, p. 739.
4. Holborn, p. 740.
5. Karl Jaspers, *The Question of German Guilt,* quoted in *Existentialism,* ed. Robert C. Solomon (New York: Random House, 1974), p. 162.
6. For "compatible with" and "authorized by," see above, chapter 4, on Hume. For "endured" and "embraced," see above, p. 152, on Pope.

in spite of its utopian content, come to play an ideological role as the moral sanction of immoral societies? What is the process that underlies the bitter plaint of so many native peoples, "At first we had the land and you had the Bible. Now we have the Bible and you have the land."[7]

At this point it will be useful to borrow the concept of "techniques of neutralization" from the sociology of juvenile delinquency. Sykes and Matza have argued that youthful criminals have essentially the same moral standards as the rest of society, but that they are able to avoid the guilt their behavior would normally produce by holding to these standards in general but rendering them irrelevant to their specifically criminal acts. There are several "techniques of neutralization" or "rationalizations" by which this is accomplished, including blaming the victim.[8] Whenever religion has taught victims of social systems of domination that they should accept their suffering as "the Lord's punishment which the subjects deserved for their sins,"[9] it has testified that the church can be as skillful as criminals in playing "blame the victim."

No attempt will be made here to be either complete or systematic in listing the techniques that neutralize essential parts of the biblical message and thereby permit Christian faith to become the opium of the people. But a variety of them will be discussed.

The first I will call Overt Espousal, for it explicitly declares that the behaviors or institutions that produce needless suffering are the will of God. When human ingenuity is combined with human sinfulness, it becomes possible to manipulate the message of God's shalom so that it seems to sanctify a sinful drive for power and wealth. In this way Christian theology publicly takes the side of systems and practices that desecrate God's image in children and women and men, its only bearers in all creation.

Thus biblical justifications for the exploitation of serfs, slaves, and wage laborers have not been lacking in the church's history — nor have theological rationalizations for the colonial domination of peoples of different color and culture, even when such domination has verged

---

7. Vittorio Lanternari, *The Religions of the Oppressed: A Study of Modern Messianic Cults,* trans. Lisa Sergio (New York: Alfred A. Knopf, 1963), p. 20.

8. Gresham M. Sykes and David Matza, "Techniques of Neutralization: A Theory of Delinquency," reprinted from *The American Sociological Review* 22 (1957), pp. 664-70, in *Guilt: Man and Society,* ed. Roger W. Smith (Garden City, NY: Doubleday, 1971). Cf. William Ryan, *Blaming the Victim* (New York: Random House, 1976).

9. See above, p. 168.

on genocide. When the Nazis made unconditional obedience to the state a solemn religious duty, they created a religion that overtly espoused their entire program.

More recently attention has been focused on the dramatic and tragic attempt of the white Dutch Reformed churches of South Africa to present apartheid as a biblical mandate.[10] Since 1986 the Dutch Reformed Church has officially moved away from this project, but there can be no doubt that it remains a powerful factor in the thinking of many white South African Christians whose orthodoxy is impeccable.[11]

In *The Covenant*, his historical novel about South Africa, James Michener writes about the battle of Blood River in 1838. The Voortrekkers, Boers on a historic migration from the Cape Colony to the Transvaal, won an overwhelming victory over the resisting Zulu armies. Three to four thousand Zulus died, but the Voortrekkers did not even suffer a serious injury. Michener reports that a troubled Dutch Reformed minister later would say, "It was not a battle. It was an execution." Then he adds this telling commentary:

> The real victor at Blood River was not the Voortrekker commando, but the spirit of the covenant that assured their triumph. As Tjaart said when he led prayers after the battle: "Almighty God, only You enabled us to win. We were faithful to You, and You fought at our side. In obedience to the covenant You offered us and which You honored, we shall henceforth abide as Your people in the land You have given us." What the Voortrekkers failed to realize in their moment of victory was that they had offered the covenant to God, not He to them. Any group of people anywhere in the world was free to propose a covenant on whatever terms they pleased, but this did not obligate God to accept that covenant, and especially not if their unilateral terms contravened His basic teachings to the detriment of another race whom He loved equally. Nevertheless, in obedience to the covenant as they understood it, they had won a signal victory, which confirmed their belief that He had accepted

10. Especially in the Landman Commission Report, approved and accepted by the General Synod of the Dutch Reformed Church in 1974, and translated as *Human Relations and the South African Scene in the Light of Scripture* (Capetown and Pretoria: Dutch Reformed Church Publishers, 1976).

11. This is possible because orthodoxy has been defined historically in terms of metaphysical issues, such as those growing out of trinitarian, christological, and sacramental debates, and terms of epistemological issues, such as those growing out of debates over the authority of the Bible, of tradition, and of the magisterium. It has not been defined with reference to the social praxis required by orthodoxy.

their offer and had personally intervened on their behalf. No matter what happened henceforth, men like Tjaart van Doorn were convinced that whatever they did was done in consonance with His wishes. The Boer nation had become a theocracy, and would so remain.[12]

Here we have the sociopolitical version of the One-Way Covenant, the psychological version of which we encountered in Salieri (see chapter 1 above), in Freud's analysis of religious renunciation (chapters 17 and 18), and in the girl who asked her mother for spankings (chapter 19). In Michener's historical fiction, there is more history than fiction. For the covenant he describes has been a powerful force for evil in the real world. Here is a 1941 version of it:

> God willed the diversity of Peoples. Thus far He has preserved the identity of our People. Such preservation was not for naught, for God allows nothing to happen for naught. He might have allowed our People to be bastardized with the native tribes as happened with other Europeans. He did not allow it. . . . He maintained the identity of our People, He has a future task for us, a calling laid away. . . . Humanly speaking, if we had had to predict what would happen to the Voortrekkers in 1838, if we had noticed the Black peril . . . each of us would have prophesied that our little People were doomed to extinction. And yet that little People remains . . . because God, the Disposer of the lot of the nations, has a future task laid away for our People. Thus let us become conscious of our calling. . . .[13]

The One-Way Covenant of the Afrikaners incorporates an element almost inevitably bound up with the technique of Overt Espousal, which is the theology of holy war. The logic is simple enough: Domination requires violence, and if that violence is to be overtly espoused in theological terms, it will have to take the form of holy war. Earlier we encountered this element, again in its psychological version, when we studied the pathetic Dr. Schreber. There we noted John Howard Yoder's account of the "egocentric altruism" involved in "being oneself the incarnation of a good and righteous cause

12. James Michener, *The Covenant* (New York: Random House, 1980), pp. 548-49. For the text of the historical Covenant Oath of 1838, see T. Dunbar Moodie, *The Rise of Afrikanerdom: Power, Apartheid, and the Afrikaner Civil Religion* (Berkeley: University of California Press, 1975), p. 179.

13. Quoted from H. G. Stoker in Moodie, p. 67.

for which others may rightly be made to suffer" (p. 75 n. 4 above; cf. chapters 10 and 16).

Law and order, and thus the police power of state, may easily become such a "good and righteous cause." In other words, the holy war mentality is not restricted to international relations. A tragic example of this is to be found in Martin Luther's role in the Peasants' War of 1525. Under feudal conditions that made a mockery of Christian love throughout Christendom, the peasants had been growing increasingly restless and were on the verge of insurrection. In Swabia, a group of them published their grievances in a pamphlet known as *The Twelve Articles,* trying to show from biblical sources that their complaints were just and that their spiritual and temporal lords were violating their rights.

Luther's response was entitled *Admonition to Peace: A Reply to the Twelve Articles of the Peasants in Swabia.* In it he first addressed the nobility, blaming them for the present social turmoil and stating clearly that the complaints of the peasants were for the most part justified. Like the peasants, he appealed to their sense of Christian duty. Then he addressed the peasants and told them that they must not resort to violence to secure their rights, quoting, as might be expected, Romans 13:1. Finally, he proposed a procedure for arbitration.

But violence broke out before this treatise could be published.[14] Luther's response is bloodcurdling. Referring to one of the peasants' leaders, Thomas Münzer, as an "archdevil," he calls not just on the authorities but on "everyone who can" to "smite, slay, and stab, secretly or openly, remembering that nothing can be more poisonous, hurtful, or devilish than a rebel. It is just as when one must kill a mad dog. . . . Thus, anyone who is killed fighting on the side of the rulers may be a true martyr in the eyes of God. . . . On the other hand, anyone who perishes on the peasants' side is an eternal firebrand of hell, for he bears the sword against God's word and is disobedient to him. . . . These are strange times, when a prince can win heaven with bloodshed better than other men with prayer!"[15] So much for salvation by grace through faith and not by works.

14. The text of the *Admonition to Peace* and a brief sketch of the historical background are found in *Luther's Works,* vol. 46: *The Christian in Society III,* ed. Helmut T. Lehmann (Philadelphia: Fortress Press, 1967).

15. From *Against the Robbing and Murdering Hordes of Peasants,* in *Luther's Works,* vol. 46, pp. 50-54. Luther's own supporters were so shocked by this treatise that he had to write a defense of it, entitled *An Open Letter on the Harsh Book Against the Peasants.*

One need not be a disciple of Frantz Fanon[16] to be deeply disturbed to see Luther abandon his own theology so easily here and support the violent perpetuation of injustice so ecstatically. By denouncing the revolutionary violence of the oppressed while supporting the repressive violence of their oppressors,[17] Luther clearly places his theology in the service of a feudal order he knows to be unjust; and it is on the path to holy war that his theology becomes ideology.

Perhaps every war tends to become a holy war. Certainly American wars have had such a tendency, which means that the two examples of Overt Espousal just discussed may not be as remote from our own experience as they seem. Presidents from William McKinley to George Bush have not been reluctant to talk publicly about how they prayed before going to war, implying quite directly that God was the true Commander in Chief who gave the ultimate order to start the killing.[18] The demonization of the enemy is, of course, another important aspect of holy war, a feature especially characteristic of American wars in the period of post-World War II anti-Communism, but still present at the "end of the Cold War" in the war against Iraq.[19]

16. Frantz Fanon's book, *The Wretched of the Earth,* trans. Constance Farrington (New York: Grove Press, 1968), is a celebration of the violence of revolutions against oppression in the Third World.

17. It is important to remember that the distinction between oppressed and oppressors here is Luther's own. I believe Luther has no answer to the Marxist who says, "To condemn the violence of the slave who revolts, is to become an accessory to the permanent violence of the enslaver." Roger Garaudy, *Marxism in the Twentieth Century,* trans. René Hague (New York: Charles Scribner's Sons, 1970), p. 151. For Friedrich Engels's account of the Peasants' War, see OR 97ff.

18. President McKinley told a group of clergy how he reached the decision to embark on the Spanish-American War (quoted by Reinhold Niebuhr in *Moral Man and Immoral Society* [New York: Charles Scribner's Sons, 1960], p. 102):

> I walked the floor of the White House night after night until midnight; and I am not ashamed to tell you gentlemen that I went on my knees and prayed to Almighty God for light and guidance more than one night. And one night it came to me this way — that there was nothing left for us to do but to take them all, and to educate the Filipinos, and uplift and civilize and Christianize them, and by God's grace do the very best we could by them, as our fellowmen for whom Christ also died. And then I went to bed and went to sleep and slept soundly.

19. It is one of the ironies of American anti-Communism, as the final paragraph of this chapter illustrates, that it provides one of the richest mines of material illustrating Marx's theory of religion as ideology. American support for repressive dictators around the world from Marcos to Somoza has been justified as keeping the world safe from atheistic Communism. To add to the irony, those who have argued this way have also decried the first principle of "Bolshevik morality," that the end justifies the means.

During the period of the Vietnam war, I often heard Joan Baez singing Bob Dylan's song that ends with the chilling words, "If God's on our side, we'll start the next war." I first really understood what it meant when I met a retired missionary to Cambodia who argued that the American war was justified because otherwise all of Indochina would be closed to the missionaries. I thought I heard the Grand Inquisitor smiling.

29 More Techniques of Neutralization

With a little talent for self-deception, it is not too hard to convince oneself that one is "the incarnation of a good and righteous cause for which others may rightly be made to suffer" (see chapter 28 above). Overt Espousal and its holy war mentality can assuage the moral pain that the beneficiaries of injustice ought to feel. The problem is that, while Overt Espousal is good at blaming the victim, it has no resources for persuading victims that the system under which they suffer is righteous. It is not easy to sell holy war theology to its intended targets, and it is hard to find a record of slaves who thought they were properly subject to the "curse of Ham." South African blacks see in the God of the Afrikaner covenant, not the Maker of Heaven and Earth, but a cruel figment of Afrikaner imagination.[1]

While half a loaf may be better than no bread at all, the need to legitimize society in the eyes of those at its bottom is a pressing one. More specifically, in a society with a Christian heritage, how can the utopian potential of the Bible be neutralized among those who have the most to gain from it? The most obvious technique is to keep them ignorant of the Bible.

---

1. There is an exception to this. One widespread argument that belongs to the Overt Espousal of slavery (and other forms of Western imperialism) is another "end justifies the means" argument. Slavery was justified because the slaves could be evangelized to Christianity. Albert J. Raboteau, *Slave Religion: The "Invisible Institution" in the Antebellum South* (New York: Oxford University Press, 1978), pp. 96-97, 159, 174. Some slaves, having been converted, apparently bought into this theory. Thus the slave poet Phyllis Wheatley wrote (Raboteau, p. 44):

'Twas mercy brought me from my *Pagan* land,
Taught my benighted soul to understand
That there's a God, that there's a *Saviour* too. . . .

This strategy was widely employed with American slaves. Since it was eventually replaced by other techniques, we have come to think of slaves as very religious. But at first there was a great reluctance to evangelize and catechize slaves, lest they become "saucy" or even, upon baptism, lay claim to liberty. Thus it was not until the nineteenth century that most slaves were exposed to Christian teaching.[2]

The same "Ban the Bible" approach is used in Gilead, the anti-utopia of Margaret Atwood's novel, *The Handmaid's Tale*.[3] Gilead is a male chauvinist's paradise in which women are completely subordinate to men and women of childbearing age are reduced to the role of concubines for older men. It is also a religiously legitimized society, as indicated by the names of the senior male rulers and the younger men whose activities made Gilead into a classic police state: They are called, respectively, Commanders of the Faithful and Guardians of the Faith. Far from being an atheistic society, this is one in which the banners announcing "WOMEN'S PRAYVAGANZA TODAY" have smaller print proclaiming (with a candor matched only by Hitler) *"God Is a National Resource."*

The handmaids of Gilead must read such signs with interest, for apart from them their only reading matter is the single word "Faith" embroidered on a seat cushion in each of their rooms. "The Bible is locked up, the way people once kept tea locked up, so the servants wouldn't steal it. It is an incendiary device: who knows what we'd make of it, if we ever got our hands on it" (p. 112).

This passage reveals the fatal flaw in the Ban the Bible technique. To the degree that it is successful the utopian content of the Bible will not be able to have any socially disruptive consequences. But the awareness among the rulers that the Bible must be banned because of its incendiary potential can only be an irritant to consciences that wish to be put to sleep. In other words, this strategy has a defect that is equal but opposite to that of Overt Espousal. While espousal helps to justify society in the eyes of its beneficiaries but not its victims, banning does the opposite. It may help in keeping the ruled pacified, but it tends to delegitimize the social order in the eyes of the rulers.[4]

---

2. Raboteau, pp. 98-99, 102, 122-25, 143, 149.

3. Margaret Atwood, *The Handmaid's Tale* (New York: Fawcett Crest, 1985).

4. The necessity to incorporate into the baptism liturgy for slaves a clause in which they stated that they sought baptism only for the good of their souls and not to free themselves from slavery (Raboteau, p. 123) testifies to an awareness on the part of the owners that the Bible is indeed dangerous to their way of life. If it is not to be banned, it will have to be broken, the way a horse is taught to serve riders.

What is most instructive about Gilead is that the Commanders of the Faithful recognize this with sufficient clarity to modify the strategy. Thus the question "who knows what we'd make of [the Bible], if we ever got our hands on it?" is followed by "We can be read to from it, by him, but we cannot read." Actually Gilead is saturated with words from the Bible, from the formal greetings the women are required to use among themselves to the "family" devotions, in which the Commander reads selected passages from the Bible to his wife and her handmaids. It takes no great ingenuity to anticipate that these texts will be those about being fruitful and about being submissive (pp. 114-19, 286).

We can call this modified technique "Edit the Bible." It is not necessary to ban the Bible entirely if a monopoly over selection can be maintained. As it turns out, slave owners did not need to go to Gilead to learn this lesson. They wanted the benefits of religious legitimation in the eyes of their slaves. As one group of them wrote, "We should protect ourselves by Law, as far as possible . . . and then we should *look at home,* and enter upon such a discharge of our Duty to the Negroes, as will meet the approbation of God and our consciences. . . . *No means will so effectually counteract evil influences, and open up our way to the proper improvement of our colored population, as a judicious system of religious instruction."* [5]

In saying this they were accepting the argument that eventually carried the day, namely that Christianity would make better slaves. Some slave churches fulfilled this hope thoroughly and even expelled members who ran away from their masters.[6] But for this to be possible, it was necessary to find *"a judicious system of religious instruction."* In what could such judiciousness consist, if not in selectivity?

No one saw this more clearly than the South Carolina planter Whitemarsh B. Seabrook. "After vehemently denying that slaves should be 'acquainted with the whole Bible,' or every doctrine therein, Seabrook argued that it was 'absolutely necessary' for them to become 'intimately acquainted' with 'the prominent portions of Scripture which shew the duties of servants and the rights of masters.' Moreover, any attempt to make the religious knowledge of slaves 'co-extensive with that of their owners' was sheer lunacy."[7] Seabrook and others drew the obvious conclusion that slaves could not be permitted to preach and

---

5. Raboteau, p. 161. In appealing to the political realm and then, more basically, to religion to support economic exploitation, they were acting as if they had been reading Marxist textbooks.

6. Raboteau, pp. 103, 145.

7. Raboteau, pp. 169-70. Cf. pp. 162, 213.

teach, just as the women in Gilead could be read to but could not read. Religious meetings by slaves alone were widely forbidden and severely punished.[8]

Ban the Bible easily becomes Edit the Bible. Just as easily, Edit the Bible becomes Interpret the Bible. For if an effective monopoly on biblical interpretation can be maintained by the power elite, it will not be necessary to hide parts of the Bible from parts of the population, something that is hard to do in any case and that has the additional drawback of rendering an awkward fact conspicuous to those who would most like not to notice it, the fact that God is being treated as a national (or class or race or gender) resource and that the Bible is being used to justify injustice. What is needed is a pattern of interpretation that will render innocuous the utopian content of the Bible in relation to contemporary social structures of domination.

In the rest of this chapter and in the next we will look at two such structures. But before doing so we might anticipate the force of the various variations of the Interpret the Bible technique of neutralization. There is a long history of links between heresy and social radicalism.[9] What can this mean except that the principles and patterns of interpretation that have defined orthodoxy in a given context have served the social status quo with the kind of consistency that Marxian theory would predict? If the ruling ideas are the ideas of the ruling class, orthodoxy can be expected to function as ideology.

What we might call ecumenical orthodoxy has defined itself in metaphysical and epistemological terms (see above, p. 175 n. 11), leaving it open for regional orthodoxies, those that have prevailed in particular times and places, to incorporate a pattern of biblical interpretation socially favorable to the powers that be. We have already seen this in the case of Overt Espousal, which is actually a variation of the Interpret the Bible technique of neutralization. The variations we are about to examine are more subtle in that they "endure" rather than "embrace" domination; they render it "compatible with" rather than "authorized by" Christian faith (see p. 173 n. 6). The advantage of this

---

8. Raboteau, pp. 170, 179-80, 195-96, 212-15.

9. See Norman Cohn, *The Pursuit of the Millennium: Revolutionary Messianism in Medieval and Reformation Europe and Its Bearing on Modern Totalitarian Movements* (New York: Harper and Row, 1961); Vittorio Lanternari, *The Religions of the Oppressed: A Study of Modern Messianic Cults*, trans. Lisa Sergio (New York: Alfred A. Knopf, 1963); Elaine Pagels, *The Gnostic Gospels* (New York: Random House, 1981); Elisabeth Schüssler Fiorenza, *In Memory of Her: A Feminist Theological Reconstruction of Christian Origins* (New York: Crossroad, 1985).

is that they have a greater chance of operating as opiates of the oppressed than Overt Espousal usually has.

The first of these we may call Vague Generality. Theologies in this vein may well denounce the evils of which the poor and oppressed are victims. But they do so in such general terms that there is no way to move from theory to practice. This is why liberation theologians have often found the political theologies of the north (Moltmann, Metz, Cox) to be far less radical than they sound. A student whose paper began, "On balance, Plato believed good was better than evil," provides an example, admittedly extreme, of the problem here. One is reminded of the South African church synod that decried racism as a sin but could not bring itself to identify apartheid as racism.

Theology enters the path of Vague Generality to avoid the scandal of specificity. Of course, one way in which specificity is scandalous is that it earns the ire (and sometimes the persecution) of those whose interests are vested in the status quo. So there is a question of courage and cowardice here.

But there are other more respectable fears at work here. It has been the liberation theologians who have joined to their emphasis on the importance of being concretely on the side of the poor and oppressed an emphasis, not only on the political risks of such involvement (of which they are keenly aware), but especially on two theological risks. The first of these is the risk of being wrong. We are, of course, never free from this possibility, but the chances of being wrong seem to increase as we get specific. It is much safer to say, "God is love and wills all people to live together in peace and justice," than it is to apply this truth to the current struggles for human dignity throughout the Third World. Since we cannot deduce from Scripture the answers to our questions about, for example, the role of corporate capitalism in Latin America, the temptation arises to remain at the level of "hoary abstract certitudes" rather than to plunge into the uncertainty of concrete political and economic reality. It is especially on the question of means that the movement from the absolutes of the biblical message to the relativities of historical situations is treacherous.[10]

Fear of the other theological risk of being on the side of the poor lures theology along the path of Vague Generality. This is the risk of what Gustavo Gutiérrez calls a "Constantinianism of the Left,"[11] the

10. Juan Luis Segundo, S.J., *The Liberation of Theology*, trans. John Drury (Maryknoll, NY: Orbis, 1976), pp. 69-72, 87, 108.
11. Gustavo Gutiérrez, *A Theology of Liberation: History, Politics and Salvation*, trans. Sr. Caridad Inda and John Eagleson (Maryknoll, NY: Orbis, 1973), p. 266.

blurring of the distinction between the Kingdom of God and historical movements of liberation that may be seeking to embody it. This makes it possible to give theological but uncritical support to historical agencies, which, however hopeful they may appear, are nevertheless human and sinful. Classical Marxism itself, a secular theology with an inadequate understanding of sin, has regularly fallen into this trap;[12] and Marxist theory has more frequently been the ideology of various tyrannical police states than a genuine instrument of liberation.

Thus Gutiérrez warns Christians that their efforts for liberation must avoid

> becoming translated into any kind of Christian ideology of political action or politico-religious messianism. Christian hope opens us, in an attitude of spiritual childhood, to the gift of the future promised by God. It keeps us from any confusion of the Kingdom with any one historical stage, from any idolatry toward unavoidably ambiguous human achievement, from absolutizing any revolution. In this way hope makes us radically free to commit ourselves to social praxis, motivated by a liberating utopia. . . . And our hope not only frees us for this commitment; it simultaneously demands and judges it.[13]

The risk of being wrong and the risk of becoming uncritically and absolutely attached to our historical choices are serious risks. But the apparently safer task is even riskier. To remain safely at the level of Vague Generality is to condemn Evil in the abstract while "enduring," both in theory and in practice, the concrete evils from which our sisters and brothers, especially the children, daily suffer and die. By making faith "compatible with" these evils, we confirm the Marxian charge that religion is the opium of the people.

---

12. For a brief sketch of the religious overtones of Marxism, see Robert Tucker, *Philosophy and Myth in Karl Marx* (2nd ed.; New York: Cambridge University Press, 1972), pp. 21-25.
13. Gutiérrez, p. 238.

30 *One Last Technique of Neutralization*

If theology is to function as ideology the utopian content of religion must be neutralized. We have named three techniques for accomplishing this task; our list looks like this:

1. Ban the Bible
2. Edit the Bible
3. Interpret the Bible
   a. Overt Espousal
   b. Vague Generality

Since we have not only three different basic techniques but also two strategically different modes of the third of these, we might ask what characteristics the best techniques will have, what makes for high-grade opium of the spirit.

Since ideology is self-deception, one obvious desideratum is inconspicuousness. Instead of hanging up banners, in effect, that say, The Bible is a national (or class, or gender) resource, it would be better if the Bible could be put to political-economic uses without either the beneficiaries or the victims noticing. By this criterion Interpret the Bible looks more promising than Ban the Bible or Edit the Bible, since to make all or part of the Bible into contraband is to announce to one and all its liberating potential and the fact that for this reason it is feared by those in power.

It would also be helpful if the social order could be legitimized in the eyes of both those at the top and those at the bottom. As we have seen, this signifies a further weakness of Ban the Bible and Edit the Bible, since their conspicuousness weakens their effectiveness for those at the top. It is also a weakness of Overt Espousal, which has little effect at the bottom of the social hierarchy.

It looks as if Vague Generality, a subtler version of Interpret the Bible than Overt Espousal, comes out the winner. It is considerably less conspicuous than the alternatives and thus better suited for generating false consciousness. And it works especially well with those at the top, since it allows them the satisfaction of being very much in favor of good and very much against evil.

Its one potential weakness is with those at the bottom. While it does not provide any clear route from theoretical opposition to evil to practical resistance of evil, it also does not place any positive barriers in the way of hearing the liberating potential of the biblical message. In Margaret Atwood's Gilead, for example (see chapter 29 above), Vague Generality would not have much power to prevent women from becoming "saucy" when they read in Genesis 1:27 that they, too, and not men only, were created in the image of God, or in Ephesians 5:21 that husbands and wives were to be "subject to one another out of reverence for Christ." And it is not at all clear that Vague Generality would have the power to produce slave churches that supported slavery by excommunicating runaway slaves.

This brings us to our final variation on Interpret the Bible. Like Vague Generality it is more subtle than Overt Espousal. But unlike Vague Generality it has the power to neutralize texts like Genesis 1:27 and Ephesians 5:21 and to produce slave churches that excommunicate runaways. In fact, historically, it has done so. We can call this new variation Dualistic Hermeneutics and add it to our list:

3. Interpret the Bible
   a. Overt Espousal
   b. Vague Generality
   c. Dualistic Hermeneutics

In this technique for neutralizing religion's utopian content, several interrelated dualities serve to separate human life into independent regions and to give religious primacy to the nonpolitical and noneconomic regions. These dualisms include spiritual vs. material, future vs. present, personal and inward vs. social and public, vertical vs. horizontal, in God's eyes vs. in the eyes of society, and so forth. With the help of these dualities the Bible's message of liberation is interpreted exclusively in innerworldly, otherworldly, and afterworldly terms, with the only social comment often being the claim that the social order is God-ordained and to be accepted.

One of the most familiar symptoms of this practice is the church's overwhelming preference for Matthew's beatitudes ("Blessed are the poor in spirit," Matt. 5:3, etc.) over Luke's ("Blessed are you poor," Luke 6:20, etc.). Next to Romans 13:1 the favorite verses of the ruling class are "The kingdom of God is within you" (Luke 17:21, KJV) and "My kingdom is not of this world" (John 18:36, KJV). Slave religion was able to be the opiate of the slaves because it bought into this dualism by building its foundation on private ecstasy and future hope.[1]

Just about the time Marx died in 1883, his friend and colleague, Friedrich Engels, wrote a couple of essays on Christianity as a slave religion. About a decade later, he added a third. In their focus on the desire for consolation in the believing soul they sound a lot like Freud (OR 202-4; cf. 334-35), and in pointing to the desire for vengeance in the believing soul they sound a lot like Nietzsche (OR 207-8; cf. 337). But in their emphasis on the role of class and of oppression they are distinctively Marxian. Engels presents early Christianity as a religion whose Darwinian survival value (OR 204) derived from its ability to satisfy the need for consolation and vengeance among slaves and all others "who had been smitten down by the levelling iron fist of conquering Rome" (OR 334, 195-202, 206, 316).

Following the lead of our old friend Bruno Bauer, Engels claims that the book of Revelation was both a reaction to Nero's Rome and the earliest book of the New Testament. More importantly, he suggests that it is the clearest expression of the joint urges toward consolation and revenge that made Christianity a world-historical religion. What is important about these essays is not the question of their historical accuracy, either in dating the book of Revelation or in

---

1. Albert J. Raboteau, *Slave Religion: The "Invisible Institution" in the Antebellum South* (New York: Oxford University Press, 1978), pp. 217-18. Not surprisingly, the twentieth-century Marxist Roger Garaudy approvingly quotes the eighteenth-century materialist Baron d'Holbach: "Religion is the art of making men drunk with ecstasy in order to divert their attention from the evils heaped upon them here below by those who govern them" (Garaudy, *Marxism in the Twentieth Century*, trans. René Hague [New York: Charles Scribner's Sons, 1970], p. 106). The ideological potential of both hope and euphoria lies in their power to divert attention. The same can be said of the metaphysical and epistemological issues that have traditionally preoccupied orthodoxy. The intellect as well as the emotions can be the locus of diversion. See my article "Orthodoxy and Inattention," *Reformed Journal* 30/1 (January 1980), pp. 13-15.

describing the sociology of early Christianity. It is rather the account they give of how Christianity was and is able to function as a slave religion.

Engels writes that in all classes "there was necessarily a number of people who, *despairing of material salvation, sought in its stead a spiritual salvation.* . . . We hardly need to note that the majority of those who were pining for such consolation of their consciousness, *for this flight from the external world into the internal,* were necessarily among the slaves" (OR 202, emphasis added). Like workers' socialism, Christianity preaches "forthcoming salvation from bondage and misery; Christianity places this salvation in a life beyond, after death, in heaven. . . . Christianity, as was bound to be the case in the historic conditions, did not want to accomplish the social transformation in this world, but beyond it, in heaven, in eternal life after death, in the impending 'millennium'" (OR 316-17). Christianity found a way out for all those who suffered from slavery and oppression, "but not in this world." It "created heaven and hell, and a way out was found which would lead the labouring and burdened from this vale of woe to eternal paradise. And in fact only with the prospect of a reward in the world beyond could . . . renunciation of the world . . . be exalted to the basic moral principle of a new universal religion which would inspire the oppressed masses with enthusiasm" (OR 335-36).

Engels's message is clear. By directing the search for salvation away from the world in which people suffer from political and economic oppression to inner and future worlds where release and restitution do not interfere with present social realities, Christianity adopts all the dualisms mentioned above and makes them the key to its interpretation of Jesus as Savior and Lord. It is by virtue of its Dualistic Hermeneutics that Christianity began as a slave religion and has continued to function as one. This is the kind of religion that could (and did) produce slave churches that punished runaway slaves. By spiritualizing, allegorizing, inwardizing, and futurizing the Kingdom of God, Christianity makes itself "compatible with" such social evils as slavery and racism; and by its capacity to "endure" them, it legitimizes them.

If the Kingdom of God is so heavenly that it represents no threat to slavery on earth, Overt Espousal is not really necessary. If, for example, I can be a slave owner and a respected elder or deacon in my church, what more need I ask of my church by way of salving my conscience? Or if I can tie up a slave for a whipping on a Sunday morning, go to church and preach to a congregation that includes her mother, and then come home and whip her,[2] my sermon need not be about the rightness of slavery to enable me to do so in good conscience. It need only observe the neat boundaries of Dualistic Hermeneutics. Similarly, slaves need not be convinced that slavery is divinely ordained in order to be convinced that their God-given duty here on earth is submission. And even if they are not convinced that obedience is obligatory, a dualistic Christianity will teach them to look for God's love only in some other (inward or future) world.

If Christianity is to avoid selling its soul to the devil in this way, it will need a holistic (non-dualistic) framework for its theology. This is why the South African Council of Churches affirms that the gospel of Jesus Christ

> offers hope and security for the whole life of man; it is to be understood not only in a mystical and ethical sense for the salvation of the individual person, and not only in a sacramental and ecclesiastical sense within the framework of the Church. The Gospel of Christ is to be understood in a cultural, social (and therefore political), cosmic, and universal sense, as the salvation of the world and of human existence in its entirety. Further, the Gospel of Christ is not only the object of our hopes; it should be experienced as a reality in the present.[3]

Archbishop Tutu insists that biblical liberation concerns sin in all its forms, not just socio-political forms. But he simultaneously insists that the latter are integral to our understanding of the gospel and cannot be excluded or made secondary. He is fond of quoting Archbishop Temple's claim that "Christianity is the most materialistic of the great religions."[4] If this is true, then a Ugandan missionary may well be right in suggesting that when we spiritualize and thus neutralize the political dimensions of the gospel

---

2. Raboteau, pp. 165-68. If I am feeling extra pious, I may wait until Monday to give my slaves the whippings they "earn" for failing to help their masters adequately enjoy Sunday as a day of rest. Among slaves, Christian masters were often perceived to be the most violent.

3. Quoted from *A Message to the People of South Africa* (1968) in *Apartheid Is a Heresy*, ed. John W. de Gruchy and Charles Villa-Vicencio (Grand Rapids: Eerdmans, 1983), pp. 154-55.

4. Desmond Tutu, *Hope and Suffering: Sermons and Speeches*, ed. John Webster (Grand Rapids: Eerdmans, 1984), pp. 169-70, 176-77. See also the quotation from Tutu in John W. de Gruchy, *The Church Struggle in South Africa* (Grand Rapids: Eerdmans, 1979), p. 163.

we have drifted back into the old polytheism against which the prophets of the Lord waged their great warfare. The real essence of paganism is that it divides the various concerns of a man's life into compartments. There is one god of the soil; there is another god of the desert. . . . All this is precisely where the modern paganism of our secular society has brought us today. Certain portions of our life we call religious. Then we are Christians. . . . We turn to another department of our life called politics. Now we think in quite different terms. Our liturgy is the catchwords of the daily press. . . . Our incentive is the fear of — we're not sure what. But it certainly is not the fear of the Lord.[5]

With sadness Adeolu Adegobola describes how in Africa "conversion to Christianity has meant, among other things, acceptance of the view that life can be divided into spiritual and material, worldly and heavenly; and God has been thought of as being in control only of the spiritual. . . . Catechumens have been led to repeat the Apostles' Creed, 'God the Father Almighty, Maker of heaven and earth,' and at the same time to behave as if the earth were outside God's sovereign control and better left in the hands of the 'princes of the world.' "[6]

Whenever and wherever this happens, it has the political and economic significance of making religion into ideological support for the status quo, however unjust. It does this not by overtly espousing the evils of the social order but by defining the Christian life without reference to them. And since the Christian faith is represented as having nothing to say about them, the message is clearly that one can be a good Christian while continuing to participate in them as perpetrator or beneficiary. The evil systems of the world sometimes demand that the church actively support them; but usually they are content with the church's silent complicity. This is why, in his 1965 call for a Confessing Church in South Africa, Beyers Naudé mentions sinful silence in the face of injustice as one of the striking parallels between the South African situation and that of Germany under the Third Reich.[7]

In the 1981 Charter of the Alliance of Black Reformed Christians

---

5. Quoted by Allan Boesak in *Black and Reformed: Apartheid, Liberation, and the Calvinist Tradition,* ed. Leonard Sweetman (Maryknoll, NY: Orbis, 1984), pp. 88-89; cf. p. 59.

6. Quoted by Manas Buthelezi in "The Theological Meaning of True Humanity," in *The Challenge of Black Theology in South Africa,* ed. Basil Moore (Atlanta: John Knox Press, 1974), p. 100.

7. See John W. de Gruchy, "Towards a Confessing Church: The Implications of a Heresy," in *Apartheid Is a Heresy,* pp. 75-76.

in South Africa (ABRECSA), we read the following: "The Reformed tradition in South Africa is seen as responsible for political oppression, economic exploitation, unbridled capitalism, social discrimination and the total disregard for human dignity. By the same token, being Reformed is equated with total, uncritical acceptance of the status quo, *sinful silence* in the face of human suffering and *manipulation* of the Word of God in order to justify oppression."[8] This *manipulation* of the Word of God is what we have called Overt Espousal. The *sinful silence* that is presented here as the powerful partner of that manipulation comes in at least two forms, Vague Generality and Dualistic Hermeneutics. In the face of social injustice, the former is silent through its refusal to become specific, while the latter is silent through its asocial spirituality. All that is necessary for religion to become the opium of the people is for religion to be silent in the face of oppression.

8. Quoted in *Apartheid Is a Heresy*, p. 164, emphasis added.

31 *Mixing Religion and Politics*

If the church is to prove Marx wrong in the only way it can, by actually being an irritant rather than an opiate in the presence of social evil, it will have to break the unconscious and unnoticed conspiracy of silence that has so often made it the silent partner of those evils. What would it mean for the church, instead of practicing and defending such silence, to seek to end it?

One recent attempt to break the unholy alliance between piety and power is liberation theology, whose Latin American and South African representatives have begun to appear in the last several chapters. We can reformulate our question in relation to this movement: What has it meant in recent decades for the church to take the lead in challenging the structures of oppression? We can begin to answer this question by locating liberation theology in relation to the secular modernism that has often held a virtual monopoly on such a challenge.

From the perspective of Marxian analysis, such opposition is a twofold task: (1) There is the task of developing a political critique of the religious ideas and practices that legitimize social structures which institutionalize oppression, exploitation, and domination, that is, of exposing the ideological function that religion plays in a particular historical context. (2) And there is the task of developing a critique of those social structures themselves, whose very heart, in the modern Western world, is capitalism. Thus both the foundation or basis and the superstructure of domination must be undermined.

Marxism has no monopoly on the first of these tasks, which has been standard fare among modern secularists whom no one would accuse of socialist sympathies. Thus Thomas Hobbes described the theocratic ideas taught by "the Roman and presbyterian clergy" as "darkness in religion," and he entitles the final chapter of his *Leviathan*

"Of the Benefit that proceedeth from such Darkness; and to whom it accrueth." By adding to the two inquiries in this title a third, namely "who they may be that have possessed the people so long in this part of Christendom, with these doctrines, contrary to the peaceable societies of mankind," Hobbes makes it clear that he is concerned with the use to which the ideas in question have been put, not their truth.[1]

Similarly, Spinoza speaks of religion as "worshipping God as [each] thought fit in order that God should love him beyond others and direct the whole of Nature so as to serve his blind cupidity and insatiable greed."[2] And John Stuart Mill speaks of Calvinism as despotism under another name.[3]

While these and other secular modernists agree with Marx in their suspicion of religion, they differ in that they do not see capitalism as the most fundamental problem. In the debate between the (liberal) followers of Mill and the (socialist) followers of Marx, it has often seemed as if the critique of religion as ideology has been the exclusive concern of secular modernists.

The liberation theologians are closer to Marx than to Mill in that they see neocolonial forms of capitalism as deeply involved in the suffering of their peoples. But they are radically different from both strands of secular modernism because their critique of both the social structures of oppression and the religious superstructure that supports them is religiously motivated and grounded. Since they are theologians it is not surprising that their thought is religiously grounded. What has caught many people off guard, however, is that they are so political, so offensively political.

From Jesus' perspective this offense is to be expected. When John the Baptist sends a delegation to find out if Jesus is indeed the long awaited Messiah, Jesus gives an extraordinarily this-worldly (materialistic, horizontal) answer: "Go and tell John what you have seen and heard: the blind receive their sight, the lame walk, lepers are cleansed, and the deaf hear, the dead are raised up, the poor have good news preached to them." There is nothing offensive about these references to the blind, the lame, the lepers, the deaf, and even the dead. But that

1. These passages come from the opening paragraphs of chapter 47 of Hobbes's *Leviathan*.

2. Baruch Spinoza, *Ethics, Book I: Appendix to the Proof of Proposition 36*, as translated in *The Ethics and Selected Letters*, trans. Samuel Shirley (Indianapolis: Hackett, 1982).

3. John Stuart Mill, *On Liberty*, ed. Elizabeth Rapaport (Indianapolis: Hackett, 1979), pp. 59-61.

the poor have good news preached to them is another matter, and perhaps this is why Jesus goes on immediately to say, "And blessed is he who takes no offense at me" (Luke 7:22-23).

That good news to the poor is a decisive hallmark of Jesus as the Christ will be especially offensive if this is understood as Mary understands the messianic fulfillment of the covenant promises in the *Magnificat:*

> You [the Lord, God my Savior] have shown strength
> > with your arm,
> > scattered the proud in their conceit.
> You have brought down rulers from their rank,
> > and lifted up the lowly.
> The hungry you have filled with good things,
> > the rich you have sent empty away.
> > > (Luke 1:51-53, adapted)

Perhaps Jesus had learned this interpretation of Hannah's song (1 Sam. 2:1-10) from Mary herself. Was it she who pointed out to him, for example in Psalms 9–10, the link between pride, power, and wealth and, most importantly, that the victims of this unholy trinity can expect God to come to their aid? Had she pointed out to him the contrast between the good king of Psalm 72, who gives justice to the poor and needy and crushes the oppressor, and the kings whom God rejects in Psalm 82, those who fail to do justice by delivering the weak from the hands of the wicked? In any case the gospel story should prepare us to find that the social meaning of the Kingdom will offend the arrogance of power and wealth.

So we should not be surprised that when a Roman Catholic archbishop in Brazil, Dom Helder Camara, and an Anglican archbishop in South Africa, Nobel Peace Prize winner Desmond Tutu, actively and articulately side with the poor and oppressed, the Pharaohs, the Herods, and the Chief Priests of the world are displeased. When these bishops (along with many other pastors) find they cannot announce the good news of the Kingdom without denouncing the political, economic, and ideological systems that sustain misery in their parishes, the beneficiaries of those systems are offended.[4]

---

4. On the link between *announcing* the Kingdom and *denouncing* the principalities and powers, see Gustavo Gutiérrez, *A Theology of Liberation: History, Politics and Salvation,* trans. Sr. Caridad Inda and John Eagleson (Maryknoll, NY: Orbis, 1973), pp. 233-34, 268-69.

They are especially offended when the archbishops denounce these systems by name. They identify the political systems that oppress their people as both military dictatorships and "democracies" that exclude the masses from effective participation and then rely on military and police violence, including torture, to repress dissent. They identify the economic systems that sustain poverty as capitalism, the neocolonial impact of multinational corporations, and the institutional framework of international trade and banking. And they identify the ideological systems that legitimize these structures as anti-Communism, the theory of development, the idea of the national security state, and Christian theology in alliance with these systems.[5]

But at this point there begins in response a loud protest against the mixing of religion and politics.[6] For example, when the South African Council of Churches (SACC) issued its *Message to the People of South Africa* in 1968, strongly denouncing apartheid and the theological legitimation of it, Prime Minister Vorster warned those "who wish to disrupt the order in South Africa under the cloak of religion" not to attempt what Martin Luther King did in America (thus Vorster acknowledges the absence of any threat of violence); they should rather "cut it out, cut it out immediately for the cloak you carry will not protect you [note the threat of state violence] if you try to do this in South Africa." In an open letter to SACC leaders he wrote, "It is your right, of course, to demean your pulpits into becoming political platforms to attack the Government and the National Party. . . . I again want to make a serious appeal to you to return to the essence of your preaching and to proclaim to your congregations the Word of God and the Gospel of Christ."[7]

We learn a lot about liberation theology by listening to its re-

---

5. A particularly good example of this kind of specificity is Dom Helder Camara, *Revolution Through Peace*, trans. Amparo McLean (New York: Harper and Row, 1971). See also José Comblin, *The Church and the National Security State* (Maryknoll, NY: Orbis, 1984); Rubem Alves, *Protestantism and Repression: A Brazilian Case Study*, trans. John Drury (Maryknoll, NY: Orbis, 1985); and *Faces of Jesus: Latin American Christologies*, ed. José Míguez Bonino, trans. Robert R. Barr (Maryknoll, NY: Orbis, 1984), especially chapters 4 and 6.

6. There is an irony in this, for when Marxists denounce the same systems they are in turn denounced as "*atheistic* Communists." But the theism of the liberation critics does not make them more welcome. Roger Garaudy has a point when he writes that the Marxist "cannot be certain that the Church rejects communism primarily because it is atheistic. He suspects that it is much more because it is revolutionary" (*Marxism in the Twentieth Century*, trans. René Hague [New York: Charles Scribner's Sons, 1970], p. 152).

7. Quoted in John W. de Gruchy, *The Church Struggle in South Africa* (Grand Rapids: Eerdmans, 1979), pp. 118-19.

sponses to this entirely typical criticism. Each of the three following replies will take us closer to the heart of these theological traditions.

The first response is *ad hominem*. It points to the double standard of those who, for example, seek biblical support for apartheid but complain about the mixing of religion and politics when others oppose apartheid on biblical grounds. Thus Archbishop Tutu writes:

> A familiar remark which has become almost a parrot cry is "Don't mix religion with politics!" . . . If the Church demonstrates a concern for the victims of . . . neglect or exploitation . . . then the Church will be accused of meddling in affairs it knows very little about. This kind of criticism will reach crescendo proportions if the Church not merely provides an ameliorative ambulance service, but aims to expose the root causes. . . . Then it will arouse the wrath of those who benefit from the particular inequitable status quo. . . . If the South African Council of Churches were to say now that it thought apartheid was not so bad, I am as certain as anything that we would not be finding ourselves where we are today. *Why is it not being political for a religious body or a religious leader to praise a social political dispensation?*[8]

In the same vein Mexican bishops expose the by no means disinterested nature of efforts to preserve the "purity" and "dignity" of religious activity uncontaminated by "political" involvement. "Frequently this false zeal veils the desire to impose a law of silence when the real need is to lend a voice to those who suffer injustice and to develop the social and political responsibility of the people of God."[9]

A second response of liberation theology to the charge of meddling in politics instead of preaching the gospel can be called the situational response. It suggests that political neutrality can never be more than a hypocritical and self-deceptive pretense because it is, at least in situations of great discrepancies of power and wealth, impossible to achieve. In such circumstances, choosing not to take sides is to take the side of the stronger.

When the U.S. State Department said that it would not take sides in the struggle between black and white in South Africa, Tutu put the point most graphically: "Admirable impartiality, but how can you be

---

8. Desmond Tutu, *Hope and Suffering* (Grand Rapids: Eerdmans, 1984), pp. 36-37, 170, emphasis added.

9. Quoted in Gutiérrez, p. 115.

impartial in a situation of injustice and oppression? . . . It is small comfort to a mouse, if an elephant is standing on its tail, to say, 'I am impartial.' In this instance, you are really supporting the elephant in its cruelty. How are you to remain impartial when the South African authorities evict helpless mothers and children and let them shiver in the winter rain, as even their flimsy plastic covers are destroyed?"[10]

Where white racism prevails, to be color-blind is to be pro-white. Moreover, it is to be morally blind. For, as Allan Boesak has pointed out, to profess neutrality where that is not possible is to adopt a naive "pseudo-innocence" that serves to "blind people so that they do not see the atrocities of the present." In one sense, he argues to Christians in the Netherlands, it is worse than openly siding with oppression. "Neutrality, as you know, is the most abominable demonstration of partiality because it means choosing the side of power and injustice without assuming responsibility for them. This you can no longer do. You, too, must make a choice."[11]

The *ad hominem* response and the situational response to the charge of mixing religion and politics are telling. But they do not take us to the heart of the matter, because the issue is theological and these are not theological responses.

After he has himself made these first two responses, Segundo takes us on to the final and fundamental response: With reference to the practice and preaching of Jesus about love, he says that to "attempt to inculcate an apolitical love today" would be "to seriously distort the gospel message."[12] The ultimate issue is the very meaning of the biblical story. When the church is urged to quit meddling in politics and get back to preaching the gospel, the most basic reply is a question: Which gospel — the gospel of white supremacy, the gospel of the national security state, or the gospel that is good news to the poor?

---

10. Tutu, p. 115; cf. p. 39.

11. Allan Boesak, *Black and Reformed: Apartheid, Liberation, and the Calvinist Tradition*, ed. Leonard Sweetman (Maryknoll, NY: Orbis, 1984), pp. 60, 134; cf. p. 75 and Boesak's *Farewell to Innocence: A Socio-Ethical Study on Black Theology and Power* (Maryknoll, NY: Orbis, 1977), pp. 3-4.

12. Juan Luis Segundo, S.J., *The Liberation of Theology*, trans. John Drury (Maryknoll, NY: Orbis, 1973), p. 71. For his version of the first two responses, see pp. 70 and 127 and pp. 13, 74, and 130 respectively.

32 Who Is the God of the Bible? Ask Pharaoh!

This question about the nature of the gospel brings us to the heart of the matter. The deepest reason why liberation theology is offensively political is the conviction that God is revealed throughout the Bible to be on the side of the poor and the oppressed. Gutiérrez writes, "Within a society where social classes conflict, we are true to God when we side with the poor, the working classes, the despised races, the marginal cultures."[1]

Liberation theologians are fond of quoting Karl Barth on this point:

> The human righteousness required by God and established in obedience — the righteousness which according to Amos 5:24 should pour down as a mighty stream — has necessarily the character of a vindication of right in favor of the threatened innocent, the oppressed poor, widows, orphans and aliens. For this reason, in the relations and events in the life of His People, God always takes His stand unconditionally and passionately on this side and on this side alone: against the lofty and on behalf of the lowly; against those who already enjoy right and privilege and on behalf of those who are denied it and deprived of it.[2]

John Calvin expresses the bond between the God of the Bible and the victims of human injustice even more strongly in his commentary on Habakkuk 2:6:

---

1. Gustavo Gutiérrez, "The Poor in the Church," in *The Poor and the Church*, ed. Norbert Greinacher and Alois Moller (New York: Seabury Press, 1977), p. 15.
2. Karl Barth, *Church Dogmatics* II/1, ed. G. W. Bromiley and T. F. Torrance (New York: Charles Scribner's Sons, 1957), p. 386.

Tyrants and their cruelty cannot be endured without great weariness and sorrow. . . . Hence almost the whole world sounds forth these words, How long, how long? When anyone disturbs the whole world by his ambition and avarice, or everywhere commits plunders, or oppresses miserable nations, when he distresses the innocent, all cry out, How long? And this cry, proceeding as it does from the feeling of nature and the dictate of justice, is at length heard by the Lord. . . . *And this feeling, is it not implanted in us by the Lord? It is then the same as though God heard himself, when he hears the cries and groanings of those who cannot bear injustice.*[3]

As Calvin says it, God does not merely side with the poor and oppressed but identifies so fully with them that their cries express divine pain. No doubt this is why Scripture teaches us to equate our treatment of them with our treatment of God (Prov. 14:31; 19:17; Matt. 25:31-46).

But how can the God of the Bible be a God who takes sides? Is this compatible with universal love? This aspect of who God is can probably best be understood through the experience of parents. The parent who insists that an older, stronger child stop bullying a younger, weaker one clearly takes the side of the one child against the other. But only the bully, while still in a pout over this, will interpret this parental intervention as meaning that the parent does not love them equally. This simple analogy helps us to see that God's "partiality," on which liberation theologians place such stress, is fully compatible with the claim that all persons are equally objects of divine love. We must not allow the message of God's love for the whole world as expressed in John 3:16 to blind us to the sustained biblical witness that God has a special concern for the widows and orphans, the little people, the victims, the excluded, the powerless.

3. Quoted twice in Allan Boesak, *Black and Reformed: Apartheid, Liberation, and the Calvinist Tradition,* ed. Leonard Sweetman (Maryknoll, NY: Orbis, 1984), pp. 23-24 and 63-64, Boesak's emphasis. Boesak also quotes Abraham Kuyper, whose theology some have sought to use in support of apartheid: "When the rich and poor stand opposed to each other, Jesus never takes his place with the wealthier, but always stands with the poorer. He is born in a stable; and while foxes have holes and birds have nests, the Son of Man has nowhere to lay his head. . . . Both the Christ, and also just as much his disciples after him as the prophets before him, invariably took sides *against* those who were powerful and living in luxury, and *for* the suffering and oppressed" (p. 91). For further discussion of Calvin and Kuyper, see Nicholas Wolterstorff, *Until Justice and Peace Embrace* (Grand Rapids: Eerdmans, 1983), chapter 4. For similar quotations from Basil the Great, Ambrose of Milan, Chrysostom, and Thomas Aquinas, see Wolterstorff's "The Moral Significance of Poverty," *Perspectives* 6/2 (February 1991), pp. 8-11.

Ultimately, indeed, it is to the Bible and not to Barth and Calvin that the liberation theologians make their appeal; and the story of the Exodus plays the role of paradigm for their understanding of who the God of the Bible is. When this God chooses a people through whom to fulfill covenantal promises to all humanity, he chooses a rabble of slaves and delivers them from their political and economic oppression. In giving the law of the covenant to the people of the covenant, God identifies himself very specifically: "I am Yahweh your God, who brought you out of the land of Egypt, out of the house of bondage" (Exod. 20:2). The formula "I am Yahweh" occurs first in Exodus 6, and "the decisive phase of history as the action of God begins here in the fact that God reveals himself to Moses with his name Yahweh, while he had appeared to the Fathers only as El-Shaddai. . . . And God will immediately reveal his most proper and characteristic essence in the fact of 'bringing out,' 'freeing,' 'releasing,' 'saving' 'with arm outstretched and great judgments' the oppressed people."[4] The author of the priestly document emphasizes in the strongest way, by God changing his own name (Exod. 6:3), the importance of this one historical intervention of the deliverance of the oppressed people of Israel from Egypt.[5] And immediately afterward, God is portrayed as saying: "Say this to the sons of Israel, 'I am Yahweh *and therefore* I will free you of the burdens which the Egyptians lay on you. I will release you from slavery to them, and with raised arm and my great justices I will deliver you. I will adopt you as my own people, and I will be your God. Then you shall know that I am Yahweh your God, he who has freed you from the Egyptians' burdens" (Exod. 6:6-7).[6]

The centrality of the Exodus motif in a theology arising among and addressed primarily to the least of Christ's sisters and brothers is due in part to its obvious relevance to their suffering. But it is not simply a matter of finding an attractive part of the Bible. Once we see the importance of this event for revealing the nature and character of God, it is easy to see its themes throughout the whole of Scripture, in the Law, the Psalms, the Prophets, the Gospels, the Epistles, and even the Apocalypse.[7]

---

4. Karl Elliger, "Sinn und Ursprung der priesterlichen Geschichtserzählung," in *Kleine Schriften zum Alten Testament* (Munich: Kaiser, 1966), p. 178, as translated in José Miranda, *Marx and the Bible: A Critique of the Philosophy of Oppression*, trans. John Eagleson (Maryknoll, NY: Orbis, 1974), p. 78.

5. As pointed out by Miranda, p. 79.

6. As translated in Miranda, p. 79.

7. For a study that does precisely this, see "Biblical Faith and Our Economic

Liberation theologians are convinced that this understanding of God comes to its climax in the Gospels, and they challenge us to learn to read the Gospels as the story of the son of the God who liberated the slaves in Egypt. In this light Jesus' identification of his mission as "good news to the poor," both in the synagogue in Nazareth (Luke 4) and in his response to the delegation from John the Baptist (Luke 7), his teachings about wealth and power, his relation to women, lepers, tax collectors, Samaritans, and so forth, and the political character of his confrontation with the Jewish authorities, including the charge that the temple trade was thievery (Mark 11) — all these parts of the story of his life and death take on new significance.[8]

What the liberation theologians challenge us to see is that the God of the Bible does not evaluate social orders by the criteria of military power or economic productivity. Nor, for that matter, is the criterion piety as the Gallup Poll measures piety, in terms of belief in God, church attendance, Bible reading, and conversion experience. The biblical criterion of social decency is the simple question, How does this society treat its widows and orphans, that is, its weakest and poorest members?

We Americans are proud of our military prowess and our economic power. We American Christians are proud that we are a more religious people than, say, the peoples of Western Europe (at least by Gallup Poll standards). But in the eyes of biblical faith none of this is worth much; and when we ask the central question of the Bible's critical sociology, the question about the widows and orphans, it is hard to be proud of being an American without lowering expectations to a shameful level relative to our resources. Economically speaking, we are preoccupied with productivity, but the prime measure thereof, the Gross

---

Life," a report of the Christian Action Commission of the Reformed Church in America, in *The Acts and Proceedings of the 178th Regular Session of the General Synod,* Vol. LXIV (Reformed Church in America, 1984), pp. 51-67. For a more detailed study of the Exodus motif throughout Scripture, see Severino Croatto, *Exodus: A Hermeneutics of Freedom* (Maryknoll, NY: Orbis, 1981). For background to the political character of Jesus' encounter with the leaders of his people, see Gustavo Gutiérrez, *A Theology of Liberation: History, Politics and Salvation,* trans. Sr. Caridad Inda and John Eagleson (Maryknoll, NY: Orbis, 1973), pp. 228-32, against the background of Richard J. Cassidy, *Jesus, Politics, and Society: A Study of Luke's Gospel* (Maryknoll, NY: Orbis, 1978) and *Political Issues in Luke-Acts,* ed. Richard J. Cassidy and Philip J. Scharper (Maryknoll, NY: Orbis, 1983).

8. For an attempt by a Marxist to read Jesus as a utopian rather than an ideological figure, see Milan Machovec, *A Marxist Looks at Jesus* (Philadelphia: Fortress Press, 1976).

National Product, is designed to ignore the very question so central in the Bible: How is the wealth distributed? We speak of productivity where the Bible speaks about justice.

Our wounded pride is likely to respond to thoughts like this by changing the subject to human rights. Here, surely, we can be justly proud. But this change of subject is of little help. Just as we can find countries less religious than we, so we can easily find countries with poorer records on human rights than ours. But if instead of comparing ourselves with others we compare ourselves with the expectations of the God of the Bible, we discover that the biblical concept of human rights is much more like Marx's than like our own. For it has an economic dimension at its heart, so much so that no wealthy country with massive poverty could be said to have a good record on human rights. And this is before the topic of racism is even mentioned.

If the biblical message is not neutralized by the techniques we have examined above, but is rather allowed to express its utopian social vision as the criterion by which societies here and now are to be judged, the biblical critique of contemporary Western societies, including American society, sounds very much like the Marxist critique. That is why it is possible for the Czech Marxist, Milan Machovec, to suggest that Marxists are the heirs of Jesus and the prophets.[9] I would like to put it the other way around and accuse Marx of plagiarism. His critique of capitalism is, in essence, the biblical concern for the widows and orphans, stripped of its theological foundation and applied to the conditions of modernity. What the liberation theologians have tried to show is that the application to modern conditions does not require the abandonment of biblical thinking.

It might seem that this attempt to rehabilitate Marx and to shake biblical Christians free from their uncritical confidence in contemporary capitalist society is badly timed. Is it not the case that the collapse of Communism in Eastern Europe has discredited Marxism once and for all and established the superiority of capitalist society?

In a word, No. It is true that European Communism has not been able to come up with a viable alternative to the democratic capitalism of the West and that the Leninist model of the state, long discredited in the eyes of all but its own "truest" believers, has collapsed. But this has little bearing on the Marxian analysis of what happens to the widows and orphans in capitalist societies, and the homeless on our

9. Machovec, p. 193. He suggests that the crucial question is which tradition best serves the utopian vision of the Bible in the modern world.

streets have been understandably muted in their celebration of the demise of the Warsaw pact.

Capitalism has shown itself to be more productive than the Leninist state. But if justice and compassion are the biblical criteria, rather than productivity, the question about the worth (and even the viability) of our own society remains an open one. We would do well to remember Israel and Judah. They could rightly point to many bad things about the cruel and idolatrous societies of Assyria and Babylon; but none of this made their own social order acceptable in the eyes of Yahweh, their God, who brought them out of slavery.

Those who benefit most from the contemporary capitalism hope that the collapse of the Soviet empire will enhance uncritical acceptance of present arrangements. They even try to build such acceptance into the definition of patriotism. My hope is just the opposite. Now that Marxist tanks, bombers, and missiles are not the threat they used to be, my hope is that we will find the courage to look more carefully at Marxist critiques of modern society and thereby discover anew the meaning of our biblical faith.

33 *Third Commandment Idolatry*

The previous chapter has suggested that biblical Christians have biblical reasons to give a critique of contemporary Western society that sounds very Marxian. But we have seen that the Marxian critique is addressed both to the political and economic institutions that make up society's basis (according to historical materialism) and to the ideologies, including religious ideologies, that make up the super-structure of society. What we need to see now is that biblical religion provides the framework for a critique of *religion* that once again sounds very Marxian. If the last chapter's subtitle might have been "The Biblical Critique of Capitalism," this chapter's subtitle could be "The Biblical Critique of Christianity."

One of the striking things about the Bible is its hostility to religion; and one of the striking things about this hostility is that it is not at all directed just against worship of other gods. It is not so much about "their" religion as about "ours." That is why Karl Barth, instead of saying that it was the Jews and not the Romans who crucified Christ, says it was the church and not the world (see pp. 3-4 above). In the New Testament we see Jesus' polemic both against the worldly disciple-ship of his followers, especially Peter, James, and John, and against Jewish legalism, focusing on the Sabbath; Paul's battle against Jewish legalism, focusing on circumcision; and, lest we abuse the Pauline message, James's critique of cheap grace. As we noted in chapter 2, these biblical diatribes against false religion are addressed to the covenant people of God in their worship (as they think) of the God of the covenant. In the case of James and Paul they are addressed to the Christian church (see especially p. 11 n. 1).

The recurrence of this theme in all these variations shows how thoroughly Jewish is the New Testament. For it occurs against the background of the Old Testament's polemic against the worship of Yahweh by the people of Yahweh, a polemic unparalleled, I believe, in the history of religion. Although it focuses on the sacrificial cult, it eventually covers virtually every aspect of Hebrew worship. This is what makes it possible for Buber to say that religion can hide the face of God from us as nothing else can (see p. 25 above).

The prophetic critique of sacrifice begins with the story of Samuel and Saul. Having kept the flocks and herds of the Amalekites, despite the explicit command from God to destroy them entirely, Saul seeks to justify this by telling Samuel that the animals are for sacrifice to Yahweh. This piety of disobedience is rejected in Samuel's familiar words:

> Has Yahweh[1] as great delight in burnt offerings and sacrifices,
>   as in obeying the voice of Yahweh?
> Behold, to obey is better than sacrifice,
>   and to hearken than the fat of rams.
>
>   (1 Sam. 15:22)[2]

Even if the intent to sacrifice had been present before Samuel discovered the forbidden flocks and was more than just a last-minute excuse, it is unlikely that it was the sole motive for keeping the flocks or that he intended to sacrifice all of them. Although the text is not fully explicit about it, it seems that the disobedience here was a case of the people of God trying to render their economic life independent of God's revealed will; and the text makes it clear that, just as the Godfather is not rendered saintly by his conspicuous philanthropy, so the believing soul manifests no true piety through the conspicuous stewardship of ill-gotten gain. God is not reluctant to look a gift horse in the mouth.

Samuel's harsh words to Saul echo throughout the Old Testament. Again and again Israel finds "the lavish cultus by which she had hoped to satisfy Yahweh's demands to be unacceptable and offensive to him."[3] Although the Torah has lengthy and detailed prescriptions for sacrifice, God is presented as uncommonly hostile to sacrifice when it is unaccompanied by obedience. Often this obedience is left generic

---

1. Here as elsewhere I use "Yahweh" in place of the Revised Standard Version's "the LORD."

2. In chapter 18 I mentioned this text in connection with Freud and noted that obedience is as ambiguous as sacrifice, or, to be more precise, that all forms of (apparent) obedience, not just sacrifice, are liable to self-serving distortion.

3. John Bright, *A History of Israel* (3rd ed.; Philadelphia: Westminster, 1981), p. 290.

and essentially undefined.[4] On other occasions, it is more specific, as when Hosea represents God as saying

> For I desire steadfast love and not sacrifice,
> the knowledge of God, rather than burnt offerings.
>
> (6:6)

On these occasions a "Marxian" theme often plays a central role. Sacrifice and other forms of worship are unacceptable to God when they are considered "compatible with" economic injustice, when they make it possible for the pious to "endure" the suffering of the poor and the needy.[5] In the next chapter we will turn our attention to such a text. But before we do, it might be helpful to add a new concept to our vocabulary for describing the kind of piety that justifiably evokes the suspicion of secular prophets like Marx and biblical prophets like Samuel.

From Freud we have learned to speak of rationalization and of wish-fulfilling illusion, including projection. From Marx we have learned to speak of mystification, opium, and ideology. And we have developed our own vocabulary. We have spoken of "instrumental religion" to signify the piety that makes God into a means toward our ends.[6] We have spoken of "possessive monotheism" to signify the attempt to make God our private property, in effect our slave (see p. 109 above). And we have spoken of the "One-Way Covenant," in which we unilaterally dictate the terms of our relation to God's power and authority. By now the overlappings and equivalences among these terms are familiar.

All these terms suggest a reduction of religion to magic, the project of learning to manipulate the sacred power for one's own purposes, personal or collective. If they grate on our ears, that does not mean that we are immune to such practices but that we will require a generous dose of self-deception to reduce cognitive dissonance whenever we fall into them.

---

4. See Ps. 40:6-8; Prov. 15:8; Eccles. 5:1; Isa. 66:1-4; Jer. 6:16-21; 7:21-23; 14:10-12; Hos. 8:11-13.

5. In addition to Prov. 21:3 and Mic. 6:6-8, see Isaiah 1, the temple sermon in Jeremiah 7, and the whole book of Amos. In Isaiah 58 it is fasting rather than sacrifice whose acceptability depends on aid for the poor and oppressed.

6. The term "instrumental religion" is derived from the term "instrumental reason" as used by members of the Frankfurt school. Since its (near) synonyms in philosophical discourse include calculative thinking, strategic action, and technology, we could extend our derivation and speak about calculative worship, strategic piety, and faith as technique.

The time has come to add to this family of concepts that of "third commandment idolatry." The kinds of religion to which the other terms appropriately apply need not violate the first two of the Ten Commandments, for they can be practiced in the name of Yahweh (or the triune God) and without the aid of graven images. But they violate the third commandment, "You shall not take the name of Yahweh your God in vain" (Exod. 20:7), for when this kind of worship is offered to the God whose will we thereby violate, we take God's name in vain.

In historical context the third commandment was a prohibition not so much of what we think of as swearing as it was of magical practices and conjuring. Commenting on this meaning of the third commandment, von Rad gives in effect a helpful definition of instrumental religion: "Israel has been assailed at all periods by the temptation to use the divine power with the help of the divine name in an anti-social manner and to place it at the service of private and even sinister interests."[7]

But the biblical God makes it abundantly clear that he is not available for such service.[8] So another way to talk about instrumental religion would be to say that what is verbally the worship of the one true God has become idolatry.[9] For when we take God's name in vain by using religion to legitimize impious practices, we worship in fact another god. In his Narnia Chronicles, C. S. Lewis has put the point succinctly. Tash is the false god of the pagan Calormenes, of whom Aslan, the true God, says, "We are opposites." But Aslan also says, "And if any man do a cruelty in my name, then though he says the name Aslan, it is Tash whom he serves and by Tash his deed is accepted."[10]

The logic of the situation is rather simple. The God of the Bible is conspicuously on the side of the poor and oppressed. When we are not on their side and when we make it clear by the juxtaposition of our lives and our worship that we attribute the same indifference (or worse) to God, we also make it clear that our worship is directed to some other god. For the god who is so heavenly minded, perhaps with help from

7. Gerhard von Rad, *Deuteronomy*, trans. Dorothea Barton (Philadelphia: Westminster, 1966), p. 57.

8. On the sanctity of the divine name and God's unwillingness to be conjured, see my *God, Guilt, and Death* (Bloomington: Indiana University Press, 1984), pp. 237-38, with notes.

9. The concept of idolatry has already put in its appearance in chapters 1, 4, 9, 18, 24, and 26 above.

10. C. S. Lewis, *The Last Battle* (New York: Macmillan, 1956), p. 165. I am indebted to Steve Evans for calling this passage to my attention.

Vague Generality or Dualistic Hermeneutics, that he is not moved to compassion and anger by what the wicked do to the weak is not the God of the Bible. And the god who is so earthly minded, perhaps with help from Overt Espousal, that he is an active collaborator in injustice is not the God of the Bible either.

What Marxian language calls "ideology," the Bible calls "idolatry." The fact that we use the biblical names for God, such as Father, Son, and Holy Spirit, does not change the idolatrous nature of our worship, for we thereby take God's name in vain.[11] The only real difference between first and third commandment idolatry is that first commandment idolaters know they worship another god, while third commandment idolaters deceive themselves about this fact. It can truly be said of them, "They know not what they do" (see chapter 16 above). Like the ideological use of religion described by Marx, third commandment idolatry is a form of false consciousness. Unless suspicion brings it to the light of day, it can be quite effective in hiding itself from itself.

11. Kierkegaard offers a helpful analysis of what it means to profess Christian faith "in vain." To all triumphalist Christians who forget that the path to victory is the way of the cross and that the consolations of faith are offered to those called upon to die away from their natural life he says, "thou hast taken God in vain" (*For Self Examination and Judge for Yourself*, trans. Walter Lowrie [Princeton: Princeton University Press, 1944], pp. 85, 95-96, 117-18). Although he does not give a sociopolitical interpretation to this dying in these texts, Kierkegaard does precisely that in a companion volume, *Training in Christianity* (trans. Walter Lowrie [Princeton: Princeton University Press, 1944]). For a look at this "Marxist" dimension in Kierkegaard, see "Inwardness and Ideology Critique in Kierkegaard's *Fragments* and *Postscript*," in my *Kierkegaard's Critique of Religion and Society* (Macon, GA: Mercer University Press, 1987). Garry Wills writes in reference to American history: "In most of our wars, as in dubious other matters like slavery, we have indeed 'taken God's name in vain'" (*Under God: Religion and American Politics* [New York: Simon and Schuster, 1990], p. 382).

34 A "Marxist" Sermon Against the Baalization of Yahweh

Martin Buber has given us an unforgettable way of speaking about third commandment idolatry. Speaking of "the degenerate sacrificial cult, in which the offering is changed from being a sign of the extreme self-devotion and becomes a ransom from all true self-devotion," he calls such worship "the baalisation of YHVH Himself."[1] One of the most attractive things about the Baalim is that they, unlike Yahweh, are not hung up about the poor and oppressed; they are willing "to let economic decisions be made on economic grounds." Religion keeps its nose out of the marketplace and lets business run its own business.

In this "baalisation" Yahweh is not (overtly) repudiated, just revised to suit our economic convenience.[2] The difference between this and the Freudian-Feuerbachian version of creating God in our own image (the essence of idolatry) is that in this case the prime function of the newly designed god is to sanctify social injustice, if not by "embracing" it, at least by "enduring" it.

The protest of the prophets against this kind of piety reverberates through their writings. Throughout the book that bears his name, Amos wages an unrelenting campaign against the worship offered by Israel to Yahweh, especially at the shrines of Bethel and Gilgal.[3] One Sunday

1. Martin Buber, *The Prophetic Faith,* trans. Carlyle Witton-Davies (New York: Harper, 1960), pp. 118-20. Buber's language presupposes that worship is not to be understood *ex opere operato.* Rather, the act is a sign, and its worth depends on what it actually, not allegedly, signifies. Buber's phrase is part of his discussion of Hosea, but it aptly fits the message of other biblical prophets as well.

2. The Baalim also have remarkably casual attitudes about sexuality. So there is a sexual as well as an economic baalization of Yahweh, though only the latter is our present concern.

3. Amos 2:8; 3:14; 4:4-5; 5:4-6; 7:9; 8:3, 10; 9:1.

morning he went to church (in effect) and preached a sermon so un-
popular that he no doubt had to preach it outside in the parking lot as
the congregation was coming to worship.[4] In his sermon he represents
God as saying:

> I hate, I despise your feasts,
>   and I take no delight in your solemn assemblies.
> Even though you offer me your burnt offerings
>   and cereal offerings,
>   I will not accept them,
> and the peace offerings of your fatted beasts
>   I will not look upon.
> Take away from me the noise of your songs;
>   to the melody of your harps I will not listen.
> But let justice roll down like waters,
>   and righteousness like an everflowing stream.
>   (5:21-24)

Something must have gone very wrong for Amos to speak like
this, and the closing lines of his short sermon identify the problem: It
was a question of justice. The anthems and organ music that made
worship so uplifting were there to drown out the cries of the victims
of social injustice, but they worked just the other way. Those cries had
turned the music sour in God's ears. This is why Amos's assault on the
sanctuaries is matched by two other themes that are equally pervasive
in his book, the plight of the poor and the luxury of the rich.[5]

In seeking to give voice to the suffering of the poor, Amos
constantly speaks of the rich as their oppressors. In seeking to give
visibility, not so much to the luxury of the rich, who have no aversion
to conspicuous consumption, but to the incongruity between their
lavish life-style and the grinding poverty of those around them, Amos
focuses on the eating and drinking habits of the rich and on their
splendid homes. His complaint is not that they enjoy good things
but that they do so in complacent indifference toward the suffering of
the poor. He notes the distinction between actively depriving the
poor of what is rightfully theirs and consuming the fruits of such
injustice without caring about the victims; but he treats this as a

---

4. I make Amos a contemporary Christian here to remind us that when we
read his sermon it is as much about us as about ancient Hebrews.
5. For the plight of the poor see 2:6-8; 3:9-10; 4:1; 5:7, 10-12, 15; 6:12; 8:4-6.
For the luxury of the rich see 2:8; 3:10-11, 15; 4:1; 5:11; 6:1-8.

difference that makes no difference. The two are equally shameful in the eyes of God.

With regard to active oppression, Amos complains bitterly that the law, at least as interpreted by the courts, is regularly the ally of the powerful rather than the defender of the weak. We are reminded of Psalm 94:20, which speaks of "wicked rulers . . . who frame mischief by statute" ("who make injustice legal," Good News Bible), and of Isaiah 10:1, "Woe to those who decree iniquitous decrees, and the writers who keep writing oppression. . . ." We are also reminded of Marx, who sees the legal system as a major instrument of the ruling class's power.

The business executives, legislators, and judges who are the targets of this critique are by no means atheists. In fact, Amos portrays them as being in church every Sunday, but his account has a bite. When those who "trample upon the poor" come to church they ask when the sabbath will be over "that we may buy the poor for silver and the needy for a pair of sandals, and sell the refuse of the wheat" (8:4-6). Their churchgoing interferes only momentarily but not essentially with their practice of injustice. Again we are reminded of Marx, as the church, through its silence, joins the state in upholding economic exploitation.

Amos records an incident that underscores this unholy alliance of church and state against the poor. Amaziah, priest of Yahweh at Bethel, tells King Jeroboam that "Amos has conspired against *you*" (emphasis added — there has been nothing overt about the king in Amos's preaching up to this point). Then he tells Amos that it would be best for him to get out of town before sundown, and "never again prophesy at Bethel, for it is the king's sanctuary, and it is a temple of the kingdom" (7:10-17).[6]

Here is the original version of historical materialism. We have as this society's basis an economic system based on class divisions and exploitation; and we have a two-tiered superstructure in its support. The state (the king and the courts) provides active and overt support to the ruling class, while the church (the priest and the cultus) provides two kinds of support: silence about the relation of prevailing economic practices to the law of God and noisy denunciation of anyone who

---

6. In 1 Kings 22 we have a paradigm for this partnership between king and prophet. Jeremiah is such a Marxist that he devotes more or less equal time to denunciation of state (king) and church (prophet, priest, scribe) as those who not only rebel against Yahweh but in so doing victimize the poor.

insists on raising such questions. If Marx had been my student and had turned in his theory in the form of a term paper, I would have searched the notes for references to Amos. In their absence I would have called young Karl in for a serious discussion about plagiarism.

I do not make this charge in order to discredit Marx. He probably never read the book of Amos. Rather, I make this charge as a way of suggesting that there is something profoundly biblical in Marx's critique of modern society. Or, to speak more generally, the hermeneutics of suspicion in the hands of modern atheists is not only a secular theology of original sin; it is also a secular version of the prophetic message. Those who profess to take biblical authority seriously can ignore (or refute) it at their peril.

Some may want to respond: "But we have Amos, so why do we need Marx?" The question is fair and deserves not one but two answers. First, we need Marx as well as Amos, perhaps Marx as a commentary on Amos, because Marx is about us in a way that Amos is not. I have been Christianizing and modernizing Amos to remind us that his message is not just about wicked people long ago and far away. We do not have that hurdle to overcome with Marx. His critique of religion is about Christians in capitalist society. We know he is talking about us. If Balaam's ass could speak the Lord's rebuke to Balaam (Numbers 22), why not a modern atheist speaking the Lord's rebuke to the modern church? Amos may understand our hearts as well as Marx does, but Marx understands our society in a way Amos could not. If we intend to let Amos really address us, we will probably have to read him with a generous dose of Marx thrown in.

The converse is equally true, and represents my second answer to the question, Given Amos, why Marx? The habits of reading and thinking that will enable us to dismiss Marx will almost certainly enable us to read Amos without noticing what he is saying.

Consider what is probably the most widely known text from Amos: "Prepare to meet your God" (4:12). I suppose it is impossible not to recognize that this is a serious warning, the biblical equivalent of "Wait till your father gets home." But anyone who has grown up in the Bible belt, which is more a complex culture than a geographical region, has been exposed to the hermeneutical practices by which this text is translated as "Get saved before you die, so you can go to heaven instead of hell."

In the book of Amos, of course, it is addressed neither to the individual nor to the irreligious. It is addressed to Israel, the covenant people of God. Its background is these scary words:

Hear this word that the LORD has spoken against you, O people of Israel, against the whole family which I brought up out of the land of Egypt:
"You only have I known
   of all the families of the earth;
 therefore I will punish you
   for all your iniquities."

(3:1-2)

God is indeed warning the wicked to repent, but the wicked are the church, and their iniquities are first and foremost the economic sins of the rich against the poor. Is it any accident that the churches most skilled in not noticing this blatant fact are churches taught and led by today's Amaziahs, devoted to celebrating America as a Christian nation but willing to dismiss questions about economic justice as "atheistic Communism" or as unpatriotic "class warfare"?

Von Rad points out that in Deuteronomy the curses of the covenant are four times as long as the blessings of the covenant.[7] Amos seems already to be in possession of this theology of the covenant, for, as the verse just cited suggests, he regularly links his message of divine judgment (already begun and about to get worse) to the special relation between Yahweh and his people. And since this relation has its most dramatic origin in the Exodus event, he uses the language of that experience to indicate that Yahweh has now become their enemy rather than their savior. There will be wailing, and mourning, and lamentation, "for I will pass through the midst of you" (Amos 5:17). "I will never again pass by them" (7:8; 8:2).[8] In this reversal of the Passover symbolism, Yahweh announces that when his people can no longer distinguish him from Baal, he can no longer distinguish them from the Egyptians.

Amos is far from being the only "Marxist" preacher among the prophets. In the first chapter of Isaiah, for example, we find an equally violent repudiation of worship in the southern kingdom of Judah (Isa. 1:10-15) and an equally economic interpretation of why Yahweh sees it

7. Gerhard von Rad, *Deuteronomy*, trans. Dorothea Barton (Philadelphia: Westminster, 1966), p. 173.

8. This theme of Yahweh as the enemy of Israel on the basis of the very covenant in which they rest complacently is so frequent and forceful a focus in James Luther Mays's *Amos: A Commentary* (Philadelphia: Westminster, 1969) that one wonders what is going on until one notices that Mays is merely reflecting the text (see pp. 6-7, 44, 53-54, 69, 76-80, 94, 99, 102-4, 113, 118-20, 131-33).

as an abomination (vv. 15-23). In the midst of this sermon we find the familiar words of verse 18:

> Come now, let us reason together,
>   says Yahweh:
> though your sins are like scarlet,
>   they shall be as white as snow;
> though they are red like crimson,
>   they shall become like wool.

This text is surrounded by Yahweh's first question about any society: Is this society good for widows and orphans? But through Vague Generality and Dualistic Hermeneutics the question has been purged of its offensively economic meaning and its address to the church as such, as the covenant people of God. The hermeneutical strategies that have sanitized and spiritualized this text need to be challenged by a hermeneutics of suspicion that is informed by historical materialism.

Or we could turn to the sermon in which Jeremiah says of the temple in Jerusalem what Amos said about the shrines at Bethel and Gilgal (Jer. 7:1-15). One interesting feature of this text is that the bill of particulars that makes up its indictment includes not only oppression of foreigners, orphans, and widows but also worship of Baal and other false gods. It turns out that third commandment idolatry is not as far removed from first commandment idolatry as it first seemed to be. For with the baalization of Yahweh the jealousy of Yahweh disappears and there is no reason not to worship other gods as well.

This is not an entirely new idea for us. In chapter 1 above we saw Karl Barth suggest that the illusory god whom we create in our own image to conform to our knowledge and our values is best called a "No-God" who, on closer inspection, turns out to be such idols as "Family, Nation, State, Church, Fatherland." In chapter 4 we saw Hume speak of idolatry and polytheism interchangeably, as if the two were synonymous. And in chapter 30 we saw a Ugandan missionary make explicit the claim, which is implicit in Barth and Hume, that idolatry is essentially polytheistic. Since this claim is true, the distinction between first and third commandment idolatry collapses.

There is no need to multiply texts. They are many, and their meaning is surprisingly clear. What seems to be lacking in the church, a church perhaps more seduced (on the right) and intimidated (on the left) by presidents and televangelists than it realizes, are pastors willing to preach and congregations willing to hear the message of the prophets. It may seem that this becomes less true as one moves from the more conservative churches to the more liberal ones. This seeming may, however, be just that, an illusion produced by the gradual replacement of the Overt Espousal and Dualistic Hermeneutics characteristic of more conservative churches with the Vague Generality characteristic of more liberal churches.

Marx's challenge to the churches is a hermeneutical challenge. It dares us to recognize in some of our most widespread rules of reading the ground of the ideological function and idolatrous substance of our faith. And it defies us to develop a hermeneutics of justice and compassion, one that seeks to hear rather than to hide what the Bible says about the widows and the orphans, the women and children in single-parent families.

IV Nietzsche and the Critique of Religion as Resentment

35 *Squintingly Yours, Friedrich Nietzsche*

Question and answer. — What is it that savage tribes
today accept first of all from Europeans? Liquor and
Christianity, the European narcotics. And of what do
they perish most quickly? Of the European narcotics.
(GS ¶147)[1]

1. Citations from Nietzsche made in the text, usually by aphorism or section
number common to all editions, signified with the ¶ sign, use the following abbreviations:

AC *The Antichrist,* in PN.

AOM *Assorted Opinions and Maxims,* Volume Two, Part One of HAH, originally
published in 1879.

BGE *Beyond Good and Evil: Prelude to a Philosophy of the Future,* trans. Walter
Kaufmann (New York: Random House, 1966).

D *Daybreak,* trans. R. J. Hollingdale (Cambridge: Cambridge University
Press, 1982).

EH *Ecce Homo* (see GM)

GM *On the Genealogy of Morals and Ecce Homo,* trans. Walter Kaufmann and
R. J. Hollingdale (New York: Random House, 1967).

GS *The Gay Science,* trans. Walter Kaufmann (New York: Random House,
1974).

HAH *Human All Too Human,* trans. R. J. Hollingdale (Cambridge: Cambridge
University Press, 1986 = the original 1878 volume, published in 1886 as
Volume One of an expanded edition).

PN *The Portable Nietzsche,* trans. Walter Kaufmann (New York: Viking, 1954).

PT *Philosophy and Truth: Selections from Nietzsche's Notebooks of the Early 1870's,*
trans. Daniel Breazeale (Atlantic Highlands, NJ: Humanities Press, 1979).

TI *Twilight of the Idols,* in PN.

UM *Untimely Meditations,* trans. R. J. Hollingdale (New York: Cambridge University Press, 1983).

These lines of Nietzsche indicate that like Freud and Marx he considers religion an opiate.[2] Also like them, he sees its narcotic function as intimately linked to self-deception. He regards human history as the story of "high-sounding stories masking the lowest of motives."[3] All three men see piety as irony in which the manifest meaning is at odds with the latent function.

Nietzsche says that it is the "epistemological skepticism" of modern philosophy that makes it, "covertly or overtly, *anti-Christian*" (BGE ¶54). But this comment follows immediately on the interesting claim "that the religious instinct is indeed in the process of growing powerfully — but the theistic satisfaction it refuses with deep suspicion" (BGE ¶53), and he is clear that his own critique is grounded in a hermeneutics of suspicion and not in evidential skepticism (see chapter 2 above). "In former times," he writes, "one sought to prove that there is no God — today one indicates how the belief that there is a God could *arise* and how this belief acquired its weight and importance: a counter-proof that there is no God thereby becomes superfluous" (D ¶95).

In his view, "Actions," including the act of believing, "are *never* what they appear to us to be!" (D ¶116) because "there come into play motives in part unknown to us, in part known very ill, which we can *never* take account of *beforehand*" (D ¶129). About the only use Nietzsche could find for Bismarck was as a model of the human mind: "*no principles but strong drives* — a volatile mind in the service of strong drives and for that reason without principles" (D ¶167). It is those strong drives that express themselves without showing themselves in the unknown motives.

It follows that "the decisive value of an action lies precisely in

---

WP   *The Will to Power*, trans. Walter Kaufmann and R. J. Hollingdale (New York: Random House, 1968).

WS   *The Wanderer and His Shadow*, Volume Two, Part Two of HAH, originally published in 1880.

Z   *Thus Spoke Zarathustra*, trans. Walter Kaufmann (New York: Viking, 1966). Following recent custom I identify the chapters by number, although Nietzsche did not himself number them.

2. Cf. p. 39 n. 1; chapter 22.

3. Hubert L. Dreyfus and Paul Rabinow, *Michel Foucault: Beyond Structuralism and Hermeneutics* (Chicago: University of Chicago Press, 1983), p. 108. This phrase belongs to their summary of Foucault's reading of Nietzsche in such essays as "Nietzsche, Genealogy, History" (in *The Foucault Reader*, ed. Paul Rabinow [New York: Pantheon Books, 1984]) and "Nietzsche, Freud, Marx" (in *Transforming the Hermeneutic Context: From Nietzsche to Nancy*, ed. Gayle L. Ormiston and Alan D. Schrift [Albany: SUNY Press, 1990]).

what is *unintentional* in it, while everything about it that is intentional, everything about it that can be seen, known, 'conscious,' still belongs to its surface and skin — which, like every skin, betrays something but *conceals* even more. In short, we believe that the intention is merely a sign and symptom that still requires interpretation" (BGE ¶32).[4] Therefore, the philosopher "has a *duty* to suspicion today, to squint maliciously out of every abyss of suspicion" (BGE ¶34).

Nietzsche comes to call his hermeneutics of suspicion "genealogy" because it inquires into the concealed origins of action and belief (GM Preface ¶¶2-3). But genealogy is to be sharply distinguished from archaeology, for it seeks no origin "*behind* the world" (¶3), nothing that would count as an *archē* in the classical sense of the word. In the case of the "moral prejudices" (¶2),[5] whose genealogy primarily concerns Nietzsche, such origins have typically been God or Reason. This is why Nietzsche treats Christianity and Platonism as the (virtually identical) twin opponents of his immoralist project of replacing the quest for transcendent origins with a quest for origins within the world, even if not exactly on its surface.[6]

The origins that Nietzsche seeks within the world are the conditions and circumstances out of which moral values emerge and of which they are the sign and symptom. This is the key to the virtually impossible question he insists on asking, What is the value of these values? (GM Preface ¶¶3, 5-6). Usually the question "What is the value of X?" calls for use of some value as the criterion by which to evaluate X. But how can we put our criteria themselves in question? (It is just because he is willing to ask this question, which many consider immoral, that Nietzsche calls himself an "immoralist.") Nietzsche's answer is simple: by asking what needs and interests underlie their adoption, by asking what they are good for, by asking what work they perform and what function they fulfill for those whose criteria they become. In other words, "Nietzsche's

4. Nietzsche repeats this language of sign and symptom in GM Preface ¶¶3, 5-6. By using the two terms interchangeably he suggests a therapeutic approach to language that is Freudian rather than Wittgensteinian. A semiotics that did not get beyond syntactics, semantics, and pragmatics would not be truly philosophical in Nietzsche's view.

5. Nietzsche's subtitle for *Daybreak* is *Thoughts on the Prejudices of Morality*.

6. Nietzsche describes himself as a "subterranean man" and a "solitary mole" who "tunnels and mines and undermines" (D Preface ¶1; cf. GM Preface ¶7). The identification of Christianity as Platonism for the masses is a recurring theme. See, for example, BGE Preface; GM III ¶24; EH (*The Birth of Tragedy* ¶2); GS ¶344. Nietzsche expresses the same link when he closely identifies the ascetic priest with the idealist philosopher. See EH (*Dawn* ¶2); AC ¶¶8, 10, 12, 26; GM III ¶10.

genealogy always comes back from the forms to the forces — whether ascending or descending — that establish them."[7]

It should be obvious that the act of adopting moral values need not itself be moral by the criteria that those values themselves represent. For example, people can make a virtue of philanthropy and even practice it quite conspicuously for reasons that have nothing to do with love of humankind. (I am thinking of the Godfather, among others. The impiety in the conspicuous piety of politicians cries out for Nietzschean irreverence.) This is why moral theory from Aristotle to Kant has insisted that the virtuous or dutiful act must not only be the right act but must be done for the right reason.

Nietzsche radicalizes this commonplace of moral theory by adding three elements: First, he includes among the actions to which this principle is applied the very act of adopting moral values as the criteria by which to judge oneself and others. Do we, he asks squintingly, embrace love out of love? Or is it part of another agenda? Second, he adds a Freudian element by recognizing that the operative "reasons" may very well be needs or drives uncontaminated by moral restraint and, for just that reason, repressed and unconscious. Finally, he adds a Marxian element by recognizing that those needs and drives are sociologically conditioned.

In order to appreciate this third element fully we need to note the sophisticated blend of ontological or metaphysical with historical or sociological elements in Nietzsche's understanding of human behavior. More specifically, this means that we need to see his theory of the will to power in conjunction with his understanding of what he calls "the morality of mores."

Nietzsche regards the most basic human drive as "the psychical extravagance of the lust for power!" (D ¶113). But he extends this beyond human behavior. The human body, including the body politic, "if it is a living and not a dying body . . . will have to be an incarnate will to power, it will strive to grow, spread, seize, become predominant — not from any morality or immorality but because it is *living* and because life simply *is* will to power. . . . 'Exploitation' does not belong to a corrupt or imperfect and primitive society; it belongs to the *essence* of what lives, as a basic organic function; it is a consequence of the will to power, which is after all the will of life" (BGE ¶259).

But Nietzsche wants to extend this principle beyond even the

7. Michel Haar, "Heidegger and the Nietzschean 'Physiology of Art,'" in *Exceedingly Nietzsche: Aspects of Contemporary Nietzsche Interpretation*, ed. David Farrell Krell and David Wood (New York: Routledge and Kegan Paul, 1988), p. 26; cf. p. 28.

organic realm. He would like to get to the place where "one would have gained the right to determine *all* efficient force univocally as — *will to power*. The world viewed from inside, the world defined and determined according to its 'intelligible character' — it would be 'will to power' and nothing else" (BGE ¶36).[8]

It is important to notice the hypothetical character of this attempt to make the will to power the all-encompassing explanation of the world. Nietzsche is an intellectual experimenter. But it is even more important to recognize the universal character of the hypothesis. It is meant to apply to everything, and thus, surely, to all humans in all times, places, and circumstances. It is an ontological or metaphysical hypothesis. Here Nietzsche sounds more like Freud than like Marx.

But when we turn to his account of the morality of mores, which also concerns how people come to have the values they have, Nietzsche sounds more like Marx. We get the conceptual tools for understanding the plurality and conflict of value systems historically and sociologically. The basic idea is quite simple. "To be moral, to act in accordance with custom, to be ethical means to practice obedience towards a law or tradition established from of old. . . . He is called good because he does what is customary" (HAH ¶96). Custom and tradition arise out of a community's need to preserve itself, its perception of what is necessary to that end, and its giving primacy to the advantage of the community over that of the individual member (HAH ¶96; AOM ¶89). Superstition, fear, and cruelty are among the important means by which mores are enforced and thus established as such. This is the origin of morality for Nietzsche, meaning, against Christianity and Platonism, that "morality is nothing other (therefore *no more*) than obedience to customs" (D ¶9). Conscience is neither the voice of God nor the recollection of the Platonic forms.

One interesting implication Nietzsche draws from this view is that one's enthusiasm for a particular morality will be inversely pro-

---

8. There is a deep affinity here with the theory of *conatus* (striving) that underlies the psychology of Parts 3-5 of Spinoza's *Ethics*. Propositions 6 and 7 of Part 3 read: "Each thing, as far as it can by its own power, strives to persevere in its being. . . . The striving [*conatus*] by which each thing strives to persevere in its being is nothing but the actual essence of the thing." In the Scholium to Proposition 9, *conatus* is specified for humans as will, appetite, and desire, and then Spinoza adds the very Nietzschean claim that "we neither strive for, nor will, neither want, nor desire anything because we judge it to be good; on the contrary, we judge something to be good because we strive for it, will it, want it, and desire it" (as translated in *The Collected Works of Spinoza*, trans. Edwin Curley [Princeton: Princeton University Press, 1985]). Quite possibly these are among the passages Nietzsche has in mind when he writes to Overbeck so enthusiastically about the five fundamental agreements between his thoughts and Spinoza's, including the denial of the unegoistic. See PN 92.

portional to the degree to which one is called on to sacrifice one's individual advantage for the sake of it (AOM ¶89). My greatest moral enthusiasm will be for principles that constrain others. Thus, for example, preachers, who have been overwhelmingly men, can have much to say about Ephesians 5:22, "Wives, be subject to your husbands, as to the Lord," but very little to say about the preceding verse, "Be subject to one another out of reverence for Christ."

A second and more important implication is that morality is inherently plural. Just as there are different communities with different (perceived) interests, so there will be different customs and traditions. Where revenge is perceived as useful to a community, it will be a virtue, whereas in different circumstances benevolence, sympathy, and helpfulness will be what custom requires. In other words, the difference fundamental to morality is not that between egoism and altruism but that between what is in accord with custom and that which defies custom (HAH ¶96). "Morality" (from Latin *mores*) and "ethics" (from Greek *ethos*) continue to this day to follow custom and tradition.

In either case, whether revenge or sympathy is the primary virtue, it is a community's will to power that is at work, so the ontological hypothesis is not violated. But depending on historical and sociological circumstances, that will to power will adopt different values. Nietzsche's suspicion focuses on the discrepancy between the religious affirmation of altruism and the will to power he detects at its origin. He does not so much adopt an ironical attitude toward morality as suggest that the prevailing (professed and preached, not necessarily practiced) morality of the West is itself ironical, a hypocrisy that can put up with itself only with the help of self-deception.

Such, in brief outline, is Nietzsche's hermeneutics of suspicion.[9] One can speak of that "false self-denial" which "looks like self-denial, but in another way it outwardly pays for itself, and so at bottom is shrewd calculation," or one can speak of contemporary culture as that which treats its "normative commitments as so many alternative strategies of self-fulfillment."[10] But in either case one invokes formulas that apply at least as well to Nietzsche as to Freud and Marx. All three are united in seeking to expose the "shrewd calculation" in the service of "self-fulfillment" that masquerades as faith.

9. For a fuller sketch see my essay "Nietzsche and the Phenomenological Ideal," *The Monist* 60/2 (April 1977), pp. 278-88.

10. The first quotation is from Kierkegaard in *For Self Examination and Judge for Yourself*, trans. Walter Lowrie (Princeton: Princeton University Press, 1944), p. 213. The second is from Robert N. Bellah, et al., *Habits of the Heart: Individualism and Commitment in American Life* (Berkeley: University of California Press, 1985), p. 48.

36 *Distinctively Yours, Friedrich Nietzsche*

The themes of the previous chapter are by now so familiar that a question becomes unavoidable: Has Nietzsche any new insight to offer us? Can he add to what we have learned from Freud and Marx? In asking what is distinctive about Nietzsche we must not look for total novelty, for at the heart of Nietzsche's thought is an atheistic hermeneutics of suspicion that has, as we have seen, much in common with Freud and Marx. And yet he is sufficiently different that some think he is clearly the most radical of the three.

For example, Gilles Deleuze, writing for a different audience than the one to whom this book is primarily addressed, says, "Probably most of us fix the dawn of our modern culture in the trinity Nietzsche-Freud-Marx. . . . Now, Marx and Freud, perhaps, do represent the dawn of our culture, but Nietzsche is something entirely different: the dawn of counterculture."[1]

Deleuze elaborates with the help of the concept of codes, the ideals of law and order, both conceptual and institutional, that inhabit modernity's self-understanding: "Modern society clearly does not function on the basis of codes." Yet Marxism and Freudianism are attempts at recodifying (reordering and thus reforming) the state and the family, respectively. They are

> the fundamental bureaucracies — one public, the other private — whose aim is somehow or other to recodify everything that ceaselessly becomes decodified at the horizon of our culture. Nietzsche's concern, on the contrary, is not this at all. . . . Confronted with the

---

1. Gilles Deleuze, "Nomad Thought," in *The New Nietzsche*, ed. David B. Allison (Cambridge: MIT Press, 1985), p. 142.

ways in which our societies become progressively decodified and unregulated, in which our codes break down at every point, Nietzsche is the only thinker who makes no attempt at recodification. . . . In his own writing and thought Nietzsche assists in the attempt at decodification — not in the relative sense . . . but in an absolute sense, by expressing something that cannot be codified, confounding all codes.[2]

Jürgen Habermas, whose sympathies lie as much with Freud and Marx as Deleuze's do with Nietzsche, agrees on the issue of what sets Nietzsche off from those two: "Nietzsche is the one among the steadfast theoreticians of unmasking who radicalizes the counter-Enlightenment."[3]

What is the meaning of this talk about counter-Enlightenment, counterculture, and decodification? Simply this: While Freud, Marx, and Nietzsche share a deep hostility to biblical religion, Freud and Marx, as sons of the Enlightenment, retain a faith in its essentially secular Reason, whereas Nietzsche sees Reason as an ersatz god through whom modern secularism seeks to salvage as much of God as possible.[4] Having directed suspicion toward religion and all its works, he continues in the direction of what Habermas calls "totalized critique" by subjecting Reason and Enlightenment to the same suspicion.[5] He suspects that Freud's faith in "our God Λόγος" (see p. 41 above), which has its strong correlates in Marx, is faith in a god not as different from

2. Deleuze, pp. 142-43. Cf. the commentary of Hugh Tomlinson in "Nietzsche on the Edge of Town: Deleuze and Reflexivity," in *Exceedingly Nietzsche: Aspects of Contemporary Nietzsche Interpretation,* ed. David Farrell Krell and David Wood (New York: Routledge and Kegan Paul, 1988), pp. 155-56. Many readers of this book may find themselves less uncomfortable with Freud and Marx than with Nietzsche for just the kind of reasons to which Deleuze points. But is not God presented in the Bible as the one who can be captured by no codes, not even the church's?

3. Jürgen Habermas, *The Philosophical Discourse of Modernity: Twelve Lectures,* trans. Frederick Lawrence (Cambridge: MIT Press, 1987), pp. 119-20.

4. It is in an entirely Nietzschean vein that Jean-Paul Sartre writes (*Existentialism and Humanism,* in *The Age of Analysis: Twentieth-Century Philosophers,* ed. Morton White [New York: New American Library, 1955], pp. 127-28):

The existentialist is strongly opposed to a certain type of secular moralism which seeks to suppress God at the least possible expense . . . and this is, I believe, the purport of all that we in France call radicalism — nothing will be changed if God does not exist; we shall rediscover the same norms of honesty, progress and humanity. . . . The existentialist, on the contrary, finds it extremely embarrassing that God does not exist, for there disappears with Him all possibility of finding values in an intelligible heaven.

5. Habermas, p. 120.

the biblical God as Freud and others allege.[6] If Christianity is Platonism for the masses, scientific objectivity is Platonism for the enlightened elites of modernity.

There is an important debate here. In contemporary language it is between modernism and postmodernism. Since the seventeenth century, the Enlightenment has joined to its critique of faith its own faith in reason.[7] In both its rationalist and its empiricist forms, it has claimed for scientific reason the capacity to transcend the relativities of particular perspectives and to transmit universal and objective truth. This claim has been under steady assault at least since Nietzsche. In other words, the debate between the modernism that wants to maintain the Enlightenment ideal of reason, even if in a humbler, somewhat chastened mode, and the postmodernism that sees Enlightenment as part of the problem rather than the cure for a society based on illusory transcendence, can be said to begin with Nietzsche.[8] Since Freud and Marx have an essentially unqualified faith in reason's capacity to rise above illusion and ideology, they are, from Nietzsche's perspective, fundamentalists of the Enlightenment.

6. For this kind of polemic, see especially "On Truth and Lies in a Nonmoral Sense," in *Philosophy and Truth;* the first of the *Untimely Meditations* ("David Strauss, the Confessor and the Writer"); the Third Essay of *On the Genealogy of Morals* ("What Is the Meaning of Ascetic Ideals"); and ¶344 of *The Gay Science,* which opens with the words *"How we, too, are still pious."*

7. On both fronts there has been an internal debate within the Enlightenment. On the question of religion, the eighteenth-century materialists, the nineteenth- and twentieth-century positivists, and others have wanted to eliminate it entirely, while others, like Kant *(Religion Within the Limits of Reason Alone)* and Julian Huxley *(Religion Without Revelation)* have only wanted to restrict religion to what could be considered strictly rational. On the question of reason, rationalists have wanted to give it metaphysical as well as empirical power, while empiricists have wanted to limit its scope to experimental science and its basis in ordinary sense experience. But both have insisted on the capacity of reason for universality and objectivity.

8. For an illuminating account of Nietzsche as the first postmodernist, see Allan Megill, *Prophets of Extremity: Nietzsche, Heidegger, Foucault, Derrida* (Berkeley: University of California Press, 1985). Cf. J. Hillis Miller, "Dismembering and Disremembering in Nietzsche's 'On Truth and Lies in a Nonmoral Sense,'" and Cornel West, "Nietzsche's Prefiguration of Postmodern American Philosophy," both in *Why Nietzsche Now?* ed. Daniel T. O'Hara (Bloomington: Indiana University Press, 1985). On the perspectivism in which Nietzsche's critique of the Enlightenment culminates see Arthur Danto, *Nietzsche as Philosopher* (New York: Macmillan, 1968), chapter 3; Alexander Nehamas, *Nietzsche: Life as Literature* (Cambridge: Harvard University Press, 1985), chapter 2; and Jean Granier, "Perspectivism and Interpretation," in *The New Nietzsche* (see n. 1 above). For the most ambitious defense of a (chastened) modernism, see Jürgen Habermas, *Theory of Communicative Action,* 2 vols., trans. Thomas McCarthy (Boston: Beacon Press, 1984, 1987).

In other words, Marxian critique of ideology and Freudian therapy are versions of Cartesian doubt, a brief negative moment on the way to clarity and certainty. They belong to the grand narrative (distressingly biblical to someone like Nietzsche) in which the light shines the darkness away. For Nietzsche, by contrast, the "curative aspect [of suspicion] is not found in an illumination of a false discourse by a true one," but in the realization that critique is itself anything but pure reason, since it is inside the ideas and practices it challenges as much as it is outside them. Thus "the aim of definitive and synthetic knowledge, the ideal of enlightenment, is destroyed by what at first appears to be enlightenment through genealogy. The latter 'enlightenment' recoils upon the unthought shadow of modern knowledge. . . ."[9]

Given the importance for the philosophical enterprise of this debate over the nature and limits of reason, it is not surprising that Nietzsche's suspicion of Reason and all its codes should seem to contemporary philosophers to be the truly distinctive thing about Nietzsche. But that need not be the case for the church, which has a different agenda. Indeed, I want to suggest that for our purposes the debate between modernism and postmodernism, as important as it is, can remain secondary.[10]

So what then is distinctively Nietzschean when it comes to the critique of religion? Putting the question that way directs us away from the perspectivism that regards truth as "illusions about which one has forgotten that this is what they are" in the form of "linguistic legislation," "arbitrary abstraction," and "canonical" or "customary metaphors" (PN 44-47) and that concludes that "Truth is the kind of error

9. Charles E. Scott, *The Question of Ethics: Nietzsche, Foucault, Heidegger* (Bloomington: Indiana University Press, 1990), pp. 62, 80. These descriptions come from Scott's account of the Nietzschean dimensions in Foucault.

10. It might also be argued that Nietzsche is distinctive in uniting the psychological perspective of Freud with the socio-political perspective of Marx. Walter Kaufmann bears witness to Nietzsche as a psychologist in the subtitle of his book, *Nietzsche: Philosopher, Psychologist, Antichrist* (3rd ed.; New York: Random House, 1968), a witness substantiated by the psychology references in the index to Karl Schlechta's three-volume edition of Nietzsche's works (*Nietzsche-Index zu den Werken in Drei Bänden* [Munich: Carl Hanser Verlag, 1965]). On the other hand, Karl Jaspers includes chapters on "History and the Present Age" and "Great Politics" in his book *Nietzsche: An Introduction to the Understanding of His Philosophical Activity,* trans. C. F. Wallraff and F. J. Schmitz (Chicago: Henry Regnery, 1965). And Tracy B. Strong's book is entitled *Friedrich Nietzsche and the Politics of Transfiguration* (expanded ed.; Berkeley: University of California Press, 1988). Perhaps in his psychologically oriented sociology Nietzsche offers us a politics of the human spirit prefigured only in Hegel.

without which a certain species of life could not live" (WP ¶493). Our attention is turned from Nietzsche's critique of Platonism with regard to the true toward his critique of Christianity with regard to the good. Here a difference from Freud and Marx emerges that is more pertinent to the present context.

With the opium metaphor, Marx begins his critique of religion with a focus on the victims of oppression, though we are immediately reminded that their violators also need an opiate for their consciences. With historical materialism and the theory of ideology, the focus shifts to this latter function, and we can say that Marx is suspicious of religion because he sees it as *power seeking legitimation*. This immediately suggests a difference from Freud, for whom religion is *weakness seeking consolation*.

But here we must invoke the distinction between metaphysical and historical thinking that we found necessary while working toward Marx from Feuerbach. The weakness of which Freud speaks is the universal, ontological weakness that all humans, regardless of their place in the political pecking order, experience in the face of guilt (the demands of culture) and death (the power of nature). By contrast, the strength of which Marx speaks is the historically specific domination of one social group over another, masters over slaves, lords over serfs, or property owners over wage laborers.[11] Since Nietzsche is like Marx in being a historical thinker,[12] but like Freud in focusing on weakness instead of strength, we can identify what is distinctively Nietzschean in the critique of religion by filling in the blanks in the statement, For _____, religion is primarily _____. Our answers would look like this:

Freud	ontological weakness seeking consolation
Marx	sociological power seeking legitimation
Nietzsche	sociological weakness seeking revenge.

11. By extension we could apply Marxian analysis to forms of domination based on gender, race, or ethnicity, all of which end up having significant economic implications. For example, see the analysis of the economic implications of gender in *Justice, Gender, and the Family,* by Susan Moller Okin (New York: Basic Books, 1989) and the question of religion and male dominance as posed in *In Memory of Her: A Feminist Theological Reconstruction of Christian Origins,* by Elisabeth Schüssler Fiorenza (New York: Crossroad, 1985).

12. This is nowhere clearer than in his famous pronouncements of the death of God. He makes it abundantly clear that this is not a metaphysical claim but a historical observation. See Martin Heidegger's "The Word of Nietzsche: 'God Is Dead,' " in *The Question Concerning Technology and Other Essays,* trans. William Lovitt (New York: Harper and Row, 1977).

On this analysis Nietzsche is not distinctive by being the most radical of the three. By virtue of going beyond metaphysical thought to historical analysis he shares that honor with Marx. But while Marx has sought to show how ugly religion can be among the rich and the powerful, Nietzsche completes the picture by showing how ugly religion can be among their victims.

I have been suggesting that the masters of suspicion are secular theologians of original sin. The short table above helps us to appreciate two strengths of their interpretation of human depravity, but only if we take them together and not in isolation. First, by taking Freud together with Marx and Nietzsche we are reminded that sin has both a universal, historically invariable nature, which we might identify as unlimited self-assertion, and a variety of localized, historically specific modes in which this self-assertion is manifested.

Second, by taking Marx and Nietzsche together we get a theology of original sin that avoids the Fonda Fallacy. Although Jane Fonda did not invent this fallacy, I have named it after her in honor of her famous trip to Hanoi. Like many antiwar liberals during the late sixties and early seventies, she thought that if one side was evil, the other side must be good. Seeing the manifest evils of the American and South Vietnamese governments, they ended up canonizing Ho Chi Minh. In doing so they were repeating and reversing the logic of their teachers, the anti-Communist conservatives who concluded that since the Communists were evil, anything done in the name of anti-Communism must be good. Both forms of the Fonda fallacy deny the Pauline claim that "all have sinned and fall short of the glory of God" (Rom. 3:23). Taken together, Marx and Nietzsche remind us of this truth. Masters may be wicked sinners, but that does not make their slaves into saints.

It has been claimed, and I have already agreed with the claim, that God is on the side of the poor and powerless. The basis of this "preference" could be that the poor and powerless are "nicer" than their oppressors only if two conditions were met: (1) They would actually have to be nicer, since God would not be fooled by appearances, and (2) God would have to be working out of a theology of works righteousness, bestowing his favor on those who have earned it by being better than others. But there is abundant empirical evidence against the first supposition and abundant biblical evidence against the second. Here again it may be helpful to remember the experience of parents (see p. 200 above). When they take the side of the child who is being bullied by a stronger, more aggressive child, they have no illusions about the holiness of the weaker child. They know that as soon as they turn their backs it is the weaker child who is likely to provide fresh evidence of original sin, probably with the self-righteous chant (sung to the only tune more widely known in our culture than the opening bars of the Hallelujah Chorus or of Beethoven's Fifth Symphony)

> Nyah nyah nyah nyah nyah nyah
> Johnny got in trouble.

It is time for us to turn to Nietzsche's account of the religious equivalent of this triumphant psalm.

37 The Big Lie

Descriptively speaking, Nietzsche is a moral pluralist. There are many different moralities. This is a direct implication, as we saw in chapter 35, of the idea that morality is a matter of mores.[1] But running throughout "the many subtler and coarser moralities" Nietzsche finds "two basic types," which he calls *master morality* and *slave morality* (BGE ¶260). Nietzsche calls the First Part of *The Genealogy of Morals*, in which he gives his most extensive account of this distinction and especially of the emergence of slave morality, his account of "the birth of Christianity out of the spirit of *ressentiment*" (EH *Genealogy of Morals*, p. 312).[2] In other words, it is here, rather than in Nietzsche's periodic announcements of the death of God, that his critique of religion is to be found. Like Marx, he directs his critique primarily to Christianity and primarily to its practical, that is ethical and political, side rather than to its theoretical, metaphysical aspects.

Nietzsche begins, as he believes human history began, with an account of master morality:

1. Nietzsche often speaks of the morality of mores as if it were a particular, prehistoric morality rather than a generic feature of the many moralities. See D ¶9; GM Preface ¶4; II ¶2; III ¶9. But a close reading of these texts shows that he actually holds that the monopoly of the morality of mores begins to be broken, not with the dawn of history, but with the dawn of modernity and the rise of the autonomous individual whose ties to custom and tradition have been substantially eroded (by such forces as Enlightenment and capitalism). But since he sees such individuals as "supramoral (for 'autonomous' and 'moral' are mutually exclusive)," morality remains the morality of mores. Even in the modern world, morality is whatever "social straitjacket" a given society feels it must enforce for its own preservation (GM II ¶2).

2. Nietzsche persistently uses the French term. Except where quoting him I will use the perfectly good English word "resentment." See Walter Kaufmann's commentary, GM Editor's Introduction ¶3.

> The concept good and evil has a two-fold prehistory: *firstly* in the soul of the ruling tribes and castes. He who has the power to requite, good with good, evil with evil, and also actually practices requital — is, that is to say, grateful and revengeful — is called good; he who is powerless and cannot requite counts as bad. As a good man one belongs to the 'good,' a community which has a sense of belonging together. . . . As a bad man one belongs to the 'bad,' to a swarm of subject, powerless people. . . . Good and bad is for a long time the same thing as noble and base, master and slave. On the other hand, one does not regard the enemy as evil: he can requite. In Homer the Trojan and the Greek are both good. (HAH ¶45; cf. BGE ¶260)

There are several things to note about this passage: (1) The phrase "ruling tribes and castes" indicates that we are dealing with a morality of mores, with the evaluational traditions and customs of a community. But not of a society as a whole. The groups that give rise to different moralities here are groups within a larger social totality, and their most important attribute in this context is power or lack of power. Thus for masters the evaluational difference between good and bad or noble and base corresponds to the sociological difference between masters and slaves. What Marx would call a class analysis of the ideo-logical stratum lies at the heart of Nietzsche's religion critique.

(2) In master morality revenge is a virtue. Nietzsche will stress the vengefulness of slave morality. But since he does not despise the former as he does the latter, the issue cannot be the mere presence of revenge, which Nietzsche takes to be an entirely natural and ubiquitous expression of the will to power. We will have to ask why Nietzsche is so hostile to the vengefulness of slave morality.

(3) Here the primary value is good/noble rather than bad/base. The basic evaluation is the spontaneous self-celebration of strength, since "every noble morality develops from a triumphant affirmation of itself" (GM I ¶10). "When man possesses the feeling of power he feels and calls himself *good*: and it is precisely then that the others upon whom he has to discharge his power feel and call him *evil!*" (D ¶189; cf. BGE ¶260; GM I ¶5). The latter half of this analysis will be Nietzsche's key to slave morality. But here the important thing is that the goodness of the good does not depend on the badness of the bad. There is no Fonda Fallacy here (see p. 230 above), but simple, shameless self-affirmation.

(4) In this respect and in that it makes revenge a primary virtue, master morality makes it clear that the identification of altruism with morality is mistaken. There is a morality of love for neighbor and even

for one's enemies, but it is only one option. The identification of morality as such with altruism or the "other-regarding point of view" is, in
Nietzsche's eyes, only the ideological blindness of those whose interests
are vested in that set of values, namely the weak, the slaves.

(5) Finally, it is important that the enemies of the good are themselves good and not evil. In fact, no one is evil in this world, divided
up between the good and the bad. To designate the weak as bad or base
is not to signify some harmful quality they possess, some essence they
exhibit, but rather to express the *"pathos of distance"* in which they are
recognized as lacking what makes life worth living for the strong, what
makes the good good (GM I ¶2; cf. BGE ¶257). Here we have the
sociological equivalent of Augustine's theory of evil as not a positive
or substantial reality but only a deprivation of good, except here this
deprivation is not called evil.

While the self-celebration of the strong that is called master
morality does not affirm the goodness of the good on the basis of the
badness of the bad, it does not entirely leave them out of view. Nietzsche
defines the egoism that belongs to the noble soul as "that unshakable
faith that to a being such as 'we are' other beings must be subordinate
by nature and have to sacrifice themselves. The noble soul accepts this
fact of its egoism without any question mark," that is, shamelessly, as
part of "the primordial law of things: if it sought a name for this fact
it would say, 'it is justice itself'" (BGE ¶265).[3]

As noted in the third comment above, those over whom the
strong exercise their power, so far from seeing this domination as "justice itself," see those who lord it over them as evil. That is the essence
of slave morality.

> That lambs dislike great birds of prey does not seem strange: only
> it gives no ground for reproaching these birds of prey for bearing
> off little lambs. And if the lambs say among themselves: "these birds
> of prey are evil; and whoever is least like a bird of prey, but rather
> its opposite, a lamb — would he not be good?" there is no reason

3. Nietzsche's use of the reflexive, *die Gerechtigkeit selbst*, "justice itself,"
echoes ironically and pointedly the language in which Plato speaks about the forms
of justice and beauty while defining the philosopher king (*Republic* 472b-76b).
Nietzsche does not believe that there is such a thing as "justice itself," but he asks
those who do, in an *ad hominem* tone, why the warrior morality Plato sought to
sublate should not have as much claim to such a discovery as Plato's idealism. It is
not an accident that Thrasymachus in the *Republic* and Callicles in the *Gorgias* are
often seen as precursors of Nietzsche, despite the crudeness of their "might makes
right" philosophies.

to find fault with this institution of an ideal, except perhaps that the birds of prey might view it a little ironically and say: "*we* don't dislike them at all, these good little lambs; we even love them: nothing is more tasty than a tender lamb." (GM I ¶13)

Here the moral distinction is between good and evil rather than between good and bad (noble and base), and Nietzsche insists that the two distinctions are indeed distinct. With reference to the slogan that became the title of his book *Beyond Good and Evil*, Nietzsche writes, "At least this does *not* mean 'Beyond Good and Bad'" (GM I ¶17).[4] In fact, he insists that "good" has two diametrically opposed meanings, depending on whether its opposite is bad or evil, or, to be more specific, depending on whether it designates the values perceived by the masters to be in their interest or those perceived by the slaves to be in theirs (GM I ¶11). The differences between the two are beginning to emerge with some clarity, but it might be useful to summarize them.

(1) The most basic difference, from which the others arise, is the difference of origin just mentioned. Master morality takes root among the strong, the confident, and the bold. By contrast, slave morality is found among "the violated, oppressed, suffering, unfree, who are uncertain of themselves and weary" (BGE ¶260).

(2) Corresponding to this difference is the basic difference of content. Slave morality speaks of love and justice, or, more generally, of altruism, because the weak see these values as in their interest. With reference to justice, for example, they cannot take more than their share in any case, but they would surely benefit from a more nearly equal distribution of wealth and power. For them justice is all benefit and no cost. But it is just the opposite for the strong, so they do not champion justice in its altruistic sense but in the sense noted above, in which justice is simply the law of the sea: Big fish eat little fish. Justice in master morality is, as Thrasymachus insisted, the interest of the stronger.

(3) Nietzsche places great emphasis on the fact that in good vs. bad, good is the theorem and bad the corollary, whereas in good vs. evil, evil is the theorem and good the corollary. The slave who creates

---

4. This is why Nietzsche can insist that he provides an alternative to nihilism. Instead of negating all values, leaving the moral equivalent of a black hole, he seeks a transvaluation of values. The new values he espouses, which are not a simple return to the master morality of Homeric Greece, are taught by the prophet Zarathustra and focus on the god Dionysus. But they are not our present concern.

a morality creates "the enemy" at the same time. "He has conceived 'the evil enemy,' 'the Evil One,' and this in fact is his basic concept, from which he then evolves, as an afterthought and pendant, a 'good one' — himself!" (GM I ¶10; cf. ¶11). Thus in slave morality the goodness of the good indeed depends on the wickedness of the wicked and we are staring the Fonda Fallacy in the face. They are evil; I am different; ergo I am good. I am a victim; therefore I am morally superior.

(4) This is the revenge of the oppressed. But how does it differ from the vengefulness that is a virtue in master morality? First of all, by virtue of the resentment in which it is grounded. "The slave revolt in morality begins when *ressentiment* itself becomes creative and gives birth to values: the *ressentiment* of natures that are denied the true reaction, that of deeds, and compensate themselves with an imaginary revenge" (GM I ¶10; cf. ¶13). This is not to say that Menelaus felt no resentment when Paris carried off his beloved and beautiful Helen. But resentment, "if it should appear in the noble man, consummates and exhausts itself in an immediate reaction, and therefore does not *poison*" (¶10). So Menelaus and his Greek buddies immediately declare war on Paris and all of Troy.

This "true reaction, that of deeds," is denied to the weak, and in them resentment lingers, festers, and poisons. They become more rather than less vengeful, but the realities of their situation limit them to a certain kind of revenge, "imaginary revenge," or, as Nietzsche calls it elsewhere, *"spiritual revenge"* (GM I ¶7). This language echoes that of Marx, who also equated the spiritual with the imaginary. Here what Marx would call ideological revenge consists in branding one's enemy as evil. If it were true that "sticks and stones can break my bones, but ugly words can't hurt me," then the slave revolt in morality would have been stillborn. Its power suggests that ideological revenge can be at least as real as it is imaginary.

We can now answer the question posed above: Why is Nietzsche so hostile to the vengefulness of slave morality, while he seems to admire the revenge of the masters? We have noted above that the latter is "shameless." The flip side of that is that it is perfectly honest. It does not pretend to be other than it is. But slave morality has reason to be ashamed of its origin in resentment and is by its very nature dishonest. It is a morality that preaches forgiveness, but whose motivation is revenge, that preaches love of enemies, but is the creation of the enemy as the incarnation of evil. It always has to pretend, to itself as well as to others, to be other than it is. Like the preacher whose concern for souls is motivated by greed for money, slave morality is a Big Lie. Of the many reasons why Nietzsche detests it, this is both the most fundamental and the one that should be taken most seriously by religious people, who rightly feel that they should be at least as strongly committed to honesty as Nietzsche is.[5]

5. Nietzsche treats honesty and intellectual integrity like a kind of Kantian categorical imperative. It is legitimate to ask whether he is entitled to do so, given his epistemology. But this question may be left for secular philosophers to worry about, as, indeed, they do. For religious thinkers to zero in on this question at the outset is to give the appearance of being too eager to change the subject. This is especially true in light of the fact that most religious philosophers are convinced that *they* are entitled to treat truthfulness as an unconditional obligation. It is *their* integrity that is at stake.

38 Jews and Priests

Nietzsche thinks he has let the cat out of the bag, revealing the true nature of Christian morality by disclosing its deepest motivation and function. Without appealing to either the Platonic Good or the biblical God he has traced altruistic values to their real origin. In so doing he has unmasked the illegitimacy of a hitherto respectable pretender to the throne by revealing for all to see "the birth of Christianity out of the spirit of *ressentiment*" (EH *Genealogy of Morals,* p. 312). Yet he makes a great deal of the fact that it is the Jews who "mark the beginning of the slave rebellion in morals" (BGE ¶195). In view of the infamous attempt of the Nazis to appropriate Nietzsche — in spite of his consistent contempt for anti-Semites — a word about Nietzsche and the Jews is necessary.[1]

In a paragraph entitled *"European man and the abolition of nations"* Nietzsche writes that "one should not be afraid to proclaim oneself simply a *good European* and actively to work for the amalgamation of nations" (HAH ¶475). In this passage he speaks of nations, peoples, and races interchangeably and explicitly focuses on the Jews as an element of the "mixed race" of Europeans he envisages.[2] Does he not, then, play into the hands of the anti-Semites, whom he so despises, when he emphasizes the Jewish origins of the slave morality, which he also despises?

Just the opposite, I believe. He is tweaking their noses. First he links the Big Lie to Jewish origins, making the bait even more irresistible

---

1. For fuller accounts, see Walter Kaufmann, *Nietzsche: Philosopher, Psychologist, Antichrist* (3rd ed.; New York: Random House, 1968), especially chapter 10; Kaufmann's introduction to WP; and Georges Bataille, "Nietzsche and the Fascists," in *Visions of Excess: Selected Writings, 1927-39,* trans. and ed. Allan Stoekl (Minneapolis: University of Minnesota Press, 1985).

2. The German terms are *Nationen, Völker,* and *Mischrasse.* Cf. D ¶205; BGE ¶¶52, 248, 250.

by calling the Jews "a people 'born for slavery,' " quoting Tacitus (BGE ¶195). Then he springs the trap. "One knows *who* inherited this Jewish revaluation" (GM I ¶7). If the Jewish slave revolt has a long and victorious history, it has it because of "Jesus of Nazareth, the incarnate gospel of love, this 'Redeemer' who brought blessedness and victory to the poor, the sick, and the sinners. . . . Did Israel not attain the ultimate goal of its sublime vengefulness precisely through the bypath of this 'Redeemer'? . . . What is certain, at least, is that *sub hoc signo* [under the sign of the cross] Israel, with its vengefulness and revaluation of all values has hitherto triumphed again and again over all other ideals, over all *nobler* ideals" (GM I ¶8).

Even within the limited confines of the First Essay of *The Genealogy of Morals*, Nietzsche is not content to make this point once. He returns to it in Section 16, where he portrays the history of the West as the conflict between the value systems represented by "good and bad" and "good and evil." "Rome against Judea, Judea against Rome. . . . Which of them has won *for the present*, Rome or Judea? But there can be no doubt: consider to whom one bows down in Rome itself today, as if they were the epitome of all the highest values — and not only in Rome but over almost half the earth, everywhere that man has become tame or desires to become tame: *three Jews*, as is known, and *one Jewess* (Jesus of Nazareth, the fisherman Peter, the rug weaver Paul, and . . . Mary."[3]

Nietzsche's emphasis on the Jewishness of Christianity is historically sound, of course, but that is not his concern. He insists on the linkage in order to embarrass Christian anti-Semites. In the process of doing so he introduces an important feature of his analysis of Judeo-Christian religion,[4] the role of priestly power. Here is another of the "anti-Semitic" passages in Nietzsche:

> All that has been done on earth against "the noble," "the powerful," "the masters," "the rulers," fades into nothing compared with what the *Jews* have done against them; *the Jews, that priestly people*, who in opposing their enemies and conquerors were ultimately satisfied with nothing less than a radical revaluation of their enemies' values,

3. Lest Protestant readers take this to be a partisan swipe at Catholics, Nietzsche adds that while the Renaissance was a "reawakening of the classical ideal . . . Judea immediately triumphed again, thanks to that thoroughly plebeian (German and English) *ressentiment* movement called the Reformation" (GM I ¶16).
4. This phrase has been challenged as one that overlooks the differences between Judaism and Christianity both in biblical and especially in postbiblical times. But here there can be no such complaint, for it is undoubted that at the heart of both traditions is an ethic of justice, compassion, and neighbor love.

that is to say, an act of the *most spiritual revenge*. For this alone was appropriate for a priestly people, the people embodying the most deeply repressed priestly vengefulness. (GM I ¶7; second emphasis added)

The inattentive Christian reader might lapse into a momentary security (or in the case of anti-Semites, even delight) at this diatribe against the Jews. But it takes only a moment of attention to realize that Nietzsche intends this passage to be a mirror for his Christian readers. For the role of the clergy in Christianity is surely not less than their role in Judaism, and Nietzsche has explicitly told us that his target here is Christianity.

Nietzsche seems to contradict himself at the very beginning of his account of priestly power. First, he acknowledges that priests are powerful. He speaks of them as a caste or aristocracy that can achieve political power and even political supremacy over its rival, the aristocracy of warrior knights.[5] But he also describes them as "the *most evil enemies*," because "they are the most impotent. It is because of their impotence that in them hatred grows to monstrous and uncanny proportions, to the most spiritual and poisonous kind of hatred" (GM I ¶¶6-7).

Here Nietzsche adds to the concept of spiritual revenge that of spiritual hatred. But which is it? Are the clergy weak or strong? They are both: They are weak with regard to their socio-psychological origin, and strong with regard to their social function. It comes as no surprise that Nietzsche interprets the priest as an expression of the will to power. But what kind of power? The references to vengefulness make the answer unambiguous: The priest emerges from "a *ressentiment* without equal, that of an insatiable instinct and power-will that want to become master" (GM III ¶11). The priest is part of the slave revolt in morals that labels its enemies evil. He has his origin among the weak, or, as Nietzsche increasingly calls them, the "sick" (GM III ¶¶13-14). When we understand "the necessity of doctors and nurses *who are themselves sick*," we understand the origin of the priest (GM III ¶15).[6]

---

5. By speaking of castes Nietzsche evokes traditional Hindu society, where the priestly caste, the Brahmins, is dominant over the warrior caste, the Kshatriyas. But he no doubt also has in mind the medieval struggle for power between church and state in the West, often personified as a duel between the chief priest, the pope, and one or another of Europe's many warrior kings.

6. I continue to refer to the priest with masculine pronouns, following Nietzsche, because throughout the history of Christendom the clergy have been overwhelmingly and often exclusively male, a point worth remembering throughout his analysis. But his reference to doctors and nurses indicates his awareness that the role can be filled by women, though the asymmetry between doctors and nurses suggests that he is not thinking of women clergy but of nuns.

But Nietzsche continues immediately to identify the role the priest comes to play as doctor (and nurse). "*Dominion over the suffering is his kingdom, that is where his instinct directs him. . . . He must be sick himself . . . but he must also be strong, master of himself even more than of others, with his will to power intact, so as to be both trusted and feared by the sick, so as to be their support, resistance, prop, compulsion, taskmaster, tyrant, and god.*" It is in the spirit of Nietzsche that Ricoeur speaks of the "clerical 'pathos' which is at one and the same time *rabies theologica* and passion for power. More often than not, it coincides with the despotic spirit and the narrowness of the field of consciousness that comes with age. This passion is all the more treacherous for it believes itself to be serving the truth."[7]

Michel Foucault, perhaps Nietzsche's truest successor in the twentieth century, notes that it is just this link to the truth that distinguishes pastoral power from royal power.[8] Knowledge of the soul generates power without the need of physical force. Stalin's contemptuous retort about the pope, "How many divisions does he have?" misses the point entirely. Mao was equally mistaken. Pastoral power does not come out of the barrel of a gun. Ofelia Schutte puts the point very bluntly: Pastoral power corrupts the notions of freedom and responsibility by placing "their use within a structure which thrives on a tyrannical use of power. The reason there is a verbal appeal to the notion of freedom instead of the physical abuse of force is that this type of structure makes use of moral approval as a tactic for behavioral control."[9]

The name that Nietzsche most often gives to the "truth" that grounds the moral basis of pastoral power is "the ascetic ideal." This name represents that cluster of ascetic and altruistic values that have been associated with the major religions of both East and West.[10] To

7. Paul Ricoeur, *History and Truth*, trans. Charles Kelbley (Evanston: Northwestern University Press, 1965), p. 179. Cf. p. 176, where the truth in question is identified as "the lie of *the* truth."

8. Michel Foucault, "The Subject and Power," afterword to Hubert L. Dreyfus and Paul Rabinow, *Michel Foucault: Beyond Structuralism and Hermeneutics* (Chicago: University of Chicago Press, 1983), p. 214; cf. *The Foucault Reader*, ed. Paul Rabinow (New York: Pantheon Books, 1984), p. 370. Foucault notes the dispersion of "pastoral power" to secular agents, including the doctor, the therapist, and the educator. His point is well illustrated by the "anticlerical" character of contemporary critiques of the (secular) university. He also points out that while pastoral power is not repressive in the usual sense, it is the context in which obedience is "a virtue that becomes an end in itself" (James W. Bernauer, *Michel Foucault's Force of Flight: Toward an Ethics for Thought* [Atlantic Highlands, NJ: Humanities Press, 1990], pp. 162-63).

9. Ofelia Schutte, *Beyond Nihilism: Nietzsche without Masks* (Chicago: University of Chicago Press, 1984), p. 55.

10. Edward Conze unwittingly illustrates Nietzsche's point with reference

remind us of the link between the priest and this system of moral values, Nietzsche often calls him the "ascetic priest."

It is through the ascetic ideal that priests are able to give "hope to desperate people by relieving them of the burden of meaningless-ness. . . ."[11] But the very ideal that makes them so useful to their people is "their best *instrument* of power, also the supreme *license* for power" (GM III ¶1; emphasis added). It is the license for power because of its legitimizing function. As its keepers the clergy can represent themselves as the earthly representatives of the Good and the True.

The ascetic ideal is the instrument of pastoral power in a some-what more complicated manner. The values that make up this ideal are those born of resentment, those that first designate the master as evil and then, by virtue of the Fonda Fallacy, oneself as good. But this concept of evil is a kind of boomerang, and Nietzsche treats it as the origin of bad conscience or guilt. In the Second Essay of *The Genealogy of Morals* he gives a long and labored account of how those who first use the concept of evil as an expression of resentment and an instrument of revenge come to apply it to themselves.[12] (It is here, incidentally, that he tries to explain the observable link between slave morality and religion. Guilt, he argues, inevitably becomes guilt before God [¶¶19-24].)

It is the guilt potential of the ascetic ideal that the priest is able to exploit, and one could say that his moral authority is simply his ability to do so. To heal he must first wound, since a religion of forgive-ness makes sense only to sinners. The priest does this when he *"alters the direction of ressentiment."* We all seek an explanation for our suffering. Resentment seeks "a *guilty* agent," one who is evil and deserves to be punished (since even if I lack the power to punish, there is satisfaction in knowing that my enemy deserves it). " 'I suffer: someone must be to blame for it' — thus thinks every sickly sheep. But his shepherd, the ascetic priest, tells him: 'Quite so, my sheep! someone must be to blame for it: but you yourself are this someone . . . *you alone are to blame for yourself!'* — This is brazen and false enough: but one thing at least is

---

to Buddhism (which Nietzsche often associates with Platonism and Christianity) when he writes, "The begging-bowl was the Buddha's badge of sovereignty. . . . Teachers often gave their begging-bowl to their successor as a sign of the transmis-sion of authority." He also describes monks as "spiritual policemen" (*Buddhism: Its Essence and Development* [New York: Harper and Row, 1975], pp. 55, 76).

11. Charles Scott, *The Question of Ethics: Nietzsche, Foucault, Heidegger* (Bloom-ington: Indiana University Press, 1990), p. 106.

12. See Gilles Deleuze, *Nietzsche and Philosophy,* trans. Hugh Tomlinson (New York: Columbia University Press, 1983), especially chapter 4.

achieved by it, the direction of *ressentiment* is *altered*" (GM III ¶15). By making the patient into a sinner in this manner (¶20), the priest gains enormous power. For, as noted above, moral approval is a splendid instrument of behavior control, and when it comes to manipulation, guilt has few if any rivals.

Nietzsche's account of pastoral power links up with Marxian analysis at several points. Though he speaks of castes where Marx speaks of classes, the awareness of sociological hierarchy is central to both. A second affinity concerns the issue of hermeneutical monopoly. Marxian analysis calls attention to the need of the powerful to control the interpretation of texts, especially texts that have anything like canonical status.[13] Nietzsche calls attention to the fact that the weak are not without their heroes in the battle for the texts. For one of the key functions of the priest is to be the authoritative interpreter of the holy texts.

Chaim Potok sounds a bit like Nietzsche on this point in his novel *Davita's Harp*. He tells of a Hebrew class in which a young girl's answer to a question about a text in Genesis seems to imply that a human author rather than God wrote the Torah. Her teacher sees this as a threat to the high view of Scripture that his teaching everywhere presupposes. "Ilana," he replies, "we do not study the Torah this way here." His explanation, in part, is this: "The Torah is God's stories. God's! The truth of God. The eternal truth given to us by the Master of the Universe. Rashi has the correct understanding of the verse. And that is the way we will learn it here."[14]

Ilana is puzzled. Why did her teacher seem "fearful of there being more than one way to understand the meaning of the Torah? Was he afraid he would lose control over our thinking? Why did he need to control the way we thought?"

We have seen that the priest needs to be both feared and trusted by his people. Nothing is as valuable toward this end as a hermeneutical monopoly over the scriptures of a community. With this tool it is relatively simple to generate enough guilt within the congregation to keep the people in fear. At the same time it is even easier to keep them trustful. All that is required are interpretations that assure the people that, while they are evil, they are at the same time good by contrast with those outside the community of faith, who are evil without

13. The contemporary debate over the canon and its interpretation in the university is another secular version of the phenomenon Nietzsche is describing. See n. 8 above.

14. Chaim Potok, *Davita's Harp* (New York: Alfred A. Knopf, 1985), pp. 270-75.

qualification.[15] The difference between the saved and the damned, which can take many forms, beginning with the most literal, is the key to pastoral power. Nietzsche, naturally, takes this distinction to be pure fiction. But that is not the point. As a "genealogist" (see chapter 35 above) he is inquiring into the uses to which this idea is put. He is giving a very direct answer to the question posed by Hobbes about Catholic and Calvinist clergy: To whom do the benefits of their interpretations accrue? (See p. 194 above.)

Max Weber defines the state as whoever "(successfully) claims the *monopoly of the legitimate use of physical force* within a given territory."[16] Marx and Nietzsche together give us a sociological and suspicious definition of the church as whoever (successfully) claims the monopoly on the interpretation of the scriptures of a given community.

Unlike Nietzsche, Marx emphasizes the role of the church in legitimizing the violence of the state. But Nietzsche's theory also illuminates, without exactly intending to, not just the difference between the priestly and warrior aristocracies but also the possibilities of alliance between priest and king. If the priest starts out impotent, he ends up anything but. While his power and that of the king may well come into conflict, they can just as well cooperate.

Ricoeur's analysis is especially helpful here:

> Reason is the supreme goal of unifying thoughts and works, unifying mankind, unifying our conception of virtue and happiness. . . .
> But as soon as the exigency for a single truth enters into history as a goal of civilization, it is immediately affected with a mark of violence. For one always wishes to tie the knot too early. The *realized* unity of the true is precisely the initial lie . . . this lie of *the* truth — appears when the goal of unifying coincides with the sociological phenomenon of authority. . . . Authority is not culpable in itself. But yet it is the occasion of the passions of power. It is by means of the passions of power that certain men exercise a unifying function. In this way, violence feigns the highest goal of reason. . . .[17]

---

15. Those who study the Torah but "not as we do here" often seem to fall into this latter category. The story is told of an ardent Calvinist preacher whose sermons always had the same three points: what the text says against the modernists, what it says against the Arminians, and what it says against the papists. Cf. Luther's critique of the religion of the Jews, the Muslims, and the Catholics (p. 5 above).

16. Max Weber, "Politics as Vocation," in *Max Weber: Essays in Sociology,* ed. H. H. Gerth and C. W. Mills (New York: Oxford University Press, 1946), p. 78.

17. Ricoeur, pp. 175-76.

Here lies the third affinity between Nietzsche and Marx. Where priests have a hermeneutical monopoly they become arbiters of *the* truth and, as such, the ideal legitimizers of violence; for violence on behalf of *the* truth can have as its enemies only the forces of evil, the damned. Where the state has the means of violence at its disposal and the church has the justification of violence at its disposal, the possibilities of a joint enterprise are strong. Each has something useful to the other, and it looks as if the priest is in the unique position of being able to serve the oppressed and their oppressors at the same time.

What Nietzsche gives us in his analysis of the priestly leaders of the slave revolt in morality is the social psychology of the Grand Inquisitor. Since Dostoyevsky makes it so compellingly clear that Christ has no more cunning competitor on earth than the Grand Inquisitor, Christian readers might do worse than read Nietzsche carefully on this matter.

39 Glittering Vices

It would be a mistake to label Nietzsche anticlerical if this were to suggest that the clergy were his primary target. He is interested in unmasking the hypocrisy of the whole system of values they help to propagate, whether it be called slave morality, the ascetic ideal, altruism, the Golden Rule, Judeo-Christian morality, or whatever. His writings thus constitute a kind of ongoing guerrilla warfare against the virtues of that morality. That warfare is sometimes overshadowed by the attention given to such dramatic doctrines as perspectivism, the death of God, the Overman, and the eternal recurrence.

In this respect Nietzsche is a kind of mirror image of Kierkegaard. The latter likes to quote the church father Lactantius, who said that the virtues of paganism were glittering vices *(vitia splendida).*[1] Nietzsche's response is that the virtues of the Christians are splendid vices. They are splendid because they represent no small spiritual achievement; but they are doubly vices, first because they mask a self-centered will to power that by their own criteria is the essence of immorality, and second, because in hiding this fact from themselves and from others, the votaries of these "virtues" engage in systematic self-deception and hypocrisy. Here again Nietzsche invokes his principle: *"To become moral is not in itself moral,"* meaning that the act of adopting certain values need not be an act instantiating those values but can just as easily violate them. "Subjection to morality can be slavish or vain or self-interested or resigned or

1. Søren Kierkegaard, *Philosophical Fragments/Johannes Climacus,* trans. H. V. Hong and E. H. Hong (Princeton: Princeton University Press, 1985), p. 53; *Two Ages,* trans. Hong and Hong (Princeton: Princeton University Press, 1978), p. 86; *The Sickness Unto Death,* trans. Hong and Hong (Princeton: Princeton University Press, 1980), pp. 46, 82; *Works of Love,* trans. Hong and Hong (New York: Harper and Row, 1962), pp. 66, 189, 251. Cf. Augustine, *City of God* XIX, 25.

gloomily enthusiastic or an act of despair, like subjection to a prince: in itself it is nothing moral" (D ¶97).

We have already seen that the key words for developing this theme are resentment and revenge, and we shall return to them in the next chapter. But just as guerrilla fighters assassinate officials one day and bomb power plants the next, so Nietzsche does not restrict himself to a single line of attack. Here we will explore a secondary strategy that Nietzsche employs, according to which the values of the weak are seen as expressing not so much their resentment as simply their weakness.

In its simplest form this argument portrays Christian virtue as "the cunning of impotence," according to which the weak say, "We weak ones are, after all, weak; it would be good if we did nothing *for which we are not strong enough.*" To make a virtue of necessity, it is treated as if it were "a voluntary achievement, willed, chosen, a *deed,* a *meritorious* act." Here weakness "is being lied into something *meritorious . . .* and impotence which does not requite into 'goodness of heart'; anxious lowliness into 'humility'; subjection to those one hates into 'obedience' . . . [and] inability for revenge is called unwillingness to revenge, perhaps even forgiveness" (GM I ¶¶13-14).[2]

Nietzsche has nothing but contempt for this "prudence of the lowest order" (¶13). He does not hesitate to speak of hypocrisy when others speak of kindness, justice, and pity and when all he can detect is weakness (Z III ¶5.2). When he is in a better mood he simply laughs at "weaklings who thought themselves good because they had no claws" (Z II ¶13).

The weakness in question here could be either physical or political: "See what a saint I am, my dear. Today I did not steal the gold from Fort Knox, did not beat up the heavyweight champion of the world, and did not even assassinate Saddam Hussein." The variations on this theme come from specifying different spiritual modes of incapacity, which all function in the same way, for instance, low self-esteem, cowardice, and laziness. In each case the goodness of the good stems from their lack of power to do what they (for that reason) designate as evil; and it is their will to power that makes this lack of power into virtue and merit.

First-time readers of *Thus Spoke Zarathustra* are bound to be

2. The element of resentment is not entirely missing here, and Nietzsche actually speaks of "the vengeful cunning of impotence" insofar as the weak are also saying, "Let us be different from the evil, namely good!" But the main point here is not putting the enemy down but finding a way to make weakness the ground of self-affirmation.

shocked by Nietzsche's hostility to love of neighbor, sometimes failing even to notice the point that he is trying to make, namely that what is passed off as neighbor love is sometimes nothing more than low self-esteem. "One must learn to love oneself — thus I teach — with a wholesome and healthy love, so that one can bear to be with oneself and need not roam. Such roaming baptizes itself 'love of the neighbor': with this phrase the best lies and hypocrisies have been perpetrated so far" (Z III ¶11.2; cf. I ¶16; III ¶5.5).

Closely related to this theme is one that Nietzsche proposes to write on under the heading "Morality as Timidity" (BGE ¶¶197-98). He believes that there is a servile altruism that counts as "selfless" among "world-weary cowards" (Z III ¶10.2). Thus what are presented as the virtues of obedience, humility, and sympathy may be but masks for fear, cowardice, and timidity, respectively (D ¶¶9, 38, 174); or again, what passes for patience may be only cowardice (GM I ¶14). Those who wish to remove all danger and "all the sharp edges of life" allow a "tyranny of timidity [to prescribe] to them their supreme moral law" (D ¶174).[3]

Love of neighbor can be the expression not only of low self-esteem but also of fear of neighbor. Where this happens we have the makings of what is to Nietzsche the dominant characteristic of modernity, the herd. He sees it expressed in the desire not to punish but to rehabilitate the criminal. " 'Is it not enough to render him *undangerous . . . ?'* With this question herd morality, the morality of timidity, draws its ultimate consequence." What speaks here is "the imperative of herd timidity: 'we want that some day there should be *nothing any more to be afraid of!'* " (BGE ¶201).

In addition to low self-esteem and cowardice or timidity, laziness can be the origin of virtue. We have already seen that the "virtue" of obedience can be the expression of either simple weakness or cowardly fear. But Nietzsche notes another species that has its birth in "a sluggish spirit" (D ¶207). He expresses his contempt for those "who call it virtue when their vices grow lazy" (Z II ¶5). Referring to the tablets of stone on which God wrote the law for Moses on Mount Sinai (Exod. 31:18), he writes that "there are tablets created by weariness and tablets created by rotten, rotting sloth" (Z III ¶12.18). It is not clear whether his satire of those whose commitment to virtue stems from the desire to sleep

---

3. In Plato's *Gorgias* Callicles says that those who praise self-control and justice do so because they lack both the power and the courage to allow their own appetites to grow and then to do what they must to satisfy them (491e-92c).

well is best understood with reference to spiritual cowardice or spiritual laziness (Z I ¶2).

It is undoubtedly all three dimensions of spiritual weakness, low self-esteem, cowardice, and laziness, that Nietzsche has in mind when he has Zarathustra teach that Overman has become necessary because humankind (read modernity) has become "a polluted stream." "Is not your soul poverty and filth and wretched contentment?" he asks (Z Prologue ¶3). The sustained polemic against the "wretched contentment" of the virtuous in and with their virtue is a protest against a certain way of trivializing the moral life.[4] What is most contemptible is the last man, for whom there is neither hope nor a goal, since he is content. Not wanting anything that would require "too much exertion," his motto is "No shepherd and one herd!" (Z Prologue ¶5).

There are no doubt many versions of wretched contentment in the moral life. Thomas Merton describes one in his account of the chaplain at his school, Oakham. "Buggy's" best sermon was on 1 Corinthians 13 and revolved around the discovery that "charity" here and throughout the Bible

> simply stood for "all that we mean when we call a chap a 'gentleman.'" In other words, charity meant good-sportsmanship, cricket, the decent thing, wearing the right kind of clothes, using the proper spoon, not being a cad or a bounder.
>
> . . . "One might go through this chapter of St. Paul and simply substitute the word 'gentleman' for 'charity' wherever it occurs. 'If I talk with the tongues of men and of angels, and be not a gentleman, I am become as sounding brass, or a tinkling cymbal. . . .'"
>
> . . . I will not accuse him of finishing the chapter with "Now there remain faith, hope and gentlemanliness, and the greatest of these is gentlemanliness . . . ," although it was the logical term of his reasoning.

Nietzsche would have smiled approvingly, in spite of himself, at Merton's conclusion:

> . . . I think St. Peter and the twelve Apostles would have been rather surprised at the concept that Christ had been scourged and

---

4. Cf. Z I ¶6; II ¶8; III ¶5.2-3; IV ¶13.3; GS ¶¶318, 338. The key terms, *Behagen* and *behaglich* are sometimes translated as "comfort/comfortable" rather than "contentment/contented." A key difference between Freud and Nietzsche is that while Freud is concerned about civilization and its *Unbehagen*, Nietzsche is concerned about the questionable *Behagen* of its prevailing morality.

beaten by soldiers . . . and finally nailed to the Cross and left to bleed to death in order that we might all become gentlemen.[5]

We can return to a passage cited earlier and, by giving it its larger context, see more clearly the positive point Nietzsche is trying to make: "When power becomes gracious and descends into the visible — such descent I call beauty. And there is nobody from whom I want beauty as much as from you who are powerful: let your kindness be your final self-conquest. Of all evil I deem you capable: therefore I want the good from you. Verily, I have often laughed at the weaklings who thought themselves good because they had no claws" (Z II ¶13). True goodness, Nietzsche believes, expresses power not impotence.

On this point Gandhi agrees with Nietzsche. He thinks only those capable of violence can truly practice nonviolence.

> A strong and self-reliant India will cease to hate . . . for she will have the power to punish . . . and therefore the power also to pity and forgive. . . . Today she can neither punish nor forgive. . . . I do believe that where there is a choice only between cowardice and violence, I would advise violence. . . . I would rather have India resort to arms in order to defend her honor than that she should in a cowardly manner become or remain a helpless witness to her own dishonor. But I believe non-violence is infinitely superior to violence, forgiveness is more manly than punishment. . . . But . . . forgiveness only when there is the power to punish. . . . A mouse hardly forgives a cat when it allows itself to be torn to pieces by her.[6]

Josef Pieper agrees with Nietzsche and Gandhi:

> Gentleness, however, does not signify that the original power of wrath is weakened or, worse still, "mortified," just as chastity does not imply a weakening of sexual power. On the contrary: gentleness as a virtue presupposes the power of wrath; gentleness implies mastery of this power, not its weakening. We should not mistake the pale-faced harmlessness which pretends to be gentleness — unfortunately often successfully — for a Christian virtue. Lack of sensuality is not chastity; and incapacity for wrath has nothing to

---

5. Thomas Merton, *The Seven Story Mountain* (New York: Harcourt, Brace, Jovanovich, 1948), pp. 73-74. I am indebted to Carol Westphal for calling this passage to my attention.

6. *The Essential Gandhi: His Life, Work, and Ideas*, ed. Louis Fischer (New York: Random House, 1962), pp. 153-57. Most of the ellipses are in Fischer's text.

do with gentleness. Such incapacity not only is not a virtue, but, as St. Thomas expressly says, a fault. . . .[7]

Now Gandhi and Pieper are what Nietzsche calls ascetic priests. The fact of this profound agreement among them is noteworthy. I have been arguing that the hermeneutics of suspicion as practiced by modern atheists draws the resources for its critique of religion from the very traditions it criticizes, leading to the conclusion that the believing soul should take them very seriously and not be in too great a hurry to refute them. When Nietzsche argues that physical, political, or spiritual incapacity to do evil is not virtue but rather, when it pretends to be, sheer hypocrisy, it may well be that he is doing something very much like what Jesus and the prophets did, protesting against a corruption of the spiritual life that disguises itself with a veneer of spirituality. Why should unbelievers have a monopoly on such a protest? More specifically, should not Christian moral instruction include "Nietzschean" warnings against making a virtue out of various forms of impotence?[8]

7. Josef Pieper, *The Four Cardinal Virtues* (Notre Dame: University of Notre Dame Press, 1966), pp. 195-96.

8. Theists would seem to be metaphysically committed to Nietzsche's central point, that true goodness expresses power rather than weakness, by virtue of their commitment to belief (1) that God is the archetype of all goodness and (2) that God is almighty or omnipotent. The kenotic goodness represented by the cross is the voluntary laying aside of power (Matt. 4:1-7; 26:47-56; 27:37-44), not the celebration of involuntary impotence.

40 Justice and the Fascists

It is time to return to Nietzsche's central themes of resentment and revenge and to the role they play in the interpretation of two central virtues of the morality he seeks to discredit: justice (in this chapter) and pity (in the next). Philosophers and theologians have often discussed the relationship of justice and love, of which pity or compassion may be considered one dimension. Recently, for example, it has been argued that justice is a vice in circumstances that call for benevolence.[1] Nietzsche's contribution to this discussion is to say that justice and compassion are two sides of the same coin, parallel expressions of the revenge of the resentful.

Nietzsche must have loved the opening of Gottfried Keller's novelette *A Village Romeo and Juliet.*[2] Manz and Marti are farmers whose long, narrow fields are separated by a similar field of uncertain ownership. Each year, by mutual agreement, each adds to his own field from the center field by plowing one furrow further into it than he had the year before. Finally, it is decided that the center field should be auctioned off, and Manz buys it. But he immediately claims that Marti has cheated him, not by shaving off part of the plot each year, as he had also done, but by not keeping his line straight in doing so. Thus a triangular piece of land is at issue between them, Manz feeling that it has been stolen from him, while Marti contends that Manz bought the

---

1. Michael J. Sandel, *Liberalism and the Limits of Justice* (Cambridge: Cambridge University Press, 1982), pp. 34-35.
2. Nietzsche speaks highly of the volume in which this story appears, *Die Leute von Seldwyla* (WS ¶109), and later, in a letter to Hippolyte Taine (4 July 1887), speaks of "that Swiss poet, whom I consider to be the only living *German* poet, Gottfried Keller." Friedrich Nietzsche, *Werke in Drei Bänden,* ed. Karl Schlechta (Munich: Carl Hanser Verlag, 1956), III, 1259.

field as it was, since anyone could see where his crops stopped and the untended field began.

Like two children convinced that the other's piece of pie was larger, the two began a genuinely Dickensian "litigation with each other, and did not rest until they were both ruined. The thoughts of these hitherto sensible men were now cut as fine as chopped straw, each being filled with the strictest sense of justice in the world. Neither could or would understand how the other, with such manifest and arbitrary injustice, could claim for himself the insignificant corner in question."[3] What Nietzsche would like best about this passage is the psychological insight that portrays justice as the very thin disguise employed by each of these men to make his wounded pride and greed appear respectable. In the process, of course, each construes the other with ever-increasing certainty as evil.

Nietzsche applies this type of analysis to both distributive and retributive justice. The central concept of distributive justice is equality. Like Hayek and Holmes (see p. 57 above), Nietzsche sees the ideal of equality as the expression of envy on the part of the have-nots. He describes the preachers of equality as tarantulas whose souls are filled with the poison of revenge, as embodiments of the "tyrannomania of impotence" whose "secret ambitions to be tyrants thus shroud themselves in words of virtue. Aggrieved conceit, repressed envy . . . erupt from you as a flame and as a frenzy of revenge." For those who distinguish between envy and jealousy, he throws jealousy into this genealogy of justice and sums it all up, "Out of every one of their complaints sounds revenge" (Z II ¶7).

The central concept of retributive justice is punishment, and in Nietzsche's eyes, quite simply, "punishment is revenge" (WS ¶33).[4] Those who have adopted the morality of altruism do not abandon the desire for revenge when they are harmed, but given their professed values they cannot acknowledge it either. The "good and the just," as they like to think of themselves, "crave to be *hangmen*." But to hide this fact from themselves and others they become "the vengeful disguised as judges, who constantly bear the word 'justice' in their mouths like poisonous spittle" (GM III ¶14). Good vs. evil becomes just vs. unjust, and those filled with the spirit of resentment call what they desire,

3. Gottfried Keller, *A Village Romeo and Juliet*, trans. P. B. Thomas and B. Q. Morgan (New York: Frederick Ungar, 1955), p. 16.
4. In this passage Nietzsche distinguishes two species of revenge that correspond quite closely, though not by name, to the difference between master and slave morality.

not retaliation, but "the triumph of *justice*"; what they hate is not their enemy, no! they hate "injustice," they hate "godlessness"; what they believe in and hope for is not the hope of revenge, the intoxication of sweet revenge (— "sweeter than honey" Homer called it), but the victory of God, of the *just* God, over the godless; what there is left for them to love on earth is not their brothers in hatred but their "brothers in love," as they put it, all the good and just on earth. (GM I ¶14)

This is why Zarathustra advises: "Mistrust all in whom the impulse to punish is powerful . . . the hangman and bloodhound look out of their faces. Mistrust all who talk much of their justice" (Z II ¶7). We begin to detect a pattern. Nietzsche warns against the "preachers of equality," against those "who constantly bear the word 'justice' in their mouths," and against "all who talk much of their justice." Those who talk most about justice, Nietzsche suspects, are those most eager to mask what their will to punish represents. As Laurence Lampert puts it, "In calling itself 'punishment' and undertaking acts of justice, revenge feigns a good conscience by means of a lie. . . ."[5]

When trying to teach these texts of Nietzsche, I often pick up on Nietzsche's linking of justice with the hangman and ask students to think about the current resurgence of enthusiasm for capital punishment in the United States. I ask them whether they can hear, thinly disguised by the vocabulary of justice, a message that runs something like this: "Let the bastards fry until our streets are safe again." They have little difficulty in doing so. I do not suggest that this is an answer to whether capital punishment is good public policy; but I do suggest that Nietzsche may well be on target in his queasiness around those "in whom the impulse to punish is powerful."

It turns out to be terribly hard to draw a clear line between punishment as justice and punishment as revenge. Nietzsche doubts whether there even is such a line and finds his own language splendidly aware of the problem. "And when they say, 'I am just,' it always sounds like "I am just — revenged'" (Z II ¶5). In German the two phrases are *Ich bin gerecht* and *Ich bin gerächt*. These two statements, easily distinguished by the eye, are virtually indistinguishable to the ear, and Nietzsche's suggestion is that the ear is more perceptive, that the concept of justice very frequently masks the vengefulness that stems from resentment. So he continues, "With their virtue they want to scratch out the eyes of their enemies. . . ."

5. Laurence Lampert, *Nietzsche's Teaching: An Interpretation of Thus Spoke Zarathustra* (New Haven: Yale University Press, 1986), p. 145.

In the same paragraph he reminds us that the discourse of justice is not only not innocent, but also not harmless. He speaks of those who "are proud of their handful of justice and commit outrages against all things for its sake, till the world is drowned in their injustice." We are reminded of Hare's claim, cited above in chapter 3, that "*The rhetoric of rights . . . is a recipe for class war, and civil war.* In pursuit of these rights, people will, because they have convinced themselves that justice demands it, inflict almost any harms on the rest of society and themselves."[6] We also hear again Yoder's warning against the "egocentric altruism" that makes of oneself "the incarnation of a good and righteous cause for which others may rightly be made to suffer."[7] Is there a better explanation of the mutual terrorism that has defined the Arab-Israeli conflict, or, to bring the matter closer to home, of Hiroshima and Nagasaki?

It is in terms of this kind of moral fanaticism that Nietzsche speaks of anarchists, Robespierre, and anti-Semites (D Preface ¶3; GM II ¶11). Had he lived in a later time he might have included the extremists of the left who bombed banks to protest the Vietnam war and the extremists of the right who bomb abortion clinics, both in the name of justice and the sacredness of life. Terrorism always speaks the language of justice. Charles Scott puts the same point just a little differently: "We can easily be fascists, for example, in the manner we apply or extend nonfascist values."[8]

Nietzsche is easy to deal with when he can be treated as a proto-Fascist whose doctrine of the will to power portends Hitler. Scott's suggestion is more disturbing. In the spirit of Nietzsche he suggests that the great gulf we have fixed between ourselves and fascism is largely wishful thinking. Far from being the Overman for whom Zarathustra longs, Hitler is the quintessential man of resentment

6. R. M. Hare, "Justice and Equality," reprinted in *Justice: Alternative Political Perspectives*, ed. James Sterba (Belmont, CA: Wadsworth, 1980), p. 119, emphasis added. Keller writes of Manz and Marti, "Thenceforward their life was like the torturing nightmare of two condemned souls, who, while floating down a dark stream on a narrow board, fall into a quarrel, thrash the air, and clinch and try to annihilate each other, each thinking that he has hold of the cause of his misfortune" (*A Village Romeo and Juliet*, p. 17).

7. John Howard Yoder, "What Would You Do If," *Journal of Religious Ethics* 2/1 (Fall 1974), pp. 82-83, quoted in Stanley Hauerwas, *The Peaceable Kingdom: A Primer in Christian Ethics* (Notre Dame: University of Notre Dame Press, 1983), p. 131; cf. p. 75 above.

8. Charles E. Scott, *The Question of Ethics: Nietzsche, Foucault, Heidegger* (Bloomington: Indiana University Press, 1990), p. 4; cf. p. 56.

against whom Nietzsche's critique (of Christianity) is directed.[9] Aryans are good and Jews are evil, deserving of whatever hell Hitler's experts can devise. Moreover, those who were best able to resist the seductions of fascism were not those we might have expected. Hannah Arendt writes, "The total moral collapse of respectable society during the Hitler regime may teach us that those who are reliable in such circumstances are not those who cherish values and hold fast to moral norms and standards."[10]

Hitler, we might say, was a gifted ascetic priest, highly skilled in the use of moral language to arouse and disguise the resentment of the masses. It was the morality of good and evil that made the Final Solution possible.

We would like to say that the fascists and the terrorists represent the distortion and misuse of the ideals of justice. Nietzsche's reply is that those ideals are in essence, and not accidentally, moral distortions because of their origin in resentment. Probably nothing makes his case stronger than comparing the fascist Final Solution with the Christian Final Judgment.

Nietzsche sees the culmination of the morality of resentment in the concept of hell. Taking over the idea from the mystery religions, Christians found in it "the most promising egg of their power," the key to their proselytizing success (D ¶72). The idea of this "spiritual torture" remains acceptable even in a time when physical torture has become disreputable, and the preaching of someone like Whitefield shows what an overpowering instrument this idea of divine justice can be in human hands (D ¶77).[11]

---

9. See Stephen Houlgate, *Hegel, Nietzsche, and the Critique of Metaphysics* (Cambridge: Cambridge University Press, 1986), p. 75, including notes 189-90.

10. Quoted from "Personal Responsibility Under Dictatorship" by Elisabeth Young-Bruehl in "From the Pariah's Point of View: Reflections on Hannah Arendt's Life and Work," in *Hannah Arendt: The Recovery of the Public World*, ed. Melvyn A. Hill (New York: St. Martin's Press, 1979), p. 16. One can say the same of American anti-black racism from slavery to the Klan to contemporary Brooklyn.

11. Catholic readers, to whom Whitefield and Protestant revivalism are not familiar, may refer to the sermon on hell in James Joyce's *A Portrait of the Artist as a Young Man*, with its emphasis on the justice of God. Ofelia Schutte writes (*Beyond Nihilism: Nietzsche without Masks* [Chicago: University of Chicago Press, 1984], p. 54):

> Nietzsche calls the official doctrine of free will a "metaphysics of the hangman" [TI ¶7]. He links the free will theory to the Christian doctrines of original sin and eternal punishment in hell. He notes in particular that whenever the instinct to punish and judge is powerful, "responsibility" is defined in such a way as to enhance the power of the judging and punishing

But Nietzsche's focus is not on hell as an instrument of priestly power. It is rather on hell as an expression of resentment and the ultimate revenge on one's enemies. In place of Dante's inscription over the gate of hell, "I too was created by eternal love," or perhaps as a commentary on what it really means, Nietzsche proposes an inscription over the gateway to the Christian Paradise, "I too was created by eternal *hate.*" In support of this suggestion he quotes Thomas Aquinas and Tertullian. According to Thomas, "The blessed in the kingdom of heaven will see the punishments of the damned, *in order that the bliss of the saints may be more delightful for them*" (GM I ¶15).[12]

The same song can be heard "in a stronger key" in Tertullian's *De Spectaculis.* This "triumphant Church Father" warns his readers against "the cruel pleasures of the public games — but why? 'For the faith offers us much more . . . *something much stronger;* thanks to the Redemption, quite other joys are at our command. . . . But think of what awaits us on the day of his return, the day of his triumph!' " Nietzsche then cites in Latin a long passage in which Tertullian describes the joy and the exultation of the faithful upon seeing their enemies in the fires of hell. Of course, it is a matter of faith and not sight for the present, and the passage cited concludes, "What quaestor or priest in his munificence will bestow on you the favour of seeing and *exulting in such things as these?* And yet even now we in a measure have them *by faith* in the picturings of imagination. But what are the things which eye has not seen, ear has not heard, and which have not so much as dimly dawned upon the human heart? Whatever they are, they are nobler, I believe, than circus, and both theatres, and every race-course" (¶15).

It is hard to deny that the spirit of resentment and the longing for vengeance burns hot in these passages. In them the final judgment makes the Final Solution seem almost moderate. Here one's enemies

---

party. Under patriarchal religion, "free will" has been invented so that the priestly class can manipulate the people with threats of God's punishment.

It should be noted that Nietzsche's use of "invented" does not mean that he had a conspiracy theory of priestly power. He was far too "Freudian" to think that the phenomena he described were conscious and deliberate.

That the move away from physical torture is not unambiguous moral progress is a central thesis of Michel Foucault in *Discipline and Punish: The Birth of the Prison,* trans. Alan Sheridan (New York: Random House, 1979).

12. Nietzsche's emphasis. Kaufmann cites the passage from *Summa Theologiae* III, *Supplementum,* Q. 94, Art. 1: "In order that the bliss of the saints may be more delightful for them and that they may render more copious thanks to God for it, it is given to them to see perfectly the punishment of the damned."

are not restricted to the Jews, nor is their punishment restricted to what Nietzsche calls *"definitive death,"* but rather is extended to "eternal torment" (D ¶¶72, 77). And the whole thing is presented as a public spectacle and source of ecstatic joy. This is possible because God's role in the whole affair makes of it the Final Justice, the ultimate triumph of good over evil, of us over them.

Just as the hermeneutics of suspicion in general cannot settle the question of God's existence, so Nietzsche's critique does not tell us whether there is eternal punishment or not. What it shows is how extraordinarily dangerous it is to believe in hell and in the concept of justice by which it is justified.

41 *Pity and the Pharisees*

In the workhouses charity has been ingeniously combined with the *revenge* of the bourgeoisie on all those
wretched enough to appeal to their charity.

KARL MARX[1]

In the new world of the asylum, in that world of a
punishing morality, madness became a fact concerning
essentially the human soul, its guilt, and its freedom. . . . It was enclosed in a punitive system in which
the madman, reduced to the status of a minor, was
treated in every way as a child, and in which madness
was associated with guilt and wrongdoing. . . . None of
this psychology would exist without the *moralizing
sadism* in which nineteenth-century "philanthropy" enclosed it, under the hypocritical appearances of "liberation."

MICHEL FOUCAULT[2]

For such a task [of psychic liberation], we place no
trust in altruistic feeling, we who lay bare the aggressiv-

---

1. Karl Marx, "Critical Notes on the Article 'The King of Prussia and Social
Reform. By a Prussian,' " *Karl Marx: Early Writings*, trans. Rodney Livingstone and
Gregor Benton (New York: Random House, 1975), p. 408.
2. Michel Foucault, *Mental Illness and Psychology*, quoted in James W. Bernauer, *Michel Foucault's Force of Flight: Toward an Ethics for Thought* (Atlantic Highlands, NJ: Humanities Press), p. 43.

ity that underlies the activity of the philanthropist, the
idealist, the pedagogue, and even the reformer.

JACQUES LACAN[3]

If Nietzsche's assault on the ideals of justice is hard to swallow, his
attack on pity or compassion is an even more bitter pill. He knows this
and makes pity the last and hardest temptation of Zarathustra (Z IV
¶2). Marx (who seems to have been reading Dickens), Foucault, and
Lacan, with their notions of charity as revenge and philanthropy as
aggression or even moral sadism, point us in the direction that
Nietzsche wants to go.

Pity is one of the virtues that make up the whole "altruistic" or
"unegoistic" morality of "self-abnegation" and "self-sacrifice" (GM
Preface ¶¶4-5). Thus "thoughtlessness" says that in pity "we are thinking only of the other person," whereas in truth we "are not consciously
thinking of ourself but are doing so *very strongly unconsciously.*" Thus
the difference between those who have pity and those who do not is
not the difference between altruism and egoism; those who do not have
pity "are a *different* kind of egoists from the men of pity" (D ¶133). We
are dealing with two different expressions of the same will to power.

There are many motives for the pity that is not genuinely altruistic (D ¶133). Thus, for example, like neighbor love, pity can arise as
a flight from oneself among those of low self-esteem (GS ¶338). But
Nietzsche's genealogy focuses on subtle revenge. The act of pity enables
me to show myself "as the more powerful and as a helper." The object
of my pity may experience it as a kind of "contempt," but for me it is
"the taste of superiority."[4] By seeking to compel *"active gratitude"* we
are able to enact "benevolent revenge" (D ¶¶133-38). For "when I
helped him, I transgressed grievously against his pride. Great indebted-
ness does not make men grateful, but vengeful; and if a little charity is
not forgotten, it turns into a gnawing worm" (Z II ¶3). Thus Zarathustra

3. Jacques Lacan, *Écrits: A Selection,* trans. Alan Sheridan (New York: W. W.
Norton, 1977), p. 7.

4. Cf. GM III ¶18, where love of neighbor is portrayed as an expression of
the will to power motivated by the "happiness of 'slight superiority,' involved in
all doing good, being useful, helping. . . ." Hegel suggests that those whose religion
makes them feel both different from and superior to others will either pity or loathe
those of other faiths (*On Christianity: Early Theological Writings,* trans. T. M. Knox
[New York: Harper and Brothers, 1961], p. 92). Nietzsche's analysis suggests that
this pity and loathing may be two sides of the same coin.

teaches, " 'Pity is obtrusive' . . . pity offends the sense of shame. And to be unwilling to help can be nobler than the virtue which jumps in to help" (Z IV ¶7).

Nietzsche's sensitivity to the paternalism in pity clarifies how it can be an act of revenge. Through my kindness I can belittle the other and elevate myself to a place of moral superiority. That is the form that my subtle, spiritual revenge takes. He would have understood why two former poster children for muscular dystrophy called for a boycott of the Jerry Lewis Labor Day Telethon on the grounds that the appeal for funds to help "Jerry's kids" is based too much on pity.

I was told of a Christian organization that sought to raise funds for the relief of world hunger. They went to the professional experts to ask what kinds of appeal would be the most effective. They were told to be sure that their appeals clearly implied the superiority of the givers to the recipients, without actually stating it. The sad part of the story, as it was told to me, is that those who asked for this advice followed it. Nietzsche would not deny that such benevolence will fill empty stomachs; but he would also insist (would Jesus disagree?) that the "compassion" and "generosity" that need to be bribed with assurances of superiority are glittering vices and no true virtues.

While the importance of moral superiority to those who may be in many other ways inferior (the weak, slaves) is central to Nietzsche's analysis of pity as revenge, it is not limited to this virtue. Any virtue can be the basis for such a feeling. Thus Nietzsche interprets humility and chastity along these lines (D ¶30; cf. Z II ¶4) and says of those who say "I am righteous" when they mean "I am revenged": "With their virtue they want to scratch out the eyes of their enemies, and they exalt themselves only to humble others" (Z II ¶5). Knowing that my enemies will be punished by an all-powerful God satisfies my cruelty, but knowing that they will be punished by a *just* God satisfies my need for moral superiority.

Thus the structure of pity is the structure of slave morality as such. Those whose weakness leaves them filled with vengefulness, rancor, and hatred desire through their virtues to achieve the one superiority available to them. "They monopolize virtue, these weak, hopelessly sick people, there is no doubt of it: 'we alone are the good and the just,' they say. . . . *They walk among us as embodied reproaches.* . . . The will of the weak to represent some form of superiority, their instinct for devious paths to tyranny over the healthy — where can it not be discovered, this will to power of the weakest!" At this point Nietzsche introduces a name, not altogether new, for this will to power whose goal is moral supremacy: Pharisaism. The Pharisees "are all men of *ressentiment* . . . a whole tremulous realm of subterranean revenge" (GM III ¶14, emphasis added). Along with the ascetic priest, the Pharisee is the personification of the morality of the Golden Rule.

Nietzsche sees the Pharisees, therefore, as those who call themselves, and themselves alone, the good and the just. It turns out that they also represent themselves as believers in the true faith. They are the confluence of moral and theological rectitude, whose God is the validator of their virtues and the avenger of their enemies.[5] Not surprisingly, Nietzsche's Zarathustra finds himself hated by the good and the just, and, although he is more nearly an Antichrist than a disciple, he reminds us that he and Jesus share this distinction (Z Prologue ¶8; I ¶21).

Why do the good and the just hate both Jesus and Zarathustra, his antithesis and would-be alternative? Because both Jesus and Zarathustra ask awkward questions about the moral life, questions that the good and the just consider immoral, and because they both stand for something new (renewal) in the moral life, while the good and the just are the quintessential moral conservatives who "already know what is good and just" (Z Prologue ¶9; I ¶¶8, 17, 19; III ¶12.26). Why should they not be? The moral status quo enables them to preach (if not necessarily to practice) a morality that gives them double vengeance on their enemies, the satisfaction of knowing themselves to be good and the satisfaction of knowing their enemies to be evil and, as such, both deserving of the most severe punishment and guaranteed to receive it.

Zarathustra tells us that "the good and the just" are the greatest danger to the future of humankind. He reminds us again of the battle between Jesus and the Pharisees, whose spirit, he says, "is imprisoned

---

5. Commenting on Nietzsche's doctrine of the death of God, Martin Heidegger writes: "The ultimate blow against God and against the suprasensory world consists in the fact that God, the first of beings, is degraded to the highest value." We understand how this elevation is a degradation when we understand that by a "value" Heidegger understands Nietzsche to mean anything that is an instrument of the human will to power. Heidegger adds that "this blow comes precisely not from those . . . who do not believe in God, but from the believers and their theologians who discourse on the being that is of all beings most in being, without ever letting it occur to them . . . that, seen from out of faith, their thinking and their talking is sheer blasphemy . . ." ("The Word of Nietzsche: 'God Is Dead,'" in *The Question Concerning Technology and Other Essays*, trans. William Lovitt [New York: Harper and Row, 1977], p. 105). Without naming them, Heidegger attributes the death of God to the Pharisees.

in their good conscience." Then he drops his bombshell: "the good *must* be pharisees — they have no choice" (Z III ¶12.26). Just in case we missed it, or are tempted to think that at least on this point Zarathustra does not speak for Nietzsche, the latter repeats the point speaking for himself: "Pharisaism is not a degeneration in a good man: a good deal of it is rather the condition of all being good" (BGE ¶135).

Surely, we would like to think, the Pharisees, like the fascists and the terrorists, are morality run amuck. Again Nietzsche challenges this as wishful thinking (see chapter 40 above). What can it mean to suggest that the good *must* be Pharisees? It is Nietzsche's way of reminding us that the morality he is discussing is the morality of good and evil, that in this morality the goodness of the good depends on the wickedness of the wicked, and, consequently, that this morality is built on the notion of moral superiority, or, to be more precise, on the Fonda Fallacy: They are evil, so we must be good. If we look closely at the way such virtues as justice and pity really operate in the real world we will see this point and learn "the danger of the desire to be better."[6]

Nietzsche thinks that the slave revolt in morality is contagious, that one sign of its triumph causes its values to prevail among the upper as well as the lower classes of society. If this is right we can expect to find Pharisees at the top as well as at the bottom of the social totem pole.

In a splendid irony, it is Marx who gives us a graphic illustration of this point in a newspaper article about the English oligarchy and its "twin sister," the church. Parliament was passing blue laws to close shops and beer halls on Sunday. While these did not affect the shopping and entertainment habits of "the privileged classes," they did affect the workers, who got paid at the end of the day on Saturday.[7] The result was a protest demonstration inspired by the Chartists, "to see how religiously the aristocracy is observing the Sabbath and how anxious it is not to employ its servants and horses on that day," as the author of one of the bills had claimed. The demonstration took place in Hyde Park, "where of an afternoon, particularly on Sunday, [English high

6. Charles E. Scott, *The Question of Ethics: Nietzsche, Foucault, Heidegger* (Bloomington: Indiana University Press, 1990), p. 65. Scott is actually speaking here of Foucault's project, but Foucault is so thoroughly Nietzschean that the comment fits equally well in either context.

7. Marx tells why he considers these laws "a conspiracy of the Church with monopoly capital," and he emphasizes the class struggle dimensions of the story. But here we are more interested in the Nietzschean than in the Marxian side of the story.

society] parade their magnificent horses and carriages with all their trappings, followed by swarms of lackeys" (OR 127-34).

The demonstrators formed a gauntlet through which the carriages had to pass. Above the "cacophony" that accompanied the drama could be heard the admonition, "Go to church!" and one lady offered her prayer book to the demonstrators. There may be a good bit of ideological bias in Marx's description of the "smiles of blissful self-satisfaction" with which the demonstrators were greeted, but these two gestures speak for themselves. In them we see a phenomenon more Nietzschean than Marxian.[8] Oblivious to the realities of working-class life, the good and the just are only able to see the workers as irreligious (i.e., evil) and as a threat to the sanctity of their Sabbath. Just as Marxian analysis evokes Amos, so Nietzschean analysis (even from the pen of Marx) evokes the confrontation between Jesus and the Pharisees.

---

8. The same phenomenon that Marx describes in an incident, Foucault describes as a historical tendency in his account of the outburst of moral indignation at the poor that accompanied the birth of modernity. *Madness and Civilization: A History of Insanity in the Age of Reason*, trans. Richard Howard (New York: Random House, 1965), chapter 2.

42 Jesus and the Pharisees I: The Sinners

The Christian Bible is surely the most anti-religious of all the world's scriptures. This often goes unnoticed because, unlike the critiques made by Freud, Marx, and Nietzsche, the biblical hermeneutics of suspicion is religiously motivated. It is not for that reason any less devastating. In the Old Testament the prophets tell the people that God cannot stand their worship. In the New Testament, Paul wages war against the religion of being good, to which James responds with a sharp critique of those who would abuse the gospel of grace.[1] But the most thoroughly anti-religious texts in the Bible are the Gospel narratives in which the piety of the Pharisees, of the Jerusalem power elite, which was dominated by Sadducees, and of Jesus' own disciples is relentlessly exposed as self-righteous and self-centered.

Our concern in this context is not the biblical polemic against the idolatry and immorality of pagan religions. Each of the instances mentioned above involves, rather, a biblical critique of what takes itself to be biblical religion. The prophets, the apostles, and Jesus himself direct their own critique of religion primarily to the covenant people of God. It is for this reason that I accuse the modern atheists of plagiarism, since they tend to repeat in their battle with biblical religion the criticisms already directed to pious Jews and Christians by the Bible. I do not make this accusation in order to silence the atheists but in order to persuade the church to read them with an eye toward repentance and renewal rather than refutation.

Since this is a book about Freud, Marx, and Nietzsche, my treatment of the biblical critique of religion is anything but comprehensive. With regard to my plagiarism charge, I am seeking an indictment, not

1. See above, p. 11 n. 1.

a verdict. My goal in discussing a few biblical passages will be achieved if I make the parallels clear enough that the reader who wishes to do so may explore the matter in greater depth and discover similar materials elsewhere. At the conclusion of the section on Marx, and with the help of liberation theology, we looked at the original "Marxian" critique of religion as found in the Hebrew prophets. It is clear from our discussion of Nietzsche that its conclusion must be a look at the confrontation between Jesus and the Pharisees.[2]

Like Nietzsche, Jesus calls the Pharisees "hypocrites" (Matthew 23). But we will misunderstand the Pharisees and the danger they represent if we take this to mean that they were cynical and cunning conspirators, consciously out to cash in on the pretense of piety. The evidence suggests, on the contrary, that they were sincerely serious about the religious life and that their brand of moral rigorism required enormous self-discipline. Nor should we impose on them our distinction between moral and ceremonial law, for in their eyes Torah was simply Torah, the command of God.

Still, we have learned from Freud's patients and from the girl who asked for spankings that the meaning of renunciation is not determined by its severity. And we have gained an understanding of the ironies of false consciousness that make conscious sincerity compatible with unconscious hypocrisy. In other words, we already realize that those who sincerely subject themselves to severe self-denial may be self-deceived about what they do and who they really are.

> The heart is deceitful above all things,
>> and desperately corrupt;
>> who can understand it?

2. I leave unexplored the critique of incipient Pelagianism in Paul and the critique of incipient antinomianism in James, and focus on only one of the three critiques to be found in the Gospels. The criticism of the chief priests and the rest of the Jerusalem establishment focused on the temple is "Marxian" rather than "Nietzschean" in character.

Two commentaries on Mark are especially helpful for developing a "Marxian" reading of the Gospels: Fernando Belo, *A Materialist Reading of the Gospel of Mark*, trans. Matthew J. O'Connell (Maryknoll, NY: Orbis, 1981); Ched Myers, *Binding the Strong Man: A Political Reading of Mark's Story of Jesus* (Maryknoll, NY: Orbis, 1988). Of these two, Myers is by far the easier to read. For him, Mark writes "more as critic than as pastor of the church, as a hedge against those in the church who would domesticate Jesus to their own ends. Jesus is not presented as 'the answer' but as the *question* to the church" (p. 106). Also helpful are the texts mentioned above in pp. 201-2 nn. 4, 7-8. See especially Cassidy's *Jesus, Politics, and Society*, Appendix III on the Pharisees and the chief priests. I will make a few brief comments on Jesus' critique of the piety of the disciples later. See also chapter 2 above.

"I the LORD search the mind
and try the heart. . . ."

(Jer. 17:9-10)

O LORD, thou hast searched me and known me. . . .
Such knowledge is too wonderful for me;
   it is high, I cannot attain it. . . .
Search me, O God, and know my heart!

(Ps. 139:1, 6, 23)

We must also, for several reasons, avoid the temptation to construe the conflict between Jesus and his enemies as one between Christians and Jews: (1) In the time of Jesus the distinction did not exist. Jesus and his disciples were part of the Jewish community. (2) The distinction between those who accepted Jesus and those who did not is not of much help here, since Jesus' criticism of his disciples (the "Christians" in the narratives) is as strong as his criticism of the Pharisees and the chief priests. (3) Most importantly, the defining characteristics of the Pharisees are not the kind of thing that could even conceivably be the monopoly of any particular community. One does not have to be a Pharisee in order to be a Pharisee.

In other words, as we approach the narratives about the Pharisees we need to hear again the words of Karl Barth, reminding us that it was the church and not the world that crucified Jesus (see above, chapter 1). Or in other words the question, Who are the Pharisees? can be answered simply with "good church people."[3] We make a terrible mistake and blind ourselves to much of the text when we identify ourselves with the disciples in reading the Gospel narratives. That identification is, to be sure, anything but flattering; but few of us are Jesus people who have left our vocations to become wandering students and evangelists. More often we are, like the Pharisees and the chief priests, comfortable members of the religious and economic establishment; or, if not, we are desperately trying to become such.

Nietzsche is surely right in pointing to the Pharisees' hatred of Jesus. Though they were the minority party in the Jerusalem establishment, which was headed by the chief priests, they were in on the final plot to kill Jesus.[4] And according to the account in the synoptic

---

3. See Carolyn Brown, *Luke's Gospel: A Personal Guide for Study and Prayer* (Louisville: Presbyterian Publishing House, 1990), pp. 14-15.

4. See John 11:45-53. The synoptic Gospels do not mention the Pharisees, but since Mark (14:1-2) and Luke (22:1-2) identify the plotters as the chief priests and the scribes (the authorized interpreters of the law, those who could be called "Rabbi") and since the vast majority of the scribes were Pharisees, there is no reason to doubt John's account. Matthew identifies the plotters as the chief priests and elders (26:1-5).

Gospels they were plotting to kill Jesus from early in his ministry (Mark 3:1-6) and to that end were continuously seeking to trap him so as to give themselves an excuse (Mark 8:11-13; 10:2-9; 12:13-17; Matt. 22:34-40; Luke 11:53-54; John 7:53–8:11).[5]

Why were these "good church people" so threatened by Jesus? Our best answer comes from the quintessential portrait of the Pharisee, given in a parable Jesus told "to some who trusted in themselves that they were righteous and despised others":

> Two men went up into the temple to pray, one a Pharisee and the other a tax collector. The Pharisee stood and prayed thus with himself, "God, I thank thee that I am not like other men, extortioners, unjust, adulterers, or even like this tax collector. I fast twice a week, I give tithes of all that I get." But the tax collector, standing far off, would not even lift up his eyes to heaven, but beat his breast, saying, "God, be merciful to me a sinner!" I tell you, this man went down to his house justified rather than the other; for every one who exalts himself will be humbled, but he who humbles himself will be exalted. (Luke 18:9-14)

Is it possible to imagine a more Nietzschean text, one in which the purpose of religious morality has to a greater degree degenerated into a device for condemning others as evil in order to enjoy the moral superiority of being, by contrast, good? Nothing more needs to be said about the Pharisee; he has already said it all himself.

But two points concerning the tax collector deserve special attention. To identify someone in Jesus' time as a tax collector was more like calling that person a loan shark, a slum landlord, or a prostitute than like calling him a garbage collector. It was not just a low prestige job but, by virtue of the way taxes were collected, a job with moral opprobrium built into it. Thus the phrase "tax collectors and sinners," which we find on the lips of the Pharisees (e.g., Matt. 9:11), really means tax collectors and *other* sinners.

---

5. The Pharisees, as a party, were much less sympathetic to the Herodians than were the Sadducees. But Mark tells us that in their original plot they conspired with the Herodians and that the attempt to entrap Jesus on the question of paying taxes to Caesar was a joint project with the Herodians. Jesus' puzzling warning about the leaven of the Pharisees and of Herod (Mark 8:14-21) comes right after one of these attempts by the Pharisees to entrap Jesus and suggests that Jesus may have been aware of their collusion with the Herodians. Mark treats the question about the greatest commandment (12:31ff.) more sympathetically than do Matthew (22:34ff.) and Luke (10:25ff.), both of whom treat it as an attempt to entrap Jesus.

The Pharisees were especially interested in distinguishing the good from the evil, or, in their vocabulary, the righteous from the sinners. Thus "sinner" came to be a sociological term used to distinguish as morally inferior at least three groups to whom the Pharisees could feel superior: (1) those entirely outside the "church," the heathen, the Gentiles, (2) those whose sins were public and conspicuous, such as tax collectors and prostitutes, and (3) even those who, while neither unbelievers nor flagrant sinners, did not follow what we might call the microlaw, as defined not by Scripture but by Pharisaic tradition. The Good News Bible captures this usage by frequently using "outcast" for the word normally translated "sinner." Jesus' benediction on the tax collector who identified himself as a sinner indicates that Jesus will be at odds with the Pharisees on their fundamental distinction of categories, the sinners and the righteous.[6]

Of equal importance is the fact that in Jesus' parable the tax collector calls *himself* a sinner. Here we glimpse Jesus' desire to go beyond the Nietzschean alternatives. In master morality, we are good, so they are bad, and in slave morality, they are evil, so we are good. In both cases we are good and the negative term is used to designate others. The only exception is the phenomenon of guilty conscience, which Nietzsche explains as the weak turning their resentment inward. But the tax collector does not seem to fit this scheme. Socially he has a great deal of power and ample opportunity to express at the expense of others any resentment he may come to feel. Yet he calls himself a sinner, giving the term a meaning not found in a Pharisaic (or Nietzschean) dictionary.

But our concern here is not with Jesus' critique of Nietzsche; it is rather with the Nietzschean dimension of the Gospels, and we see that dimension dramatically in the dispute between Jesus and the Pharisees over their moral caste system, the righteous and the sinners. There are four key texts:

Mark 2:13-17 (Matt. 9:9-13; Luke 5:27-32). Having called Levi (Matthew), a tax collector, to follow him, Jesus and his disciples are having dinner with "many tax collectors and sinners." The Pharisees

6. By calling this distinction a fundamental category of Pharisaic perception I mean that it functions for them somewhat like the distinction male-female does for us: Whenever we meet a person we immediately notice which gender he or she is. When we cannot tell, we feel somewhat uncomfortable, and when we discover that we have misclassified someone, the change in gender classification is often accompanied by other changes of attitude or affect. We do not feel nearly as strong a need to classify dogs, cats, or parakeets by gender.

object. Noting that the well do not need a doctor, but only the sick, Jesus replies, "I came not to call the righteous, but sinners" (Good News Bible: "respectable people," "outcasts"). Jesus does not explicitly repudiate the righteousness of those who classify themselves as righteous, but he says that the kingdom he brings, its healing and its banquets, are not for them but for those to whom they feel morally superior.

Matthew 21:23-45 (Mark 11:27–12:12; Luke 20:1-19). After Jesus' triumphal entry into Jerusalem and his cleansing of the temple, the collective religious leadership challenges his authority.[7] He parries with a question about why they did not accept the baptism of John, to which they astutely reply, "No comment." Then Jesus tells two parables. The first is about two sons whose father asks them to work in his vineyard. The son who was a "sinner" at first said no, "but afterward he repented and went." The "righteous" son answered, "I go, sir," but did not. On this occasion Jesus' capacity for subtlety abandons him. To his already hostile audience of "good church people," he repeats the message of the previous paragraph and adds an explanation. "Truly, I say to you, the tax collectors and the harlots go into the kingdom of God before you." The reason? The former repented at the preaching of John, while the latter did not.[8]

The second parable is about a farmer who let out his vineyard to tenants while he was out of the country. When he sent servants to collect the rent, the tenants beat or killed them, eventually killing the son whom the owner sent as his final emissary. They thought that in this way they could have the vineyard for themselves, though the owner himself returned and foiled their plot. Again, with a total lack of indirection, Jesus says, "Therefore I tell you, the kingdom of God will be taken away from you and given to a nation producing the fruits of it."

---

7. Matthew at first identifies the challengers as the chief priests and elders but at the end of the sequence refers to the chief priests and Pharisees. Mark and Luke identify the challengers as the chief priests, the scribes, and the elders, the three major components of the Sanhedrin. Since the vast majority of the scribes were Pharisees, there can be little question that Pharisees were part, though not all, of Jesus' audience on this occasion, which was not the only confrontation between Pharisees and Jesus over the question of authority. See also Luke 5:17-26. In asking about Jesus' authority they and the others acknowledged that Jesus was a threat to the legitimacy of their own power. In other words, the challenge is motivated by their will to power.

8. This story is recorded only in Matthew, but the question about Jesus' authority and the parable about the rebellious tenants are found in all three synoptic Gospels.

Those who seem to be the proper vicars of the vineyard turn out to be rebellious rather than faithful stewards of their trust, willing to kill in order to steal, willing to defy the master in order to take his place as owners. The eschatological dimensions of the story suggest that such rebellions can be expected in the vineyard as long as the master is away (cf. Luke 19:11-12). Matthew adds that on hearing these parables, "the chief priests and the Pharisees . . . perceived that he was speaking about them." He was indeed, but he was also speaking to all their Christian successors, who often fail to perceive that Jesus was also speaking about their desire to own the kingdom, making its rules and reaping its benefits.[9]

Luke 7:36-50. Simon the Pharisee invites Jesus to dinner. A woman "who was a sinner," presumably a prostitute, anoints Jesus' feet with her tears and with ointment. Simon objects, saying that if Jesus were a prophet he would know what sort of woman she was. The unstated implication is that if Jesus knew she was a sinner he would have nothing to do with her, especially at table. Jeremias is helpful here: "For the oriental every table fellowship is a guarantee of peace, trust, or brotherhood. Table fellowship is a fellowship of life." Thus Jesus' contemporaries "would immediately understand the acceptance of the outcasts into table fellowship with Jesus as an offer of salvation to guilty sinners and as the assurance of forgiveness. Hence the objections of the Pharisees . . . who held that the pious could only have table fellowship with the righteous. They understood the intention of Jesus as being to accord the outcasts worth before God by eating with them, and they objected to his placing of the sinner on the same level as the righteous."[10]

---

9. Ekkehard Stegemann writes of the Markan version of this story, "It is said here that God will take the vineyard from Israel and give it to others because Israel has always mistreated God's messengers and finally even put his Son to death" ("From Criticism to Enmity: An Interpretation of Mark 2:1–3:6," in *God of the Lowly: Socio-Historical Interpretations of the Bible,* trans. Matthew J. O'Connell [Maryknoll, NY: Orbis, 1984], p. 114). But both the eschatological dimension of the parable and the explicit reference to the chief priests and Pharisees as Jesus' immediate target argue against making the nation of Israel in any primary sense the referent of the story. Stegemann's warning not to draw anti-Semitic conclusions from the story (pp. 116-17) should have been unnecessary.

10. Joachim Jeremias, *The Eucharistic Words of Jesus,* trans. Norman Perrin (London: SCM Press, 1966), pp. 204-5. Cf. Geoffrey Wainwright, *Eucharist and Eschatology* (New York: Oxford University Press, 1981), p. 28: "Certainly the meals which Jesus deliberately took with publicans and sinners and which earned Him such notoriety . . . were to be seen as embodying the divine offer of salvation for sinners: it was in this context that Jesus declared that He came to call . . . not the righteous, but sinners (Mark 2:17)."

"Hence the objections of the Pharisees." The implication is that it is an unwillingness to forgive that underlies the unwillingness to eat with "sinners." Those unwilling to share God's salvation with others become unwilling to share a meal with them. But how could I forgive those on whose wickedness my own goodness depends? How can I share salvation and thereby put myself on a par with those whose moral inferiority is the basis of the moral superiority that is my ticket, not just to the kingdom, but to a place of prominence and power within it?

Thus it is appropriate that Jesus' reply is entirely in terms of forgiveness. By declaring the woman forgiven Jesus again employs the distinction between the righteous and the sinners in such a manner as to undermine it. He tells Simon that it is the degree to which we have experienced forgiveness, not the degree to which we persuade ourselves that others need it more than we, that is our ticket to the kingdom ball.

The story of the woman taken in adultery (John 7:53–8:11) is pertinent here, for it contrasts Jesus' willingness to forgive with the Pharisees' desire to condemn and to punish, especially those most vulnerable socially.[11] They bring to Jesus a woman who had been "caught in the act of adultery," remind Jesus that according to the law of Moses she should be stoned, and ask what he thinks. "This they said to test him, that they might have some charge to bring against him." Jesus' response, "Let him who is without sin among you be the first to throw a stone at her," directly challenges the distinction between the righteous and the sinners. But before Jesus gives it, he writes on the ground with his finger. What did he write? I like to think he wrote "Where is her partner?" For the law of Moses commands that both the man and the woman should be stoned to death (Lev. 20:10; Deut. 22:22-24). Those who brought the woman claim to have caught her in the act. But they only brought her and not her male partner. Why? Because they were not so much interested in upholding the law of Moses as they were in exposing the woman as a sinner and in embarrassing the upstart rabbi who challenged their favorite sport, distinguishing the sinners from the righteous.

Luke 15 (Matt. 18:12-14). The scene is already familiar: "Now the tax collectors and sinners were all drawing near to hear him. And

---

11. This episode belongs among the illustrations of Nietzsche's suggestion that punishment is a public festival of cruelty (GM II ¶¶6-7). Similar scenes can be found in the opening chapters of Hawthorne's *The Scarlet Letter* and of Foucault's *Discipline and Punish*. See above, p. 256 n. 11.

the Pharisees and the scribes murmured, saying, 'This man receives sinners and eats with them.' " Jesus responds by telling three parables. The first, the parable of the lost sheep, ends with the pronouncement that "there will be more joy in heaven over one sinner who repents than over ninety-nine righteous persons who need no repentance." A heaven that finds its joy, not in the righteousness of the righteous, but in the repentance of sinners has a different sense of what makes for a good party than the Pharisee has. This is because it has a different morality. The distinction between good and evil has not vanished, since repentance is valued, but its purpose is not to exclude from God's celebrative love those whom "good church people" like to look down on. The story of the lost coin, which follows, simply repeats the theme of heaven's joy over repentant sinners.

Most of the chapter is given over to the story of the prodigal son. Heaven's joy over the repentant sinner is given graphic earthly portrayal. But Jesus does not linger at the party; he rather hurries outside to the pouting elder brother. Up to this point Jesus has used a coin, a sheep, and a son to portray the sinner. Now he uses the other son to portray the righteous. Like the Pharisee praying in the temple, he recites his rectitude. "Lo, these many years I have served you, and I never disobeyed your command." The father does not challenge this but only asserts, "It was fitting to make merry and be glad, for this your brother was dead, and is alive; he was lost, and is found."

In response to the Pharisees' objection to his eating with sinners and forgiving even tax collectors and women guilty of sexual sins, Jesus contrasts this father's willingness to forgive with the son's unwillingness to share in either the forgiveness or the festive meal that signifies it.[12] In Jesus' eyes the righteous are more deeply alienated from God than are the sinners.

Walter Brueggemann calls attention to the fact that compassion plays a key role in both of Jesus' best-known parables, this one and the story of the Good Samaritan. "Both the Samaritan and the father are Jesus' peculiar articulation against the dominant culture, and so they stand as a radical threat. . . . The ones who pass by, obviously carriers of the dominant tradition, are numbed, indifferent, and do not notice. The Samaritan expresses a new way that displaces the old arrangements in which outcasts are simply out. . . . In similar fashion the father by his ready embrace of his unacceptable son condemns the 'righteousness

---

12. To celebrate the eucharistic feast in a Pharisaic spirit would surely be to take God's name in vain, a form of third commandment idolatry.

of the law' by which society is currently ordered and by which social rejects are forever rejected."[13]

In other words, in Jesus' two most familiar parables we find both a Nietzschean critique of the Pharisaic distinction between the righteous and the sinners, and a compassion that may escape the bounds of the paternalistic pity that Nietzsche deplores.

13. Walter Brueggemann, *The Prophetic Imagination* (Philadelphia: Fortress Press, 1978), pp. 87-88.

43 Jesus and the Pharisees II: The Sabbath

Much of the friction between Jesus and the Pharisees concerned the failure of Jesus and his disciples to observe the sabbath to the satisfaction of the Pharisees. Although Jesus was regularly to be found in the synagogue on the sabbath, he had the disconcerting habit of healing people on this holy day. The Gospels record five such healings and the conflicts they generated.

Mark 3:1-6 (Matt. 12:9-14; Luke 6:6-11). Jesus heals a man with a withered hand in the synagogue on the sabbath. Before doing so he asks: "Is it lawful on the sabbath to do good or to do harm, to save life or to kill?" The Pharisees refuse to answer, but immediately afterward begin their plot with the Herodians to kill Jesus.

What is at issue is not the sabbath as such. Jesus' question is not whether we should take the fourth commandment seriously or not. It is a question of interpretation. Shall we understand healing as the kind of work forbidden on the sabbath? Underlying this specific question, of course, is the more general question, What spirit should shape our hermeneutics?

The contrast between doing good and doing harm is a bit puzzling. It is easy to identify healing the sick with doing good, but what is the meaning of doing harm in this context? Was not the alternative between doing good and doing nothing? To make Jesus' words fit the situation we need to think in terms of James 4:17: "Anyone, then, who knows the right thing to do and fails to do it, commits sin" (NRSV). Jesus is arguing that an interpretation of the law that leads me to do nothing when I could do good thus leads me to do evil, to commit what are sometimes called sins of omission.

The contrast in Jesus' words between saving life and killing is even more puzzling. Neither this illness nor any of the other four in

275

stories of Jesus healing on the sabbath is in any immediate sense life threatening. Jesus seems to be interpreting the sixth commandment not merely as prohibiting murder but as requiring a positive concern that the lives of others flourish; he also seems to be suggesting that our interpretation of one commandment needs to be guided by our understanding of the others.

But it is the Pharisees themselves who give the most dramatic meaning to the contrast between saving life and killing. For on the same sabbath when Jesus gave back to the man that part of his life that was lost when his hand withered, the Pharisees plotted to kill Jesus. Their interpretation of the fourth commandment put them afoul of the simple, negative meaning of the sixth.

Why?

Luke 13:10-17; 14:1-6. These two episodes, recorded only by Luke, are so similar that they can be treated together. First Jesus heals a woman who has been unable to stand up straight for eighteen years. Then he heals a man with dropsy. In the latter case Jesus himself raises the issue, repeating his question whether it is lawful to heal on the sabbath. In the former case the ruler of the synagogue indignantly tells the people to come for healing on the other six days, but not on the sabbath.[1] In both cases Jesus gives what we might call the ox and ass defense. He notes that the Pharisees have no qualms at all about untying their livestock to lead them to water on the sabbath or about pulling an ox or an ass that has fallen into a well to safety.[2] They interpret the law as permitting this work for the welfare of their animals but as prohibiting the healing of their human sister and brother.

Why?

John 5:1-18. Jesus heals a man by the pool of Bethzatha (or Bethesda) who had been lame for thirty-eight years. The man is told that he is breaking the sabbath by carrying his pallet, and the plot to kill Jesus gains momentum because he healed on the sabbath and defended this by saying, "My Father is working still, and I am working." In defending himself further (7:22-23), Jesus gives a variation of

1. The ruler is not identified as a Pharisee, but we can assume he was since the synagogues were the strongholds of the Pharisees and the objection he raises is elsewhere regularly associated with Pharisees. Similarly, in John 5 the objectors are not identified as Pharisees. While they most likely were, what is important is the Pharisaic character of their concerns.

2. Matthew has Jesus make the same point in terms of sheep in connection with the healing of the man with the withered hand: "Of how much more value is a man than a sheep! So it is lawful to do good on the sabbath" (12:12).

the ox and ass defense. He notes that his enemies interpret the law as permitting circumcision on the sabbath but not as permitting the healing that gives a man new life.

Why?

John 9:1-41. Jesus restores sight to a man blind from birth. Much of the chapter is given over to the debate between, on the one hand, the healed man and others who think Jesus must be a prophet from God and, on the other hand, the Pharisees, who insist that Jesus is a sinner.[3] In reply to their "we know that this man is a sinner," he replies, "Whether he is a sinner, I do not know; one thing I know, that though I was blind, now I see."

By giving the back of his hand to the Pharisees' passion for publicly singling out sinners, this newly sighted man answers the question we have been asking about their hypocritical hermeneutic: *Why* is their interpretation of the sabbath so generous to animals and so hostile to human flourishing? Because in their hands the law in general and the sabbath in particular have become an instrument of their will to power, a means of guaranteeing their goodness by identifying others as evil. Jesus is a threat to them because he understands religious obligation in a completely different way. Because he sides with Jesus, this man is also a threat. So they declare him a sinner as well and cast him out of the synagogue. In their hermeneutical and sociological circle, "sinner" and "outcast" are indeed synonymous.

Mark 2:23-28 (Matt. 12:1-8; Luke 6:1-5). This final confrontation over the sabbath does not concern healing, but otherwise is the same old story. The disciples are hungry, and, as they pass through the grain fields, they pluck some of the grain to eat. The Pharisees complain that this "harvesting" violates the law. Jesus defends the disciples by referring to what David did "when he was in need and was hungry, he and those who were with him": They ate the "bread of the Presence" from the house of God, "which it is not lawful for any but the priests to eat." He concludes, "The sabbath was made for man, not man for the sabbath. . . ." In Matthew's version Jesus gives a different punch line to the story. Drawing on one of the anti-sacrifice texts from the prophets (Hos. 6:6), he says, "And if you had known what this means, 'I desire mercy, and not sacrifice,' you would not have condemned the guiltless."

---

3. The Pharisees' need to explain Jesus' exorcisms as signs of a partnership with Beelzebul, the prince of demons, closely parallels their eagerness to label him a sinner in this instance. See Matt. 12:22-32. Anyone who challenges their labeling as sinners all to whom they feel morally superior automatically becomes a sinner.

The two endings agree. In their eagerness to condemn others, the Pharisees have become blind to human need, in this case hunger,[4] in the other cases the need for healing. They have put the cart before the horse in their understanding of the sabbath so that the sabbath oppresses and condemns rather than refreshing and renewing human life. In doing this, they have parted company with mercy, which is not surprising, since the deepest motivation of their morality is to set themselves above their neighbor, not to love their neighbor.

A similar motif arises in Jesus' critique of Pharisaic tithing in his diatribe against the hypocrisy of the scribes and Pharisees (Matthew 23). They are superscrupulous tithers, giving ten percent of their "mint and dill and cummin." It is as if they were careful to give a tithe of the change they found in the coin returns of pay telephones and Coke machines. Jesus commends them for this but complains that at the same time they have "neglected the weightier matters of the law, justice and mercy and faith." He finds that their attention to tiny details has left them oblivious to the larger issues concerning their neighbors that a genuine concern for justice and mercy would raise and the larger issues of their relation to God that a genuine concern for faith would raise. So he calls them "blind guides, straining out a gnat and swallowing a camel!"[5] An interpretation of the law that makes people merciless is an interpretation in the service of resentment and revenge.

The sabbath was not the only bone of contention between Jesus and the Pharisees when it came to interpreting the law. There was also the Pharisees' concern for cleanliness. It seems that in their symbolic system good vs. evil, righteous vs. sinner, and clean vs. dirty were more or less interchangeable. They were a bit like that ardent, old-style housewife whose favorite Bible verse, so she averred, was "Cleanliness is next to godliness," though she could never find it in the Bible. In their world there were only two kinds of people, themselves and the great

4. In the diatribe in Matthew 23 Jesus calls the Pharisees blind (vv. 16, 17, 19, 24, 26; cf. John 9:39-41). By cultivating the ability to see others as sinners, the Pharisees have lost the ability to see the things that matter most to Jesus, in this case as in the healings, human need. Luise Schottroff and Wolfgang Stegemann are right in emphasizing this dimension of the story and linking the episode with the Lukan claim that the kingdom Jesus announces is good news to the poor ("The Sabbath Was Made for Man: The Interpretation of Mark 2:23-28," in *God of the Lowly: Socio-Historical Interpretations of the Bible*, trans. Matthew J. O'Connell [Maryknoll, NY: Orbis, 1984], pp. 122-27).

5. For a more detailed discussion of this text, see my essay "New Covenant Tithing," *The Church Herald* 36/22 (November 2, 1979), pp. 4-7.

unwashed. On this point as with regard to the sabbath, what has come to be known as the ceremonial law was helpful in enlarging beyond the scope of tax collectors and harlots the group to whom they could feel morally superior.

Mark 7:1-13 (Matt. 15:1-9). Again the disciples are eating. This time the problem is that they do so with unwashed hands. The Pharisees, it seems, have very strict rules about ritual purity and thus about washing hands, cups, pots, etc. So they complain to Jesus once again about his disciples' eating habits.

Jesus replies with a biblical quotation:

> "Well did Isaiah prophesy of you hypocrites, as it is written,
>> 'This people honors me with their lips,
>> but their heart is far from me;
>> in vain do they worship me,
>> teaching as doctrines the precepts of men.'
> You leave the commandment of God, and hold fast the tradition of men."

There are four things to note about this response: (1) The contrast between the lips and the heart is between publicly observable behavior and that which gives meaning to that behavior without itself being publicly observable. Just as Nietzsche thinks that what is really important in our actions is not to be found on their visible surface (see above, chapter 35), so Jesus insists that the heart of the matter is to be found in the human heart.

This is a major theme of his polemic against the scribes and Pharisees in Matthew 23. Referring to their ritual washings, he compares them to cups and plates that have been cleansed on the outside but inside are full of "extortion and rapacity" and to whitewashed tombs that are outwardly beautiful "but within they are full of dead men's bones and all uncleanness." Just in case they miss the point, he adds, "So you also outwardly appear righteous to men, but within you are full of hypocrisy and iniquity" (vv. 25-28).

It seems that the need to feel morally superior leads to making appearance and reputation more important than the actual attitudes of the heart. So Jesus warns against the scribes and Pharisees that they "do all their deeds to be seen by men . . . and they love the place of honor at feasts and the best seats in the synagogues, and salutations in the market places, and being called rabbi by men" (Matt. 23:5-7).

(2) Most of Jesus' complaints against the Pharisees come down

to whether they take seriously the command to love their neighbor. His responses to their attacks highlight their indifference to pressing human need and the absence of compassion and mercy from their piety. But here attention is shifted to the greatest commandment of all, the command to love God with all one's heart. Having shifted attention from outward behavior to the heart, Jesus also shifts attention from the neighbor relationship to one's relationship with God. It is the voice of God that says, "Their heart is far from me."

(3) This means that Pharisaism, which makes the whole of life into the most strenuous project of obedience to the law of God, is an instance of third commandment idolatry. They constantly speak of God, but they take God's name in vain. They embody the systematic failure to love God with all their heart and to love their neighbors as themselves. Perhaps the saddest words in the entire New Testament are Jesus' verdict on these "good church people," when he applies to them the words of God as presented by Isaiah: "In vain do they worship me."

(4) The essence of idolatry is the human usurpation of the divine. This is why Jesus' own commentary on the quotation from Isaiah focuses on its last phrase, "teaching as doctrines [divine truths] the precepts of men." He not only reiterates the distinction between "the commandment of God" and "the tradition of men," as we saw above, but he goes on to illustrate the point with the Pharisaic interpretation of corban (cf. Matt. 23:16-22). He begins with the charge, "You have a fine way of rejecting the commandment of God, in order to keep your tradition!" and concludes with "thus making void the word of God through your tradition which you hand on" (Mark 7:9, 13). The irony is that those who seem most concerned with obedience to the law of God turn out to be those who "leave" and "reject" it. At issue is not an occasional lapse but a systemic flaw in their project of obedience. Its deepest motivation renders it hypocritical.

No fewer than seven times in this passage is the rule to which the Pharisees appeal identified as a human tradition. As before, the dispute is over the right interpretation of the law. A major distinction between the Pharisees and Sadducees is that the former regarded the oral tradition that had grown up around the law as part of the law. Knowing this, Protestant readers of this text are tempted to say, "Look. Jesus is a Protestant, at least through the Prolegomena of Systematic Theology. He rejects the Catholic appeal to Scripture and tradition as normative, elevating Scripture clearly above tradition."

But Jesus is not doing Systematic Theology, and the question is not about theories of theological norms. The question concerns the practice of treating human interpretations of Scripture as if they were the voice of God, thereby co-opting that voice to the service of whatever motivations govern those interpretations. One need not know much about the history of Protestantism to know that nothing in the theory that subordinates tradition to Scripture prevents reversal of that subordination in practice.

It can be argued quite persuasively that the Gospel narratives give a very one-sided picture of the Pharisees. There was much about them deserving of praise and admiration, but the Gospels paint a consistently dark picture. It is to account for this that I have spoken of their "systematic failure to love God . . . and neighbor" and of the "systemic flaw in their project of obedience." The Gospel accounts are single-minded to the point of being one-sided. The reason is the belief that at the heart of the Pharisees' project is a heart given over to a vice that makes of all their undeniable virtues only glittering vices.

As they wait for the appearance of his father's ghost, Hamlet muses to Horatio:

> So, oft it chances in particular men,
> That for some vicious mole of nature in them,
> As in their birth . . .
> . . . .
> By the o'ergrowth of some complexion,
> Oft breaking down the pales and forts of reason,
> Or by some habit that too much o'er-leavens
> The form of plausive manners, that these men,
> Carrying, I say, the stamp of one defect,
> Being nature's livery, or fortune's star,
> Their virtues else, be they as pure as grace,
> As infinite as man may undergo,
> Shall in the general censure take corruption
> From that particular fault.
>
> (I, iv, 23-36)

Hamlet was not thinking of the Pharisees, but he might as well have been. For their virtues else *were* quite considerable; and yet they were all corrupted by one particular fault, the need to use religious morality as a tool to lower others and thereby raise themselves.

44 In Conclusion: The Dangers of Suspicion

[Secular moral] theories may challenge and judge certain claims made on the basis of Scripture. Scripture has, after all, been used to justify racial and sexual discrimination; it has been used to justify "holy wars," crusades, and inquisitions; it has been used to justify the abuse of power and the violation of the rights and integrity of others in order to pursue what has been taken to be God's cause. Secular moral wisdom, and especially the principle of justice, has sometimes challenged such uses of Scripture and led the church to reconsider particular practices and to repent of them. We must note that it is not the authority of Scripture itself that comes under criticism and review here, but authorizations for the use of Scripture in moral argument and moral claims made employing such authorizations. In the churches Scripture itself has sometimes finally corroborated the judgments of secular morality and been vindicated against both its detractors and its so-called defenders in such cases.

ALLEN VERHEY[1]

. . . one of the characteristics of a community of wise readers [of the Bible] is an openness to outsiders. . . .

1. Allen Verhey, *The Great Reversal: Ethics and the New Testament* (Grand Rapids: Eerdmans, 1984), p. 193.

Without ears to hear the voices of outsiders, we can
forget that now "we know in part and we prophesy in
part . . . now we see in a mirror dimly" (I Cor. 13.9, 12).
Our interpretations can take on pretensions of permanence. When our communities fall prey to this
greatest of interpretive temptations, it is often only the
voice of outsiders that can set us right. If we have not
taken the time to cultivate the skills, habits and disposi-
tions that allow us to hear the voices of outsiders, we
will fall into a situation of interpretive arrogance. That
is, we will deceive ourselves into thinking that our
words are God's word. The exercise of power and coercion will characterize our communities. Conformity
rather than faithfulness will be the standard used to
judge our lives. If nothing else, then, our awareness of
our own tendencies towards interpretive self-deception
should compel us to learn to listen to outsiders.

STEPHEN E. FOWL AND L. GREGORY JONES[2]

Sometimes, when our best friends will not tell us what we very much
need to know, our enemies lack the love to be tactful and therefore go
ahead and tell us the truth. When our holiness has halitosis we need
someone to let us know, and on such occasions those who wish us no
good can be helpful. So I have been arguing that we should listen
carefully and humbly to the critiques of three of the Christian church's
most formidable foes.

But this advice is dangerous because suspicion is dangerous. The
difference between courage and foolhardiness is that, while both engage
the danger that only cowardice would avoid, foolhardiness is oblivious
to danger, while courage is fully aware of its peril. Suspicion is dangerous, but that does not mean that we should suspend our suspicions. It
means, rather, that we should suspect our suspicions, knowing of their
danger.

In concluding my plea for a religiously motivated hermeneutics
of suspicion, I want to highlight three dangers that can make the cure
for self-deception as deadly as the disease. The first is that we could

---

2. Stephen E. Fowl and L. Gregory Jones, *Reading in Communion: Scripture and
Ethics in the Christian Life* (Grand Rapids: Eerdmans, 1991), p. 110. This is an important
theme for Fowl and Jones (cf. pp. 42-43, 104, and the whole of chapter 5).

become merely skillful at seeing through the false consciousness of others. As David Tracy has wisely noted, "To suspect the presence of ideology is one thing. To face the actuality of the ideologies in ourselves and even in our most beloved classics is quite another."[3]

It is easy, for example, to become a Pharisee in the process of unmasking Pharisaic hypocrisy. Consider the Sunday school teacher who taught a lesson on the Pharisee and the tax collector who went up to the temple to pray and then said, "Now children, let us fold our hands and close our eyes and thank God that we are not like that Pharisee." It is a sad insight as well as a sparkling wit that leads Peter DeVries to have one of his characters say as he watches the faithful flocking to worship, "There, but for the grace of God, go I."[4]

Thomas Merton warns us of this danger by calling attention to Dostoyevsky's contrast between "the rigid, authoritarian, self-righteous, ascetic Therapont, who delivers himself from the world by sheer effort, and then feels qualified to call down curses upon it; and the Staretz, Zossima, the kind, compassionate man of prayer who identifies himself with the sinful and suffering world in order to call down God's blessing upon it."[5] It is much easier to become a Therapont than a Zossima, especially if we become skillful at practicing the hermeneutics of suspicion on others while exempting ourselves from its scrutiny.

The examples of false consciousness given in this book that each reader finds most convincing will most likely be those that are (or seem to be) farthest removed from his or her own life. Thus I suspect that many readers, like me, will have no difficulty seeing attempts to defend apartheid biblically as ideology or in detecting the will to power that shaped Pharisaic piety in Jesus' time. But we find it much more difficult to detect the apartheid in our own view of the world or the ways in which we work to keep Jesus from upsetting our own religious status quo. Yet the latter is the whole point of the exercise. The goal is not to develop skill in suspicion in order to become more incurably Pharisaic but just the opposite, to find, if not a cure, at least a diagnosis of our own Pharisaism.

3. David Tracy, *Plurality and Ambiguity: Hermeneutics, Religion, Hope* (San Francisco: Harper and Row, 1987), p. 69.
4. Peter DeVries, *Comfort Me With Apples* (Boston: Little, Brown, 1956), p. 35. I am indebted to Fowl and Jones, p. 65, for this reference. They in turn took it from Ralph Wood's *The Comedy of Redemption* (Notre Dame: University of Notre Dame Press, 1988), pp. 244-46.
5. Thomas Merton, *Contemplative Prayer* (Garden City, NY: Doubleday, 1971), p. 28.

Insofar as I learn suspicion by learning to see through the self-deceptions of others, this can be helpful to me rather than harmful only if I go on to employ this skill against myself. The same can be said in the first person plural, for *we* can be Pharisees as easily as *I* can be. "Let *us* fold *our* hands and close *our* eyes and thank God that *we* are not like that Pharisee."

I know of no surefire protection against using suspicion to make myself look good by making others look bad, or to make us God's elect while placing others outside the pale, if not of God's love, at least of God's inner circle. But we need to remind ourselves constantly that Jesus thought it was more important to get at the log in our own eye than to worry about the speck in someone else's eye, that in saying this he taught us always to see our own spiritual defects as more serious than those of our neighbors, and that this is the meaning of "Judge not, that you be not judged" (Matt. 7:1-5).

The second danger of suspicion is that it will degenerate into cynicism, into the view that false consciousness is so pervasive, so ineluctable, so "natural" that there is really no point pothering over it.[6] The cynic bursts the bubble of naive self-consciousness and then only laughs at efforts to resist or escape. Cynicism is the complacent confidence that suspicion reveals the whole story of human ideals and idealism. There is nothing but self-interest, self-righteousness, and self-deception.

Erich Heller takes Nietzsche to be a cynic and in doing so describes cynicism with a very vivid image:

> Psychology was the weapon — the deadly weapon, as he believed — that Nietzsche wielded in the subsequent war against idealism, metaphysics, and religion; psychology informed by the persistent suspicion that all "higher values" are merely satisfactions of psychological needs. . . . Nietzsche's is the eye that now sees through everything until there is nothing left to see through, nothing except blank nothingness; and even then this eye would turn around, fairy-tale like, and see through the seer. (Introduction to HAH, p. xiii)

Actually, Nietzsche warns against cynicism. It is, he writes, "the only form in which base souls approach honesty" (BGE ¶26). It is also a danger to the noble soul, whose temptation is not to become one of

---

6. Philosophically speaking, this is the besetting danger of postmodernism, while Pharisaism is the besetting danger of modernism.

the good but to become "a churl, a mocker, a destroyer" (Z I ¶8). Still, Heller's account is helpful in highlighting the reductionist character of cynicism. For the cynic, "higher values" are "merely satisfactions."

No doubt there are times when our modern atheists talk that way. But we need not follow them, for they have surely not argued in support of such a claim, which would be, by virtue of its negative character, the hardest of all to establish. If there is a purple elephant on the front lawn, it is not too difficult to point it out. But it is very difficult to show that there are no purple elephants to be found anywhere. Similarly, it is easy to show that religion is easily and often corrupted by self-deceived self-interest; but it is very difficult to show that in the hearts of the faithful there is nothing else to be found.

Foucault warns against taking his own genealogical exposures cynically when he insists that his point "is not that everything is bad, but that everything is dangerous. . . . If everything is dangerous, then we always have something to do. So my position leads not to apathy, but to a hyper- and pessimistic activism."[7] Everything is dangerous. This does not mean that religion is nothing but the will to power dressed up in its Sunday-go-to-meetin' clothes, that there is never any genuine love of God or neighbor. It does mean that every piety, whether of belief or of practice, whether of the individual or of the community, whether of worship or of ethics, is human, all too human. If we look closely enough we are likely to find it serving as the instrument of interests that it was meant to constrain. So no piety is exempt from scrutiny.

Theologically speaking, human life is good insofar as it is created, and evil insofar as it is fallen. The hermeneutics of suspicion insists that our religious life is not exempt from the second, the evil. This hermeneutics becomes cynicism only if it forgets or denies the first, the good, in the process.

The third danger of suspicion is that in remembering our sinfulness we forget the grace of God. Every attempt to become holy, including the project of reading Freud, Marx, and Nietzsche as a Lenten exercise, has built into it the double danger of this forgetting. (Everything is dangerous.) On the one hand, there is the temptation to think that God will love us (and that we can therefore love ourselves) only

---

7. Michel Foucault, "On the Genealogy of Ethics: An Overview of Work in Progress," 1983 Afterword to Hubert L. Dreyfus and Paul Rabinow, *Michel Foucault: Beyond Structuralism and Hermeneutics* (Chicago: University of Chicago Press, 1983), pp. 231-32.

if we become truly good; there comes with this thought, on the other hand, the belief that we can actually make ourselves truly good, if only we try hard enough. In the present case, the twin temptations are to think that we must and can rid our lives of self-deception.

Just as we needed to remind ourselves of the doctrine of creation to ward off cynicism, so we need to remember the doctrines of justification and sanctification so as not to forget the grace of God. In other words, we need to remember that God's love is a gift and is not conditioned on our having already become truly good, and that any progress we make in that direction is at once incomplete and not merely our own doing but a sign of God's work within us.

In calling Freud, Marx, and Nietzsche the great secular theologians of original sin I have suggested that the hermeneutics of suspicion belongs to our understanding of human sinfulness. The self-deceptions they seek to expose, like those exposed by Jesus and the prophets, are sins and signs of our fallenness. If we are to deepen our understanding of our sinfulness with their help, we need to remember at the same time the larger theological context in which the doctrine of the fall is properly placed, between the doctrines of creation and redemption.

Although I have described it last, the danger of forgetting God's grace is really the most basic danger. If we succumb to it, it is almost certain that we will succumb to one of the other two, becoming either a Pharisee or a cynic. Either we will persuade ourselves (proudly) that we, unlike others, are capable of becoming truly good and have very largely done so, or we will persuade ourselves (despairingly) that the possibility of moral and spiritual growth is illusory. If, on the other hand, we remember God's grace, then we lose the pride that would make us a Pharisee and the despair that would make us a cynic.

Suspicion can be a kind of spirituality. Its goal, like that of every spirituality, is to hold together a deep sense of our sinfulness with an equally deep sense of the gracious love of God. Freud, Marx, and Nietzsche will have become fruitful Lenten reading for us when they have helped us learn to pray the following hymn individually and together, free of pride or despair:

> Not for our sins alone thy mercy, Lord, we sue;
> let fall thy pitying glance on our devotions too,
> what we have done for thee, and what we think to do.
> The holiest hours we spend in prayer upon our knees,
> the times when most we deem our songs of praise will please,
> thou searcher of all hearts, forgiveness pour on these.

And all the gifts we bring, and all the vows we make,
and all the acts of love we plan for thy dear sake,
into thy pard'ning thought, O God in mercy take.
  Bow down thine ear and hear! Open thine eyes and see.
  Our very love is shame, and we must come to thee
  to make it of thy grace what thou wouldst have it be.[8]

8. Henry Twells, "Not For Our Sins Alone" (1889), *Rejoice in the Lord: A Hymn Companion to the Scriptures*, ed. Erik Routley (Grand Rapids: Eerdmans, 1985), no. 506, stanzas 1-3, 5.

Index